How Did I Get Here?

How Did I Get Here?

a memoir

Bruce McCall

blue
rider
press

NEW YORK

blue
rider
press

An imprint of Penguin Random House LLC
penguinrandomhouse.com

Images on pages xiv, 26, 58, 98, 122, 152, 174, 202, and 232 are courtesy of the author.

Library of Congress Cataloging-in-Publication Data

Names: McCall, Bruce, author.
Title: How did I get here? : a memoir / Bruce McCall.
Description: New York: Blue Rider Press, 2020.
Identifiers: LCCN 2020011842 (print) | LCCN 2020011843 (ebook) |
ISBN 9780399172281 (hardcover) | ISBN 9780698178991 (ebook)
Subjects: LCSH: McCall, Bruce. | Cartoonists—United States—Biography. |
Illustrators—United States—Biography. |
Television writers—United States—Biography.
Classification: LCC NC1429.M466 A2 2020 (print) |
LCC NC1429.M466 (ebook) | DDC 741.5/973 [B]—dc23
LC record available at https://lccn.loc.gov/2020011842
LC ebook record available at https://lccn.loc.gov/2020011843

Printed in the United States of America
1 3 5 7 9 10 8 6 4 2

Book design by Lorie Pagnozzi

Dedicated to my brother Hugh

Contents

Introduction

Every life, experienced from inside, feels like a failure. Even Shakespeare, from the evidence of the sonnets, retired thinking that he had wasted too much time on all those popular plays (in retirement, he was going to focus on his poetry), while Mozart's final frustrations were off the charts. Only a very few lives, however, benefit from an articulate underestimation of their own accomplishment, since they make us ironically aware of the actual processes of artistic triumph. All of which is an unduly fancy way of saying something simple: Everyone I know thinks Bruce McCall is a genius, except for Bruce, who hardly thinks he's gotten much past dunce.

This is not disingenuous, on either party's part. What *we* mean by "genius" is that he has a style, a vision, that is both instantly recognizable and entirely ineffable—it can't be reproduced by anyone else—and also that the satiric points he lands in this unique style are always on the money. His marriage of a century's worth of virtuoso commercial illustration styles with a first-class satiric imagination creates both delighted laughter and uncanny truth. Looking at what we have to call, since the 1980s, Trump's New York—an insane place that looks plausibly real but hides its madness within it—well, only McCall has shown us its tall, slick, demented shapes.

Yet, reading this book, the reader comes away knocked sideways by the sheer painstaking study that led to the wild flights of surreal fantasy. Throughout, in describing his formation as an artist, he emphasizes skill, fidelity, mastery, *truth*. "Realism" is his principle and "detail" his watchword. From the first, one sees that McCall instinctively understood the great Surrealist principle: The more detail an image contains, the more dreamlike it becomes. Getting everything maniacally right drains mundane reality from a painting or drawing, and lets it enter into the realm of the visionary. A diagram is the most fantastic kind of image ever created. Reducing and describing—cutting away in cross sections and footnoting each labeled part—it overlays a wistful logic on the sheer chaos of actual life. The more encyclopedically detailed a car or a skyscraper is, the more unreal it seems.

This is very partially a perceptual effect—as McCall says, we all work with a varying failure of optical focus: we don't see a world of even microscopically exact detail, except in illustration. But this perceptual effect is more a result of the way that the styles of illustration participate in desires even as they summon up descriptions—the realist illustration that McCall grew up on makes fantasies real (the car with the proportions of an aircraft carrier, the luxury motel on Mars) and in so doing makes the real fantastic. Not the least of the many pleasures of reading this, the second volume of autobiography he's offered, is to see him for the first time lovingly inventory the great illustrators, almost all names unknown to anyone but aficionados, who influenced him. My own Google image search worked overtime to discover, and let me for the first time fully appreciate, such extraordinary figures as Robert Fawcett, with his tweedy atmospheric interiors; the astounding Art Fitzpatrick, whose Edenic images of Pontiacs with grilles as wide as a sixties expense account are hard to credit as anything except Pop Art parody advertisement (they weren't); and above all the great Chesley Bonestell, the visionary science fiction illustrator, who showed a view of Saturn from the planet's largest moon, Titan, as though it were a view across a fifties back fence. The imagery that fed Bruce's style, we learn in this book, was not mass produced, but particular, made by masters.

But his underestimation of his own gift is completely sincere—all he sees, like any artist, is work and failure. Because of the aplomb of his cheerfully pessimistic and self-deprecating nature—not a contradiction, more a Canadian national trait—we can therefore learn something about how genius really operates, exactly through the strength of his self-denial. McCall tells us that he has taken as his subject for this book the nature of the "Little Bang"—the explosive interior moments in a life when suddenly an ordinary Joe becomes an expressive fountain.

And what McCall reveals here is the secret of all bangs, big and little. It is the capacity for commitment. To a degree that he himself hardly seems to understand is exceptional, in this beautiful memoir he recalls, hilariously, what feels like *every* landing place, every teacher, every drawing desk where he has worked—every assignment to draw a car, every boss whose generous appreciation helped, every job praising a long-forgotten Corvair or Corvette—and we learn from the journey that art is just work taken to another dimension of purpose. He isn't trying to push the artisanal foundation out of his story, from his perch of a now-legendary *New Yorker* artist. He moves it to the very center, with an eye to how even a modest job can teach a major lesson. McCall persistently underrates his own gifts, the gifts that overwhelm his friends. But this modesty also presents a path, one of persistence and sanity. A lesson learned in two ways: both that mastery of a craft is a springboard to art, and that without a genuine appetite for art, craft becomes mere labor. He writes of a not-untalented colleague that "Rudy practiced art without being an artist. His was the perfect example of that approach. No other art form interested him. The richest artistic rewards—pride, satisfaction, a sense of achievement, the joy of creativity—were of zero interest to him. He didn't have to set aside his artistic nature because he didn't have one. Rudy was distanced from any emotional connection with his work, which liberated him from anxiety, second-guessing, and self-doubt. I envied this bastard relative of mental discipline, but not enough to emulate it."

And then there is the gruff, acerbic generosity of his writing! Sentence after sentence rises up, not, as with some of us, in polished preening but in a style as distinctly disillusioned as it is painfully funny. As when he writes of his family's fatal relocation from their first home in Simcoe, Ontario, to a nasty new apartment in gray Toronto:

On a sunny and cold Thursday morning in November 1947, the car carrying most of the McCall family from Simcoe to their new life in Toronto (a life, the kids expected, that would be a whirl of unending action, fun, and pleasure) trundled to the far side of the city and crash-landed on the dark side of Pluto.

Not *that* Pluto, but since it was a featureless wasteland with no signs of life and a distinctly alien atmosphere, it could have been . . . It sat on Danforth Avenue, a miles-long East End corridor lined with modest storefronts, used-car lots, greasy spoons, and off-brand churches.

Many good humorists might have arrived at "the dark side of Pluto." There is a spark of genius about "off-brand churches." Again and again in this memoir, we are knocked sideways by sentences that manage to combine a misanthropic refusal to overrate reality with a gentle urge to be generous to the generous. This is, as much as it is a chronicle of many bangs, a story of shared loyalties with wife and children and friends. McCall's perpetual underestimation of his own capacities allows him to overstate those of his companions—he writes reverently of the legendary first crew of editors at *National Lampoon*, without stopping to think that the only one with a real legacy is the older, more watchful man now writing this book.

His alcoholic mother and unreliable father and many siblings who shared the ship with him are honestly but never cruelly described, and one is left again with the conundrum of genius: How does it rise from such resistant ground? The one truth seems to be that his parents, for all their faults, knew good writing from bad, had a standard of excellence (even unto subscribing to *The New Yorker*), and infected their children with that knowledge. An uncanny natural ability to discriminate—to see the world sharply and cleanly—seems, for all their unhappiness, to have been a core McCall family virtue, and, however hard won from life, remains a Bruce McCall singularity. No one sees what Bruce does the way he does. Now we are lucky he has created this plausible diagram of the mechanisms that connect eye to mind, and mind to hand, and both to heart.

—Adam Gopnik

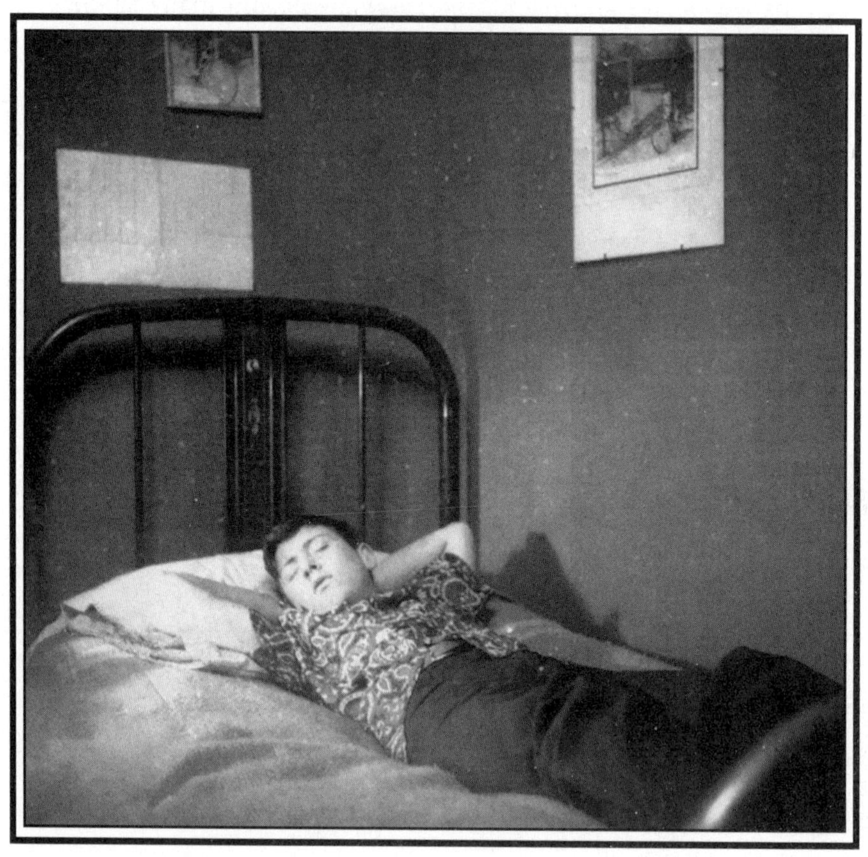

My life, and my dreams of being an artist, began in Simcoe, Ontario.

Chapter 1

Be Careful What You Wish For

Colonel John Graves Simcoe delivered the first valentine card in North America. A century later, another colonel, James Sutherland "Buster" Brown, Simcoe born and bred, drafted Defence Scheme No. 1, the Canadian government's secret 1921 plan to invade key U.S. cities in the event of war.

That about covers the claim to fame of Simcoe, Ontario. I was born there when it was a town of six thousand; now it's more than doubled, a bedroom community for Hamilton and Toronto. Simcoe prospered with a rich agricultural base, and tobacco was the big industry when I was a boy. No Ontario town was ever nominated to be sister city to Florence, and there were good reasons why Simcoe was among the nonstarters. Scottish conservatism is as close to the opposite of Florentine culture as can be imagined. Piano lessons and church choirs sufficed as culture, which otherwise had no role in the life of the town.

Kids like me avoided Sunday school and regular church attendance. We were unwitting cultural morons who couldn't miss what we never had. As did all heathens, we wallowed in an idyllic freedom. This got a huge boost from the Second World War, which removed innumerable dads and further loosened the controls on our behavior. Domestic life and disciplining kids became, by default, the duty of wives, and wives of that era seldom ruled households harshly.

The McCall family was big—five boys and, eventually, one girl: Mike, Hugh, me, twins Tom and Walter, and Chris. I attribute my lifelong shunning of group activities to this. My antipathy took a brief time-out when I was suckered into Lord Baden-Powell's Boy Scouts as a Cub, at the bottom of a hierarchy of ranks not unlike the arrangements in the Vatican. Boy Scouts patiently climbed up in modest increments: at the summit stood the Sea Scouts, as elite as the King's Mounted Household Guards. I never saw a Sea Scout. I still suspect they were a gaudy invention, like Jesus, to keep all Boy Scouts striving.

I salivated when I landed on the Sea Scouts section of the official Scouts catalog. What greedy kid wouldn't want that inventory? There were silken neckerchiefs. An over-the-shoulder leather Sam Browne belt. A steel canteen. A second belt around the waist, its clasp ingeniously mating two halves to form the Boy Scouts escutcheon. A small leather case clipped to the belt for fishing lures, small change, the odd whistle or rubber band. A hornpipe dangling from the same belt. Over the left shoulder, a set of semaphore signaling flags in a cylindrical leather case. There were pockets and flaps on the official Sea Scout shirt. Binoculars on a strap slung around the neck. Knee socks. A pair of waterproof Sea Scout brogans. Sewn onto the shirtfront and sleeves, resembling a horde of caterpillars, were cloth Sea Scout badges of merit: bed making, swimming, diving, drowning-cat rescue, tree felling, completion of an anti-seasickness course. Badges commemorating a fire extinguished, a torpedo assembled, a torpedo disassembled. And in the

Sea Scout model's hand, a silver whistle so powerful that when blown in Cairo it could be heard in Johannesburg.

Only the sons of mining company CEOs, arms dealers, and senior officers of secret banks could afford the complete Sea Scout uniform. I grieved for my fundlessness: my bilious-green, beanie-like peaked cap, cut to the pattern of every English public school boy's cap since *Tom Brown's School Days*, was my only item of Cubs regalia.

Ill fortune soon proved good fortune shortly after my enthusiasm for Lord Baden-Powell's mild outdoor adventuring, feeble at the start, crashed. Our pack leader was exposed as a pederast and fled town on his Harley-Davidson with sidecar. I hadn't the money for Sea Scouts gewgaws, and had already tired of sitting on my haunches in some ratty clubhouse, imitating a talking wolf by shouting, "A-Kay-LUH!" I slipped away. The Cubs cap hung around the house, a reminder of the dangers of joining up, until someone (me, legend has it) fed it one day to Billy Perkins's dog, Tip.

▪ ▪ ▪

The toys and tools of a happy boyhood circa 1943 demanded improvisation more than cash. While American kids feasted on tons of magnificent plastic junk, Canada couldn't produce toys in war-time conditions beyond a handful of crude pot-metal Hurricanes. In Simcoe, fifty cents could buy the indiscriminate kid a tommy gun cut out of a chunk of wood that resembled a folded umbrella. Some of our improvisations:

- The green steel pot Mother used to boil potatoes made a perfect Japanese Imperial Army helmet for Pacific jungle skirmishes in the lilac bushes.

- The flour canister in the kitchen became a snowbound hell for the five plastic British soldiers—unfazed by their gas masks—sent to ambush Nazis in the wastes of Norway. Mother later discovered a Brit soldier buried deep in the flour, perfectly preserved.

- Rich brown horse chestnuts, tied by strings to hankies, subbed for a band of Wehrmacht parachutists floating down from a second-story sunporch window to land on Crete.

A working cap gun bestowed prestige—and what felt like real killing power—on its owner. A mouth-made firing noise might spray a foe with spittle, but no firing noise from a human source could beat the three or four eardrum-puncturing *bang-bang-bang-bangs* in a cap-gun blast. A functioning gun cost an eight-year-old partisan big money. A discarded cap gun retrieved from the battlefield, sans trigger and missing its fake-pearl celluloid handle, was as close as I ever came. Even rarer than a working gun were the dirty-red rolls of caps required to make it go *bang!* and emit an acrid aroma. These were forever in short supply. Maybe the army maintained an elite Cap Gun Brigade that claimed top priority—another damn casualty of wartime restrictions.

Weekly Saturday matinees ran war movies. Fifty-two weeks' worth per year exhausted the supply, leaving us to sit through Durango Kid westerns, Boston Blackie detective junk, and the odd stale box-office hit, usually a musical. In retrospect, while certain Hollywood war flicks charged the imagination and lifted the soul, many were so cheaply made that footage of a World War I Spad was suddenly spliced into the frenzy of World War II dogfights. The best war movies were British: *Target for Tonight*, *In Which We Serve*, *Five Graves to Cairo*, et al.

Authenticity was the difference. They seemed more realistic than the stagey, broad American fare like *Edge of Darkness* or *Desperate Journey.*

▪ ▪ ▪

Toboggans rocketed us down Simcoe's steepest grade, off the first tee of the Norfolk Country Club. Snowshoes had been supplied by our boisterous cousins, the Stewart boys. I never got good at snowshoeing, which requires control and is more like walking hard than sliding along on a pair of skis. A bunch of skis reposed in the shadows but were seldom used, because Simcoe lacked the gradients they were meant for.

The substantial Jackson house sat on a hill directly facing our peeling stucco home across Talbot Street. Daredevil kids lugged their sleds up to the Jacksons' front lawn, then dived downhill belly-first on the sleds. A Flexible Flyer, with glass-smooth steel runners, was the ride of choice. Victory went to the sledboy who eked out energy enough to keep his momentum as he reached Talbot Street and his path flattened out. He summoned the last erg of sledpower as he and his mount transected the slippery street and crossed the finish line in a controlled crash. On winter afternoons in Simcoe, darkness fell around four o'clock with an almost audible thud. Cars, headlights blazing, arrowed past. No walkie-talkies linked sledboy and headquarters. A shouted "*Look out!*" curbed—or tried to curb—sled and pilot as the operator mentally calculated time and distance, how many seconds would be left after the sled burst through the snow-shrouded bushes to lie squarely in the path of the onrushing Studebaker or Nash. That no sled ever collided with a moving vehicle was pure luck—and light traffic, is my theory.

Hockey was a cultural signifier in Canada, and a further reason to not be American. The winter pastime made perfect sense: a sport for fans who adored the fast and graceful game while also secretly adoring the cretinous physical violence inherent in it. Canadian hockey fans had it both ways.

The national pastime was crucial to the Canadian sense of identity. Playing hockey was a ritual like the Japanese tea ceremony, except for the broken noses. Everybody wanted to play, but there was only one indoor rink in town, and it was devoted to skating parties for people who probably wouldn't leave tracks of blood on the ice. Although Simcoe produced NHL players, few of them were graduates of ponds and backyard rinks. There were twenty wannabe players for every gifted one: How could anyone stand out when pickup games regularly placed thirty skaters on the ice—on both teams? For every ace—some lucky bastard who actually had a puck on his stick for a fleeting instant before vanishing under the human wave of defensemen—there were scores of wretches, drafted by neither team, who had no stick or who couldn't find, borrow, or afford a pair of skates.

I came perilously close to being a hockey have-not. The solution, for me, was more like a part solution: in the pile of skates jumbled into a small mountain just inside the kitchen door in the McCall household at 101 Union Street (we moved there in 1942), I literally stumbled on a pair that fit. I hurriedly laced them up in case the owner happened by, and hobbled out in that weird wobble-walk even NHL players had to perform when negotiating a surface other than ice. I skated in circles, to demonstrate skills my older brothers had ridiculed me for. They ridiculed again. My newfound skates were for a girl. I should have detected that fact by looking at them: White. With tiny jingling bells.

The front lawn of 101 Union Street was big, but more important, it was level. Run a hose over a rectangular patch of dead grass long enough and by next morning there was a sheet of ice, a hockey rink (in Simcoe parlance, a hockey "cushion," one thing it definitely was not). Snow was piled around the cushion as the boundary. What in November had been a gleaming white border carefully leveled to a uniform height was by early May a dark gray ruin of unevenly melting ice boulders.

▪ ▪ ▪

Growing up during World War II made my contemporaries and me richer for the experience. I was four years old at the start and had just attained my first decade when they finally pinned and hog-tied Nazi Germany. There were twenty-point newspaper headlines, fire trucks marauding down side streets blasting their horns and jangling their bells, and a school shutdown. It was a day so hysterically noisy that no American would believe it was coming out of Canada.

That gaudy episode, in a culture allergic to overstatement, shook even a ten-year-old kid. My classmates, neighbors, and friends were glad to hear that Hitler was kaput—although that villain out of central casting left a gaping hole in our schoolyard pantheon of evil.

What the war meant to most Simcoe kids was the nonstop entertainment of movies, radio dramas, comic books, and *Terry and the Pirates* comic strips. One strip starred a freelance squadron of hero pilots who flew a matching set of Grumman Skyrockets, elevated by the sorcery of fiction from the real-life scrap heap to murderously fast, maneuverable fighter planes. The war was a tumultuous party, exciting enough to produce a prepuberty high. No wonder every shortpants warrior was secretly dreading a world at peace. What would life in Simcoe be without the drama of a really smashing war?

No more scrap drives, blood banks, Armistice Day parades. Worse yet for the platoon of neighborhood kids in volunteer armies, runty dogfaces all. No more campaigns fought in the war zone of the McCall grounds: thick bushes, copses, alleyways, the broad lawn favoring suicide charges by classmates–turned–Japanese soldiers screaming, "*Banzai!*" until mowed down by two Yanks-for-the-day and their imaginary machine gun firing from a nest obscured by a fanciful stack of sandbags. We fought an equal-opportunity war. British commandos or Afrika Korps tank drivers, Axis regiments bent on killing innocent civilians in Singapore or whatever Allied heroes were featured in last Saturday's World War II matinee, against a handful of Axis rats stealthily nesting in the leafy umbrella tree edging the side porch that doubled as Allied HQ and my home. Nazis and Imperial Armed Forces constituted ninety-nine percent of all enemies fought and clobbered from the start to the finish of WWII.*

▪ ▪ ▪

Dad was home on weekends from his job in Toronto from 1937 until he joined the RCAF and shipped overseas in 1941 at age thirty-one, when I was about six. He returned to Simcoe at thirty-

* But wait! What about the third Axis power? Mussolini had mugged and stomped around throughout the 1930s, bragging about creating an army worthy of its name, the New Romans. Fascist Italy and the New Romans invaded Eritrea and Ethiopia in 1935, bombers versus spears, and barely squeaked out a win. But where were the Italian armed forces after the real war began? A few Italian bombers hit Britain when she was down, fled back home, and stayed. The New Romans landed in North Africa just in time to surrender en masse to anyone who'd take them. If he'd created the New Romans, Hitler probably would have killed himself in 1941.

three, battered by depression after a ringside view of the war, especially the death over France in mid-1943 of his closest friend, Wing Commander Chris Bartlett, on a night bombing raid. Nerves scraped raw, he underwent a brief recuperation at home, then went back to Toronto and a civil service job. Back to being an absentee father. A distant figure, anxious to see his brood grow—as long as we didn't spoil his weekend golfing dates.

He was no hypocrite. He never pretended to be a doting dad. I hadn't expected much and wasn't disappointed. We barely knew each other, then and in the years to come. This mild estrangement, and his absence from my daily life, allowed the freedom I had come to take for granted to continue. He could radiate what felt like hostility, Mr. Murdstone barely tolerating David Copperfield.

His father, Walter Sydney McCall, would leave his family for months to go adventuring—i.e., gambling—turning up in parlors as far away as Texas. Dad's strict moral code was probably fashioned at this point. He was not amused by his father's exploits and held a grudge, spurning him in later years. And as his mother's loyal defender-protector, he was steadfast until she died of cancer in 1938.

Dad married my mother, Helen "Peg" Gilbertson, in 1930. The core mystery remains: Why did they have half a dozen kids? Dad had to work 120 miles away to earn enough to make ends meet, starting a split family life that lasted from 1937 to 1947. By sheer numbers, six kids means family life. In spirit, we were barely a family. Particularly when it was clear that he didn't even like kids. Mother paid the bill—six kids to care for, no money for anything except the kids, and the daily burden of heavy housework with no help. Worst of all, the darkness of loneliness. Drinking was a side door for a bit of relief. She was petite and not particularly robust to begin with. She was a living billboard for nice folk making themselves dizzy-drunk, and soon enough, full-fledged alcoholics. Neither Dad nor a town harboring its fair share of serious addicts lifted a finger to intervene. She graduated to alcoholism as a way of life, further tearing apart the pretense that this was a normal family raising normal kids.

Before he left Canada for his wartime stint in Yorkshire, Dad managed to send RCAF-style wedge caps to Mike, Hugh, and me. *Captains of the Clouds* was printed on both sides—he had been the RCAF liaison with the Hollywood team. They shot some footage nine miles away at the Jarvis Air Training base, and he attended the premiere in New York. *Captains of the Clouds*, led by Jimmy Cagney, saluted Canadian bush pilots. It failed to be nominated for an Oscar. It failed, period.

Thereafter, every few months a package arrived from overseas: war treasures from Dad. I snared a U.S. 8th Air Force shoulder patch. A rattling box full of Canadian and British military badges got snatched up before I could strike. A creepy weirdo from down Talbot Street managed to pry every one of them out of McCall hands for the equivalent of twenty-four wampum beads.

Dad had bequeathed a genuine RCAF "Mae West" life preserver to my siblings and me before marching off to war. Such prestige was showered on whatever McCall kid was bobbing around the municipal swimming pool in that balloon-like butter-yellow souvenir. That Mae West was coveted by its owners—but apparently not as much as by the footpad who one night stole across the lawn to grab the prize resting on the ground where it had been carelessly flung. It was never seen again.

Military affairs never inconvenienced Simcoe. Almost daily, Harvard and Fairey Battle training planes howled overhead. Sunday afternoons a motley mob of airmen and soldiers in mufti wandered

Norfolk Street, the town's main artery, looking for fun. If they ever found it, they never spread the word. Hugh and I sometimes stayed at our aunt Eva's house, situated diagonally across the street from the Governor Simcoe Hotel. On summer evenings we slept out on the porch—or tried to: across the way, the windows of the hotel's lounge were wide open, the room packed with airmen, some of them freshly graduated pilot trainees, ready to muster for duty overseas.

Melancholia shouldn't afflict innocent kids, so I must have been precocious: in the loud babble and the sing-alongs of ancient and familiar old marching songs, male voices raised and rolling into the dark summer night, I sensed a sadness beyond my ability to comprehend. This was my first overpowering feeling. That hotel lounge, with the babble of party talk and, stabbingly, the lusty singing of male voices belting out "We'll Meet Again," "I've Got Sixpence," and endless other songs. Young men, mixing memories and premonitions and feeling a bittersweet sense of loss. They'd remember this evening, aswim in Labatt's beer in the humid, smoky lounge of an elderly clapboard hotel in a town in the middle of nowhere. The sound of the singing, the feelings of belonging, the premonition of never knowing another moment like this: that night would tug at the heartstrings for . . .

My sleepy mind lost its grip; the thread slipped away and vanished. I woke up Sunday morning and saw the Governor Simcoe deserted. A sense of loss clung to me for weeks.

▪ ▪ ▪

Musical prodigies like Mozart have no literary equivalents. The ear is a lightning-quick organ. Contrarily, the brain develops language only gradually: thus, the caves at Lascaux are studded with perfect animal cartoons—and no captions. Kid novelists are scarce. Françoise Sagan, anyone? That French writer hit the big time at age eighteen. She may have peaked early: none of her work after *Bonjour Tristesse* wowed the literary world.

My writing career began inauspiciously, with a sixth-grade class assignment to compose a fire safety essay. Before exposing my draft to the teacher and the class, I asked Mike to read it over. He'd barely started before his loud cackle contradicted my serious intent. A blunt question was the powerful opening line. "How would you like to loose your life?" I had written. I've seldom made a spelling mistake since.

The setback failed to quash my growing urge to write, an urge that accelerated the day I discovered Dad's portable Royal typewriter where he'd stashed it on a closet shelf. Typed drivel gained five thousand times more authority than the same drivel written by hand. The act of feeding a page into the machine thrilled me: What would emerge when I finished? Mere twaddle, when it marched across the page in rigid straight lines of typeface, gained weight. Unlike a schoolboy's lumpy scrawl, a typed page deserved attention and, until it was found to be senseless blather, respect beyond the dreamy hopes of a ten-year-old author.

The typewriter was a free pass into the sober world of letters. It forced me to imitate published writers, to advance my spelling, to pull back from uncouth language and sloppy-looking work. Typing elevated the writer; readers wouldn't stand for careless scrawling. I loved the rituals involved: Rolling sheets of paper into place. Tapping the keys, watching each stroke pounded onto the page, then seeing intent magically turn into words and sentences. Hearing the little bell and nudging the next line into being with that perfect ergonomic carriage return.

My typing was done in brief bouts and called for stealth. Like a

Free French operative hidden under the kitchen floor of a Paris boîte in 1941 furtively transmitting coded messages to London under the nose of the Gestapo, I dreaded Dad discovering his machine in my sweaty hands. He didn't need to officially forbid anybody sharing his Royal. Sharing wasn't in his DNA.

▪ ▪ ▪

Any kid could trace Mickey Mouse off a comic book page. Far fewer kids could write down quickie stories for classmates facing a deadline with their scribbler pages blank. Soon enough I was doing a brisk trade in book reviews and story-writing exercises in English class. A dime bought a single-page review of *Tom Sawyer* or *Kidnapped.* A quarter got a taut story—setting, plot, characters, the works. A sideline to this sideline was a page of lurid U.S. Civil War battlefield carnage in blue ballpoint ink, price determined by body count.

Literary fame was clearly nigh. If a ten-year-old author churned out neat little mini-novels that sold on the spot, how much more fame and coin, in increments of more than two bits, was waiting up there with the big boys? Protecting my bottomless ignorance, I shoved under the rug such concerns as the fact that I was unpublished. Nor was I as informed as an author ought to be about the odds of a ten-year-old boy being contracted to write a bestseller. So, like any famed writer needing to shield himself from rabid fans and autograph hounds, I decided I needed a nom de plume.

The Bell Telephone directory for Simcoe yielded as many noms as a plume-pusher could ever require. I drove Mother nuts, day after day, reciting likely choices. Eventually, the hunt was abandoned: the town directory fatally lacked the brand of aristocratic French and Russian names, sleek with grandiosity, that my pre-success now pre-justified.

■ ■ ■

At an early age books and magazines pumped high-octane stimulation, available nowhere else, into my cerebral cortex. My vocabulary ballooned. My horizons expanded. Reading at that hungry developmental stage, when your head is an empty vessel, acts almost like a drug: the more you ingest, the more you want, until it's become a full-blown craving and is ultimately needed to maintain mental equilibrium.

The McCall living room shelves were a cross section of literature of the late twenties and early thirties: Michael Arlen, Edmund Wilson, H. L. Mencken—a variety of literary genres. I read them all (well, to be honest, I passed my glazed eyes over some), from Hector Bolitho's deferential biography of King George VI to the weirdly comic, including Don Marquis's unjustly neglected *Archy and Mehitabel* and an early effort at parody by Corey Ford, *Salt Water Taffy,* with witty photographic illustrations. Our parents had taste and discrimination, not the result of being wellborn or highly educated but because curiosity had driven them to reading, whereupon reading led to learning, kindling a passion that never faded, indeed remained a necessity and a pleasure for as long as they lived.

Their mutual attraction, arguably aided by each discovering the other's intelligence from reading books without pictures or talking vermin, began in Simcoe High School. Their dueling class newsletters, one edited by Tom McCall and the other by Peg Gilbertson, put aside classroom news and useful school-related fare. They featured feigned personal attacks, disguising tender feelings within insult-charged cannonades of mockery and teasing throughout the school year.

I still ponder why our parents' literary enthusiasms were withheld from us. Mike, Hugh, and I—with Walter coming up fast—

had forsaken comic books; all of us wanted reading that meant something. We were soul mates to our parents, and it would have immeasurably enriched our reading lives to talk books with Mother and Dad. It would also have helped close the vast gap of intimacy between our parents and us. Given Tom and Peg McCall's allergies to meaningful contact with their offspring, maybe that explains this disinclination. Living among the collected wisdom and sophistication conveyed by a sea of books, in a rare small-town home where the life of the mind was recreational and educational, we were excluded from the blessings of such good fortune. Left to devise my own solution for enlightenment, I plugged away regardless. I kept reading for selfish pleasure. Consequently, I didn't know what an autodidact was until I'd become one.*

I grew up assuming that writing and drawing originate in the same synaptic boiler room and split only when one or the other is deliberately left behind. I couldn't (and even today can't) grasp why it is that—despite the fact that writing and drawing share so much creative DNA, so many neurons flashing through the same network of muscles, veins, and nerve endings—this creative duality coexists so seldom that the term "writer/artist" almost always means "self-described hack." (Which is why "I'm an artist-writer" has been voted the dreariest charade of all time.)

I've virtually always written and drawn simultaneously and can offer no scientific reason for it. I'm an artist and a writer—maybe better defined as a writer who draws and paints. My first act in making an illustration is to pepper a page with free-form,

* I wonder how Dad and Mother would react today to the fact that to date, Walter, Chris, and I have published thirteen books among us. My daughter, Amanda, lists six publications.

stream-of-consciousness phrases. Not notes, exactly, but blurts about color rules, the mood, things to avoid: in sum, pep talks to myself. A blank page is a terrifying thing to an artist. Words help diminish the fear of losing oneself in a vast white emptiness. Or maybe that's just me. At any rate, I can't get traction without this step.

An insufficient art education bars me from enjoying museum shows and retrospectives. After a lifetime of toiling in art, that admission should haunt me. It doesn't. I'm the sum total of a bundle of instincts, and gaps and mistakes in shaping them. That mess is my style.

My artistic tools in the early phase were a short step up from caveman levels of sophistication: an HB pencil, a bottle of Higgins india ink, a crow quill fine-point drawing pen and a big flat Speedball pen for lettering, stubs of Crayolas excavated from chesterfield cushions and under beds, and an early Scripto ballpoint pen that leaked ink like a busted pump. From somewhere materialized a small black tin box of used watercolor paints, a dozen tiny cakes scoured down to crusty remnants by a previous owner. One sable watercolor brush, stiffened by age and too much use into a point, completed my tool set. It's a measure of my cluelessness that I was content with it. In any case, if an art supply store had existed in Simcoe circa 1946, I wouldn't have known what to ask for. Or even what to want.

▪ ▪ ▪

Why do so few kids continue to push forward with art after kindergarten? Interest trails off; of my many Simcoe classmates, for instance, I was the only one to keep on drawing after art ceased being mandatory in school. Other diversions eclipsed the slow, solitary act of making pictures. My preference for sitting alone, pulling images out of my brain and seeing what happened when I transposed the intellectual to the visual, excited me. Whether this was fired by genes or by talent and boredom, I still haven't a clue. Whatever. An engine in my prefrontal lobes—or is it the hippocampus, the amygdala, or for all I know the Christmas tree lightbulb—was revving up and driving me onward.

Millions of pencil sketches in the early years represented an investment in training the tendons and muscles in my right hand to precisely record what my brain so effortlessly visualized. Fine-motor control, taming dumb digits to obey commands relayed by the central nervous system, spiral far beyond Malcolm Gladwell's dictum of ten thousand hours to proficiency. (Artists don't count practice hours.)

Of course, no artist can so smoothly link brain, eye, and hand that the intended rendering is realized every time. I've only once or twice even come close to fully capturing a mind's-eye image on paper. That's okay by me: defeat is no reason to stop. In fact, ninety percent of the pleasure of a creative act is in the chimerical pursuit. Next time I'll hit the center of the bull's-eye. Never have, never will. Yet a certain delusional quirk cons the artist into slaving away, through one screwed-up effort after another. That frustration can't be borne by the normal mind. The sanest course is to surrender, whereupon the would-be artist turns to some pastime that offers better odds, leaving a few misfits to persist in their creepy obsessions.

Like every other lad on earth, I craved instant, or at least satisfyingly prompt, gratification. But the written word demands an investment of time to absorb and cogitate. And rewrite. Thus, when temporarily sated with wordplay, I'd set aside my pads of lined paper and ten-pound encyclopedia and commence to draw. My chosen subject was—now, what the hell else but the one and only subject a seven-year-old kid in 1942 knew was worth his time and effort—the war.

It was difficult, not to mention sure to produce an inevitably lengthy, ragged end result, to verbally describe a dogfight between a Spitfire and a Messerschmitt Bf 109 over the Channel in the epic days of late summer 1940. Words can function brilliantly, but who can write and keep pace with sentences and punctuation good enough to capture a fury lasting seconds? How much easier, and more gratifying for the originator, to grab a bunch of pastels and romp high in a cloudless cerulean sky, the Channel a flat gray mat far below, to follow the hot pursuit of an Me-109, the evil flying jackal of the Luftwaffe, by a svelte RAF Spitfire!

No profundity snuck into this and the hundreds of other aerial scenes I did. The point was to discharge emotional ammunition. So transitory was the pleasure of the image, so fleeting the feeling, that unless the drawing hit a bull's-eye in both composition and rendering, its meaning and its value shriveled and died on completion: another ball of paper dings off the wastebasket and rolls off to a corner of the room. Next?

Whatever drawing and writing I churned out in those wartime years barely differed from daydreaming: embryonic creative impulses, fashioned by hands still mulishly uncooperative and still only sporadically coordinated, attempting to immortalize on paper scenes inspired by movie moments colliding with my imagination. Whether my drawing skills rated equal to, or even better than, those of any other wannabe artist—in my class, my town, my country—I neither knew nor cared. Begun in early boyhood, my drawing stayed deeply private and personal, and had never been seen as a public contest for supremacy.

Art wasn't a conscious ambition. It ran deeper: something, part hobby, part self-expression, part ideas, that I wanted and soon needed to record in a closed-loop system dependent on no external factors. This solitary aspect was just as well. Nobody praised me or even much noticed what in hell little Brucie was doing, holed up in that bedroom all day. My ego would eventually swell with the flattery of praise and attention, but not for a few years.

It was a dire fact of wartime life that paper didn't grow on trees. (Well, yes, it sort of does, in fact, but not in this particular context.) Access to exotic extras like tracing paper was almost impossible, a reality that inspired a frantic household ransack. I'm ashamed now to confess that I unearthed pay dirt on the bottom shelf of a battered old cabinet, where expired books, like ailing Eskimo elders, were put out to die. I found and hefted a weighty hardcover tome published late in the nineteenth century: Sir Walter Scott's smash bestseller of 1814, *Waverley*, donated by some now-forgotten family friend who had wildly overrated the McCalls' literary tastes. What it offered—and what I quickly tore out—were two dozen or so unblemished pages of transparent vellum, each laid over a fine engraving bound into the book.

Tardily but sincerely, I hereby apologize to the shade of Sir Walter for having desecrated his classic. And for failing thereafter to read a single word of it.

■ ■ ■

Week after week all through my boyhood years, *The Saturday Evening Post* was nudging me toward the craft of illustration. There was no real competition: we had no art books, and I saw no art shows and thus had no chance to aspire to some legitimate niche. Thanks to this magazine I was soaked in colorful, antic imagery fifty-two weeks of every year, bewitched by samples of America's most famous living illustrators. The idea that drawing and painting vivid pictures to run in the *Post* was the royal road to artistic success controlled my work. It fought with no competing forces. Temptation—the study of art, its history, its evolution over the centuries from the Romantic to Realism to Impressionism to Surrealism to Modernism—never distracted me.

My admiration for the illustrators who brought stories to life in memorable paintings every week was aesthetic and nothing else. Prosodic excellence, originality, the quality of the story, lay off to the side. It was only years later, when I started recognizing the critical differences between superior writing and workmanlike prose, that the fiction featured in *The Saturday Evening Post* was revealed to be steadfastly lowbrow, deliberately so. The magazine's editors knew what they were doing, and it wasn't capital-*L* Literature. It was entertainment, pitched to a readership of eighteen million.

Norman Rockwell painted 322 *Saturday Evening Post* covers between 1916 and 1963. For much of that time he ruled as America's most famous artist, most beloved artist, and finest artist. He was sui generis, so confoundingly skilled that no artist ever tried to copy him. Rockwell was tall and skinny, his face arguably better known than that of many movie stars. He wasn't handsome, but he conveyed an inimitable decency.

I adored Rockwell's work. Any Rockwell cover stimulated an afternoon's fond, inch-by-inch examination. The "corny" charge, the jeering criticism of his work as trafficking exclusively in a mythical America, the world Rockwell populated with clichéd characters—the lovable kid making harmless mischief, the benevolent small-town cop, the gawky young GI, the bashful couple getting their wedding license from a grandfatherly clerk, ad infinitum—all of it was provably true, upsetting to neither the *Post* readers nor to me. These were incidental elements.

His characters couldn't exist in the real world, but Rockwell documented the places, things, and rituals of everyday American life with absolute, sometimes stunning, fidelity. He had no identifiable "style." His scenes looked found, natural. Tricks of composition were ingeniously buried. Rockwell studied every detail he placed in his pictures; should you find an error anywhere—even a tiny prop of zero importance to the picture—the entire illusion of reality he slaved to create would collapse. So he never erred.

Rockwell seemed a regular guy. No airs, a dedicated painter, happy to patiently work alone in his studio, day after day. I sent him a fan letter in October 1946, wrapped around a few pencil drawings. I had no motive other than perhaps earning a pat on the head. Two weeks later the mail brought a note and a pat on the head, signed *Norman Rockwell.*

The Rockwell romance continued for five or six years, before a wider perspective and budding maturity combined to identify additional heroes. *Collier's*, the only serious rival to the *SatEvePost*, had its own Rockwell, Robert Fawcett. Fawcett was a more cerebral artist than Rockwell. Each illustration was a feast of detail. He seemed incapable of leaving an inch of space unfilled. His characters moped, grimaced, and sneered like a cast of British stage actors strutting their stuff with grace and energy, exaggerating their movements for those up in the balcony.

Fawcett was a great draftsman: that is to say, he could really draw. His illustrations in a 1953 *Collier's* series of Sherlock Holmes stories show him at his peak. You could almost smell the horsehair and macassar in the stuffy rooms where Holmes, the veiled young mystery lady, and tweedy Inspector Lestrade have reached a dramatic turn. Fawcett wasn't a painter like Rockwell. He stripped away the merely decorative, worked in a blend of ink and aniline dyes, and grabbed the reader by the balls.

Robert Fawcett was great. C. G. Evers, on the other hand, was sublime. He conjured dense scenes for steamship lines, the U.S. Navy, and Philadelphia Electric Company, among others. Evers wasn't an editorial illustrator; his work was watercolor reportage in advertising and in navy wardrooms. His subject was water: stormy water, calm, cool water. Evers wasn't celebrated. His scope was too narrow to make his name a household word. C. G. Evers was only the greatest marine artist of the twentieth century.

Austin Briggs, Bernie Fuchs, Peter Helck, Bruce Bomberger, Mead Schaeffer, and Chesley Bonestell held and still hold niches in my personal pantheon. Bonestell was the first postwar space artist. His haunting depictions of Mars and Venus and other planets on his fanciful tours of the cosmos were one-quarter science and three-quarters conjecture. (NASA and space satellites were still years away.) His bold visions of worlds beyond ours lifted my visual imagination into another dimension. Brilliant pioneering work, Chesley: space and its mysteries caused hearts all over the world in the late forties and fifties to pump faster. He was the Merlin who opened the world's eyes.

The styles of these illustrators of course varied widely, but I recognized an underlying consistency that united them and shaped my approach to art and illustration. They stuck to realism. Their work looked at the world, at life, intelligently: No bogus sentiment. No fakery. Just life, unretouched.

■ ■ ■

I'd dreaded the end of the war because without it, what could be the theme of life? Kids like me had grown up inside a giant bubble that was rapidly deflating: our enemies gone, our kill-the-Nazis play now pointless. The sky overhead was suddenly empty of aircraft that were no longer needed as the military was dismantled. "Peace"—what did it mean, what did it portend? How would I fill my days?

An interim few months let us taper off from World War II. The atomic bomb in August finished off Japan but furnished nothing a kid could turn into play. The Nuremberg trials entertained us, especially in the aftermath, as one Nazi rat after another died a painful death, then vanished from the earth, leaving me with no archvillains until 1946 and Winston Churchill's Missouri speech. We'd never warmed up to the Russians; now the Commies were officially the skunks. The Cold War was on.

It's doubtless a matter of mind coloring memory, but I'll forever remember 1947 as one long spring day, bright with yellows and dynamic orange under a cloudless peacetime sky. It was a palette that had been in storage since September 1939 (December 1941 for Americans). Now peacetime was in the air everywhere. To kids like me, the gray, grimy, worn-out world had just been washed clean.

"The United States peers into a crystal ball," writes Verlyn Klinkenborg in *The Last Fine Time*, his sensitive book about life in postwar Buffalo, "and what it sees is Kelvinators. It sees relief from patriotic abstinence, a whole continent beginning to untruss. . . . Postwar ads paint a future succulent enough to redeem with interest the drab, self-sacrificing years just past. As paradigms for national life in a new age, advertising's benign, iconic predictions are perfect."

Amen to that. The same euphoric release from grim regimentation gusted through Simcoe, Ontario, eighty-six miles southwest of Buffalo, New York. Much had stood still during the war. The word "new" was, in fact, new. In no time I developed a raging thirst for new experiences and new anything. The cornucopia of postwar affluence hadn't dumped big changes into McCall family life. To Dad, as to millions of others, it didn't really matter very much. Infected by the dream virus of postwar promise, he shared his grand plans: An amphibian flying car. A new DeSoto. A house in ritzy Rosedale, the Beverly Hills of Toronto. Hugh and I would be enrolled at Royal Roads, the military prep school in faraway British Columbia. We kids slavered and nodded and dreamed our own dreams.

Dad's dreams soon deflated, of course, but it would have been petty to begrudge his expulsion of hot air. In any event, two years of peace and prosperity had yet to produce bounty trickling down to the McCall household, still languishing in its wartime state of suspended decay. The one advance we kids recognized concerned bubbles. The labs of military science had devised a revolutionary product: a tougher breed of bubble, balloon-size and pop-resistant. Even sissy kids could now blow spherical miracles skyward as stupefied bullies stood by.

▪ ▪ ▪

Simcoe had been the McCall family hearth for almost two hundred years when, in the summer of 1947, Dad moved us to Toronto. It isn't that we never returned. Mother's three sisters, my grandfather Walt and his second wife plus their two kids, and squads of friends dating back to high school days in the twenties ensured that we'd continue to return to our former hometown.

In Toronto we certainly didn't feel isolated. Air-conditioning was still a luxury, and at least theoretically, an electric fan cooled the occupants of a room. Never my room, though. Our top-floor apartment at 2377 Danforth Avenue became a broiler thanks to the effect of sunshine on a flat roof three feet above us. Our apartment always lacked serenity; now it was unlivable. Summer heat bred some chemical reaction that also made it a stink box. And so in those first summers we fled Toronto like Brits fleeing the 1857 Sepoy Massacre.

Dad and Mother took over her sister May's austere house in 1948, 1949, and 1950. May was a teacher who taught me in grade six. She lived her entire life as a spinster and traveled in summertime. Back in Simcoe I tried unsuccessfully to revive friendships interrupted by the Toronto move. Out of sight, out of mind; now the one hospitable refuge in life had turned alien.

Our aunts May and Eva were older sisters with little in common with our mother. Her eldest sister, Netta, lived on a small farm in Lynn Valley, four miles from town, with her husband, Ed. Poor all their married lives, they never bitched about it. Warm and generous Netta, beloved by everyone who knew her, exactly defined what a mother could be and our mother couldn't.

Leaving Simcoe was easy. Living in Toronto would be harder than our sheltered lives had prepared us for. In the four months between Dad's announcement and the actual move, I floated in gorgeous daydreams of the life awaiting us in the big city. Somehow, for inexplicable reasons, an abrupt elevation in our social status was my constant delusion. Picture a tall old elm tree in a huge manicured park on a sunny summer afternoon. A group of schoolmates—in school blazers and caps, like me—sits in the shade, listening enraptured as I recite tales of my Simcoe boyhood.

I can't imagine what idiotic notion made me equate the move to Toronto with my enrollment in a private school. Nor could I possibly have spellbound a gang of acolytes about Simcoe and my adventures there. Everything about that fantasy is egregiously stupid. But it takes more than that to explain why it remains vivid through the decades. It's a long leap into a distant past. And a rendezvous with myself, in my final days of innocence.

As my life became more complicated, my drawings offered an escape.

Chapter 2

Underground Artists

On a sunny and cold Thursday morning in November 1947, the car carrying most of the McCall family from Simcoe to their new life in Toronto (a life, the kids expected, that would be a whirl of unending action, fun, and pleasure) trundled to the far side of the city and crash-landed on the dark side of Pluto.

Not *that* Pluto, but since it was a featureless wasteland with no signs of life and a distinctly alien atmosphere, it could have been. Confronting us was a formation of redbrick buildings housing thirty-two identically sized apartments that had been slapped together by a federal government agency to give overseas Canadian veterans places to live until the housing crisis slowed. Danforth Court was its name. It sat on Danforth Avenue, a miles-long East End corridor lined with modest storefronts, used-car lots, greasy spoons, and off-brand churches.

Culture shock socked the innocent McCall kids in their solar plexuses: we had just vacated a drafty, roomy old barn of a house on a quarter-acre corner lot in a leafy neighborhood in a small town. What we now had to call home was a third-floor walk-up in which eight humans were crammed into three cell-like bedrooms. The "Court" in Danforth Court was a stingy rectangle of grass surrounded by three-story buildings and was soon beaten down to mud. Even greenery was rationed: Albert Speer probably saw more foliage from his cell window at Spandau.

The sickly-sweet odor of fresh paint permeated our apartment and mixed with the perplexity and mild terror I felt in those first, woozy hours. That olfactory insult replayed itself for years. Another pungent aroma—of fresh horseshit—wafted on hot summer nights from the Acme Farmers Dairy stables next door. The dairy still used horse-drawn wagons, a somewhat uncommon holdout.

Escaping the toxicity of Danforth Court for school wasn't a relief so much as a variation on the theme of ugly surprises. Gledhill Public School was an ugly revelation in itself: a brownish-black stone fortress in that unlovely Victorian Gothic architectural style favored for every British prison, asylum, orphanage, and workhouse, faithfully copied for Canadian schools in order to terrify students before they even passed through the doors.

I made no friends right away, founding a tradition of social self-isolation that would persist for years. I did, however, attract an enemy in my first week at Gledhill. The school playground was larger than certain Polynesian islands, a vast open space modeled on the Alcatraz exercise yard. Making enemies at Gledhill was easier, I realized, than making friends. What provoked the enmity I never knew, but when I sidled out to the yard at recess, scanning the milling throngs in search of a friendly face, an eggplant-shaped thug waddled up to welcome me with a hearty smash on the shoulder. "Fuckin' little sissy," he explained.

■ ■ ■

I had been drawing, like every other young kid near a paper supply, almost from the day I realized that the little pink rubber thingamajig at the top end of a pencil wasn't nearly as good as the pointed graphite tip at the other end for making marks on paper. Nobody in the family, the school, or Simcoe had yet detected an embryonic Michelangelo (the artistic talent scouts hadn't reached Norfolk County). Reducing the circle to my family, I was a prodigy. Too bad if artistic merit in my neck of the woods conferred prestige only to those whose talents lay somewhere between carving a good jack-o'-lantern and accurately spelling the name of Prime Minister Mackenzie King.

I never flattered myself that my drawing and writing amounted to anything but a hobby, private and pleasurable. I could use this creative energy as a bathysphere to explore the deep mysteries of my life hidden below the surface. My vessel bore no relationship to the *Good Ship Lollipop*. The route to understanding my world, and my place in it, was oblique. I crept up on truths, spun my wheels, invented detours that led to more detours. I spent more time in the psychic muck than in sunlit uplands. My subject matter differed from those of the standard exercises: I went slumming. My fledgling artwork limned no pastoral vistas or still lifes of fruits and flowers. My instincts led me to a dark, humid, nasty subterranean world.

I had never seen a Hogarth or Cruikshank engraving, yet one of my earliest renderings was uncannily similar: I drew a dank stone cellar. A scrum of lowlifes were brawling to grab chunks of garbage tumbling down a chute. What in hell was my point? I didn't know or care. Maybe it was fascination with the underclass. Maybe panoramas of human desperation raised the creative stakes: it's harder to show misery than happiness. My ideal was perfected through practice in lovingly rendering armies of cretinous bums in mildewed rags. The most Neanderthal one stands in a mud puddle, waiting for a lightning strike.

No such scenes of misery could be found near Danforth Court or anywhere else, even in the slums. My life had never intersected with society's dregs. Our family was never Norman Rockwell–content with life or with one another, yet despite all the tears and tantrums, we never came close to the brink of patri-, matri-, or infanticide. And even with six kids to feed and succor, our parents managed to squeak by financially. So then why on God's green earth had I plunged my gifts into despair, sought out scenes of abject poverty, and then populated my entire netherworld with human flotsam comfortable in their rotting domain?

It seems that I wasn't entirely happy with the circumstances of my life and expressed my disaffection by declaring war on what I perceived to be the enemy. Drawing and writing were my weapons. The tragic truth was that my weapons couldn't change anything. Couldn't win this war within the family, nor out in the real world. But the purpose was in fact internal. I drew and wrote to vent my feelings, to explain to myself what was going on. The psychology of it is revealing: I was afraid to openly criticize Dad and Mother, from whom I believed all the unfairness, frustration, and evil flowed. So I disguised them, and my most urgent beefs, in a world so weirdly strange that neither they nor anybody else could detect my purpose. I felt at the time so unworthy, so powerless, and so low on life's totem pole that the slums and hopelessness, the failed lives I created, radiated from one source: me.

When I began my descent into defeat and depression in my early teens, I felt that we were six siblings without parents—even though our parents actually lived in the same apartment. Mother, upon whom all McCall siblings depended for food and a soft refuge, had begun drinking during her lonely nights in Simcoe; in Toronto she slipped from tipsy to slightly drunk to a state near stupefaction. The creepy sense of our mother living with us while we had no mother agonized us all. Dad ignored—or pretended to ignore—Mother's alcoholism. He never intervened. His weekends in Simcoe had been devoted to his selfish hobby, golf. He had all but rejected his paternal role long before the war, which supplied a plausible alibi to continue leaving Mother alone with their brood. She was a ghost. From ages three to eleven, when I felt I needed them most, I lacked the benefits of a mother and a father. This was a gap that was never closed.

Dad was too busy and too tired, when he was finally pinned down and cohabited with his offspring, to make quality time for his kids. Now and then after dinner we'd play catch in the alleyway beside our apartment block. And he often took two or three volunteers on Saturday-morning drives to the Liquor Control Board to pick up Molson's and Labatt's. Otherwise he was unavailable. Stingy as he was with his attentions to me, Dad seemed to actively dislike the twins, Tom and Walt, from the minute they were born. He was no baby kisser. Kids made him nervous. His—and Mother's—cold rejection of these two sweet-natured young boys was lifelong. Apparently the twins were being punished for existing, and this neglect amounted to child abuse.

The parental vacuum created a noxious side effect. Kids need attention, love, and a decent home—normality. We siblings never got these things. But every day in a desperate kid's life starts out hopefully. Every school day was another exercise in willed optimism. At the three o'clock dismissal I started for home, lifted by self-generated images of a fresh start. These foolish fantasies were exposed the instant I closed the door behind me. The bedroom door was shut. Mother was in bed, privately trying to will her hangover away. The apartment was as I had left it early that morning: dirty dishes in the sink, a peanut butter jar, an empty cardboard orange juice container, and other breakfast leftovers littered the kitchen table. The place was permeated by the stale funk of cigarette smoke from the night before. Moments of warmth, brief breaks in the clouds, now and then relieved the tension. But frustration, estrangement, and that chilling absence of affection made daily life miserable for most of us kids, most of the time. Neither Tom nor Walt ever spent a day alone with their father. Walt's 1950 Christmas gift to his mother was signed *Your Friend, Walter.* Tom wet the bed and stuttered. "He just wants attention," Dad sneered.

High school provided no relief. None of us succeeded in shucking off the gloom of life in that apartment enough to gain traction. All of us struggled with learning; studying demanded concentration, which we could muster only erratically. Outside of school, we all dwelled in perfect social emptiness. Hugh, Tom, Walt, and I had two or three friends apiece. (Mike was in the navy at this point; I steered clear of Chris's nascent romantic affairs.) None were girls. The idea of any of us ever dating a female person was a bizarre notion: none of us had the poise, the clothes, the confidence, the social skills. None of us could dance.

▪ ▪ ▪

Dinnertime. All eight McCalls are crammed around the kitchen table. The dull clack of working mandibles only emphasizes the tense silence. Dad reigns, too preoccupied with some grievance too private, too important, to share with strangers, i.e., his kids. And anyhow, the unwritten code forbids anyone asking what's ailing him. Dinner drags on and finally ends. A gust of relief emanates from the kitchen.

It was during this period, before high school, I started becoming an artist. I'd hurry from the dinner table to the bedroom desk to once again squeeze through the cracks in reality and try to fathom the confusion I felt. Drawing and writing were a kind of lens through which I could narrow my focus. What I was doing with pen and ink and paper had nothing to do with art. My creativity was too intimate to share. And nobody would understand what this continuous flow of seeming nonsense meant. I had adapted creativity as a survival therapy, not a calling. Nobody except an absolute narcissist could keep examining his own belly button and feel satisfied with the result. The early sprinklings of humor in my creative efforts did not represent aspirations to entertain a mob. They started out as an intensely private communion with myself, for mental comfort and to lessen the chronic fantods. The technique was not to use "humor" in a broad sense, like a network radio comedian, but to shave an idea down to a sharp point and stick it into my tormentor. Satire demonstrated an intellectual jujitsu, a way of bringing villains down with ridicule. And even if it couldn't topple the antagonist, the revenge felt deeply satisfying.

Lacking identifiable examples to emulate, my initial version of satire was crude, but that cast of mind affected almost everything I produced. It was a weapon the powerless could use to ridicule the overstuffed, the phony, the bully, the pretentious everybody and everything. Nothing was so invulnerable that it couldn't be mocked. Satire so suited my temperament and my emotional needs that it became a habit of mind—so much so that I began seeing my life and world through a satirical lens. My perspective skewed off to the side, oblique, slightly skeptical, somewhat jaundiced. Or maybe that trait had been in me always, and satire simply drew it out.

What can an unsophisticated thirteen-year-old know of the world? He works his way inside his targets like a termite, and once he's there, his close observation, guided by a mischievous intent, mocks what nobody noticed before. Close observation, indeed. The latent satirist sharpens his wits out of self-protection. He feels he's on a precarious perch. To him, survival depends on reading the tiniest clues to escape being ambushed.

Now, looting the archive, tracing ancient fragments of work from the era just before puberty, I've uncovered my first attempts to make satire not simply a flavor but the formal purpose of a piece. Wild exaggeration, excusable in a kid whose world is already arguably half made of stupendous lies, runs through this early work like a locomotive through a straw hut. It would take time to acquire the restraint and maturity to give up pounding points home with a rhetorical mallet, making triply sure that the joke wouldn't be missed.

Toronto only stubbornly released its charms. I sensed that there must be some differences between a town of six thousand and this mighty metropolis, but I was cautiously slow to experience them. Walking tours made sense: Toronto held the distinction of being Canada's largest city, and that surely guaranteed *something.* And on a gray Sunday morning in January, I wasn't drowning in things to do. Movies, plays, imbibing spirits in a public space, sports of most kinds—all were proscribed on Sundays by way of the Lord's Day Alliance, Toronto's self-appointed God cops, Protestant protectors of civic virtue.

Touring neighborhoods revealed only streets and houses, so Mike, Hugh, and I headed downtown. That's Maple Leaf Gardens; now we're in Queen's Park, home of the Ontario government; a few blocks north lay the Royal Ontario Museum and the University of Toronto. The city's main stem, Yonge Street, looked deserted, as if there'd just been a bomb threat; the Lord's Day zealots had made certain that Yonge Street's almost wholesome vulgarity was suspended every Sunday. Even in the commercial heart of the city, the paucity of fellow pedestrians suggested that all Torontonians were still in church, had been kidnapped by Roman Catholics, or had expired from boredom. Sunshine was illegal on Sundays.

It's not incidental to this story to note that although the McCall household was starved for parental love, the act of reading thrived, independent of our day-to-day relations. By age nine I was spewing words and sentences, symbolically twinning my two creative pursuits by drawing on the reverse side of a failed prose masterpiece, or writing on the reverse side of a drawing gone stale. All my meaningful reading occurred outside the classroom. Reading was the key, the one reliable means of understanding the world. And at this juncture it was a pleasure without consequences. I read not in order to get smarter than everybody else or to bone up on exotica. Living in that troubled home made reading ideal: it cost nothing, and it was selfish, shared with nobody. Whatever information or pleasure, whatever exciting boost it gave, was a gift to a solitary person: me. And amid the squabbling mob that six siblings could become simply by being in the same room at the same time, solitude was an escape.

Canadian culture mixes aspects of a British sensibility with the dominant presence of the United States. It's a form of hybridism that can affect reading, writing, and values—in my case, just enough to amuse the Americans and occasionally piss off the Brits. The British version of the English language permeated those years when, as with music closely heard, subtle differences alter the pace and rhythm. I'd love to go about drawling in that inimitable Mayfair accent, dripping with class. It's all bullshit, this use of accent and speed of delivery, but I don't care. It sounds the way every English English-speaker should speak.

It's a secret craving of mine. I owe it to the cache of British boys' weekly magazines stashed years ago at the back of a closet by Dad, bound into a volume as thick as a brick. An embossed cover depicted a bronco about to buck the cowpoke on its back into the next dimension. The magazine was *Chums*. The *Chums* I had excavated were dated 1922 and were natural fare for a thirteen-year-old kid. But why did Dad drag this oddity along when he and Mother changed homes many times before he laid it in that closet? It's another regret that I never got the chance to hear the *Chums* story. Perhaps it was his Rosebud. No other mementos or souvenirs from Dad's adolescence survive.

Devouring hundreds of *Chums* stories, which were devoid of the female gender, that year may have further postponed my sluggish sexual awakening. Maybe. But the weird genius of *Chums* was to so lather up the preadolescent in the noble pursuit of enemies and protection of the British Empire that girls and sex were irrelevant. Nary a slinky Oriental spy, nor a temptress from the Argentine, nor even a peaches-and-cream English Mata Hari could get into *Chums* with a Luger in each hand and Mills bombs in her trench-coat pockets. These lads had a more urgent mission: save Britannia. The Imperial High Noon was clouding up. The Great War just ended had killed seven hundred thousand Tommies. The exchequer was drained dry by the cost. A worldwide depression stalked the land.

Wherever the Union Jack was imperiled, whether in 1678 on the Spanish Main, or 1857 at Sevastopol, or 1916 on the Western Front, penny-a-page hacks devised tales of derring-do to fit any war by these volunteer upright young public school military geniuses: Reggie. Algernon. Roger. Plus, trailing behind, fat and permanently famished Tubby, the reliable dunce, good for a chuckle, while Napoleon's cannons lob fire and steel over their heads. These brave boys sallied forth to foil Evil, always in unstinting loyalty to King and Country. And, of course, playing the game the British Way.

The exploits of these precocious juniors ran a distant second to the real attraction: a prose style baked in Victorian formality, burnished with Kipling-quality touches—"That worthy, for his part" . . . "Twixt Law and Outlaw"—written for a reading experience chewier and more nourishing than the monosyllabic grunts that served as the dialogue in American comic books. Mimicry was a reflexive act in my youth, so it's hardly surprising that a preference for the literary high road seeped into my writing style, veering into fancy-pants verbiage that added nothing but length. Just before some more literate friend suggested that I knock it off, I knocked it off.

My art career developed slowly. (I should put it that my art career "cautiously advanced.") School offered tiny bites—a weekly class in the ninth grade, and later, a weekly fifty-five-minute spare period in an empty classroom, drawing anything I fancied, sans teacher. One teacher, Mr. McKenzie, had an imagination. For one project he challenged us to design a swatch of wallpaper for a modern living area. I dived in. The next class required a sample of the design and a brief sell. I stepped to the front of the room and faced the class.

"These are dangerous times," I mumbled, facing the floor. "Soviet Russia is threatening atomic war. I thought the wallpaper in a Russian home would look something like . . . *this!*" I hoisted my sample to show the class: raining down in a diagonal pattern against a flat, butter-yellow background were fat little red bombs bearing the Communist Party hammer-and-sickle insignia. Mister and Missus Red Russia, I surmised, supported the Kremlin's threat to annihilate the capitalist warmongers and honored it on their living room walls.

My exposition elicited silence, then some polite coughing interrupted by the bell signaling the end of the period. I figured it out on the walk home: these kids, my classmates, clearly didn't read the papers or listen to Edward R. Murrow's nightly radio newscast. Once more the world was out of step with me.

No other kid I knew, or knew on sight, had the drawing or writing bug in their system. They were consumers, and I produced. Art wasn't taught or talked about in public school. Once a month or so, Mrs. Coombs broke out sheets of poster stock, placed a dozen jars of poster paint on the table at the back of the room, and watched an Oklahoma land rush of kids racing to grab a jar of paint and start slathering. My fame as an artist was mild, but enough to attract attention. I'd drawn my usual Spitfires and piles of dead Nazis, but that wasn't what my clique wanted. "Draw Mickey Mouse!" "Naw, do Donald Duck!" "Or Donald Duck and Huey, Louie, and Dewey!"

When some crossed parental wires brought a well-meaning but totally wrong gift to me under the tree on Christmas 1950, I curbed the instinct to vent and pretended surprised gratitude. "You must have been reading my mind!" I lied. My gift was an oil-painting starter kit. To date I had painted exclusively in watercolors: simpler, cheaper, faster-drying than oils. But I refrained from bitching. I'd try the medium of Rembrandt.

My first—and last—venture into this new medium would be a cinch in any contest for World's Worst Oil Painting. A thick smearing of linseed oil all but obliterated the paint. I ignored the instruction book, which was clearly insulting to a master craftsman such as me. Compounding the missteps in the wrong order, I attempted a battle scene in the War of 1812; you could tell this by the red coats of the British army. I set the scene in a barnyard. The skirmish appeared to have been fought during a partial eclipse. Human figures of various height stand around, helpless victims of my troubles with perspective. Many more are sleeping or dead. So grudgingly is the oil paint applied that more canvas than paint is visible. I never did take to oils.

▪ ▪ ▪

Rainy Saturday afternoons sent me by streetcar on a straight line to the Royal Ontario Museum. I'd pull a wad of blank paper, a few HB pencils, and a gum eraser from various pockets and sit down to draw—mostly beasts from Africa, fantastically lifelike, posed in dioramas. (I admired those ingenious fakes that somehow defied reality by turning a cave-shaped space into a view of the Serengeti Plain receding to a horizon miles away.) The point of these drawings was the accuracy of line that drawing from life can instill. What I learned tended to go from my brain to my synapses to my fingertips. By the time I got home in the late afternoon, the three or four finished drawings were wrinkled and smudged and unceremoniously chucked. They had served their purpose.

In the spring of 1952, Hugh was stricken with appendicitis, rushed to the hospital, and consigned to bed to recover. McCalls weren't the flowers-and-candy type. My hand-delivered get-well card flirted with no cutesy sentimental mush. In fact, it had nothing remotely to do with Hugh's condition or his medical ordeal. Aviation—airplanes, and especially military airplanes—were mutual enthusiasms. My gift to Hugh was a small stack of bubblegum cards, sans the gum. I drew satirical flying idiocies—the Avro Churchmouse trainer, the hideous Blowmouth Gumby bomber powered by twin orange juice–cooled engines. (Looking back now, I realize that the planes constituted my first foray into the form that could be the shorthand for my "style.") On the card's reverse side I added a text description. I found that even a dry couple of paragraphs could be satirized. Hugh almost laughed his stitches out. Jeez, I wanted to entertain him, not kill him.

Our sister, Chris, age eight, spent a couple of weeks in the Sick Children's Hospital at about the same time. Her case was rheumatic fever, a childhood disease that came on quietly, then became alarming. Chris gamely tried to lift a spoon at the dinner table; she fumbled with it, and it clanked to the floor while the rest of us sat, fighting back tears. While she was in the hospital I made an effort to amuse her, avoiding dolls and other sickroom clichés. I drew and wrote a series of comic strips featuring a squat masked hero in a wrinkled crimson costume. He was Captain Puff. Explosions, fires, and train wrecks surrounded him. Captain Puff coughed into his hankie, muttered, "Hem-hem," and did nothing. Chris lapped it up.

Most of my creative effort in the middle Toronto years involved such jokes or satirical caricatures for a small group of friends. The research was my imagination. Every pencil drawing was crammed with idiotic detail, then inscribed on a sheet of typing paper with a fine-point crow quill pen. A light watercolor wash tinted the scene. An innovation I prized (because it was mine) was to place the drawing on a flat surface and run over it with a steam iron, locking in the colors, protecting the masterpiece from peanut butter and strawberry jam smears, and turning a sheet of cheap typing paper into a stiff parchment heirloom suitable for framing. This innovation, as with so many others, successful or not, arose from the continuous bedroom experiments conducted by Hugh and me.

▪ ▪ ▪

My prolific production of art slowed to a crawl—not because I'd lost interest, but because I had segued into an intense new phase. Drawing and painting took longer: I had fallen madly in love with detail. Detail for its own sake. The challenge of injecting everything visible into everything shown in an illustration became primary. I wasn't furnishing information so the picture would be crammed with detail that told the story. Rather, I'd sold myself the alibi that this obsession was propelled by the artist's solemn sense of duty. I thought it was the job of the artist to fill in all the details. Give the viewer not a mere suggestion, but a scene so complete that no interpretation was possible other than the one so painstakingly, exhaustively provided. There lurked a second consideration: there could be, should be, sufficient detail to allay a viewer's suspicion that this house, that airplane, and the car purporting to be a 1946 New York taxicab, weren't real. One careless mistake could smash the viewer's confidence. Therefore, the artist—at least, this artist—was honor-bound to capture absolute realism.

Pulling back from my intense concentration on getting every detail correct was a necessity. The need for an overview, a step back, to read the composition of the picture, to see how the individual elements worked together and balanced, was urgent. Alas for my obsession with photographic realism, that way lay madness. As a telephoto photograph flattens depth and perspective, my approach was to render the background as precisely as the foreground. But fine focus needed a break: a background was a background for a reason. It wasn't really necessary, for instance, to painstakingly trace individual treads on the tires of a car that was supposed to be a thousand feet away. I forgot the workings of the human eye. Learning to convey depth as seen by the eye—to separate foreground from deep background, overcoming my detail mania and letting my pictures breathe—was a process that would take years.

When the gum-eraser crumbs had been swept aside and the picture unpinned and lifted off the drawing board, a piece of art filled me with pleasure. Making art was not often a mellow experience.

Rage at my right hand and its five fingers' mulish refusal to guide the outline in my brain onto paper could probably be heard a block away, climaxing in hot tears and a howling vow to swear off art forever.

Forever recycling in my YouTube of memory is the anguish of trying, failing, trying and failing again, to capture the exact curves of the nose of the Douglas DC-3. Though I'd memorized it with blueprint exactitude in my mind's eye, my intent was then sloppily betrayed with shapes too curved, not curvy enough, too clumsily inept to accurately portray it.

Exposure to objective teaching might have telescoped my agonies into a few days instead of squandered weeks of DIY fumbling. I was educationally shortchanged. Perhaps a proper art education would have inspired worthier ambitions and produced a conventional artist who obeyed conventional rules. Perhaps. But what I achieved by teaching myself, ignoring the rules, working around the gaps, was a style. Eccentric, to be sure, but whatever my style could be called, it was unique. Entirely my own.

The autumn of 1948 brought a large envelope with a Simcoe postmark addressed to me. I had swept the Norfolk County agricultural fair's art show. Three large prize tickets were proof. Mostly I felt embarrassed. My prizewinners were a trio of weak umber watercolor tints over a lake in a dark forest. They went for the cheap trick of a canoe reflected in the water. The honor of winning wasn't diminished by the fact that the ag fair art contest was no revival of the 1913 New York Armory Show but mostly a titanic struggle to decide the finest swine in Norfolk County.

■ ■ ■

The family dynamic took a torpedo amidships in the summer of 1952. Big brother Mike was twenty-one and restless. He was studying to be a chef at Ryerson Institute of Technology in Toronto. The future failed to excite him. One afternoon he heard a navy recruitment radio commercial in the tiny bedroom he shared with Hugh and me. Within two weeks he was gone, now a midshipman. Mike would eventually become a pilot, landing on aircraft carriers and, in classic naval fashion, seeing the world.

His departure was less good for the siblings he left behind, knocking out the props that shored up our rickety relationships with Mother and Dad. As the eldest, closest to both parents because he was the firstborn and that novelty never faded, Mike had been our ambassador and advocate for the defense of us younger siblings. He had lubricated the hinge of the door between Them and Us. That task fell to Hugh and me, now seniormost among the young McCalls. We adjusted and did well enough, but things would never be the same.

Mike's absence left a hole in my way of life. I'd depended on him for a strong defense against Dad's occasional explosions generated by some idiotic and/or wrongheaded charge. Mike, being four years my senior, could be a sympathetic audience for grievances; an encyclopedia for answering questions and giving advice; a neutral arbiter of internecine disputes involving money and Monopoly. All sibling issues temporarily benched, Mike came closest to normality than anybody in the family. He was cheerful and witty. He must surely have sometimes chafed at his role as Big Brother, but Michael Scott Cameron was the one McCall everybody liked. I also admired him, and still do.

I had no candidate for a replacement Mike. Then, in my final high school year, I fell into the original Gang of Four within the school: me, Dave, Maurice, and Tony. We formed a loose group based on no mischievous pranks and no aggression. Dave smoked, he laughed at my humor, and he lived in a drab household. Dave was in an art class under false pretexts; he was almost spectacularly ungifted. But that didn't matter to me. He lived in a world more interesting than mine, and he knew his way around. I envied his cool gravitas; he seemed the kind who's seen it all, who's never surprised, maybe because he's learned to expect the worst. He kept to himself, a taciturn type who used words sparingly. Dave and I hung out on Danforth Avenue. We'd lock ourselves in conversation in the Gainsworth, a huge eat-o-drome where I wolfed down strawberry shortcake, or in a struggling little Greek greasy spoon. Spring came; growing restless, we got to Avenue Road, took the elevator of the Park Plaza Hotel to the top floor and the outdoor roof garden. This was, we'd heard somewhere, a favorite spot for young people to hang out and hook up. Maybe so, but as two high schoolers with nothing to say and too timid to initiate a conversation, we were in over our heads. We fell back on our specialty, sneering at these pretentious jerks, pretending to be enraptured by the view, and soon shuffling off.

■ ■ ■

Making some money and escaping the alternating drudgery and terror of life in our apartment furnished two powerful incentives to find summer employment. Pressure from Dad added urgency; he expected us to live like other teenagers, a view that was closer to an Archie comic book than to reality. I quickly realized that I wasn't cut out to be an adult: anxieties I'd been grooming since I first learned to worry rattled me. My lack of self-esteem turned the prospect of meeting strangers and bargaining for employment into a moment in the Spanish Inquisition; the would-be employer would know in an instant that I was a screwball loser.

Luckily, no opportunity to shame myself popped up. But Hugh and I did find lucrative summer employment after all. We applied for and were accepted into the Royal Canadian Air Force Reserve program for high school boys, a summerlong program. When we arrived, way past bedtime, at the Trenton air base, we were still vibrating from the bus ride with the small mob of fellow Reserve recruits. We'd been isolated from our age group when we arrived in Toronto. Now, in one fell swoop, we were plunged into a mayhem of barbarian tumult. These were our peers? Hugh and I cowered in our seats amid the noisy anarchy. I never mastered the language in which every verb was a sexual thrust, every noun a private female part. That five-hour bus ride was a sudden, merciless dunk in a living cross section of male Toronto teenagers. Witless, ill-equipped to interact with our fellow summer airmen, Hugh and I had no contributions to make to the evening's entertainment: filthy jokes racketed around, as did beloved old songs with obscene new lyrics. Swear words machine-gunned through the assembled. An unseen performer recited a poem of sex and misogyny and bestiality, while verbal cross fire from some other corner sang of killing Jews, lynching Negroes, and raping nuns. The hilarity depressed both of us. Homesickness tripped up both Hugh and me. We couldn't fathom why, but that sickly form of misery hung around for the first several days, until the clouds finally lifted.

The familiarization program, held at the Trenton air base, combined deep boredom (World War II–era films warning new inductees about social diseases and how penicillin could save your life) with genuine excitement (as in my first airplane flight: eight minutes circling the Trenton base at a low altitude in a battered old DC-3). In the end, Trenton gave me more than training. It was there that I met a couple of brothers who appeared to be as bemused as Hugh and me by the swamp level of civilization around us. Frank Levay and his brother, John, while not officially part of the Gang of Four, were a godsend: funny, fearless, the brainiest guys I'd ever met—and baseball fans more rabid even than I was starting to be. The pair lent much-needed polish to the Trenton experience, and we kept up a friendship for years afterward. Frank knew literature, had a skeptical view of modern life, and was a devout Roman Catholic whose religious dedication eventually gave him a career. I now realize that if not for Frank Levay, I could all too easily have slid down into the mire with the Snopeses of the RCAF Reserve.

▪ ▪ ▪

After two years in Toronto, I found that nothing in my life was better than it had been in Simcoe. Small wonder: Simcoe had expected nothing of me. No challenges, no unfamiliar feelings. Toronto threw everything at me, and my resources were shallow. I tried to thwart or duck most challenges, until I realized that I had been trying to live a Simcoe life in big, strange, uncomfortable Toronto. The minute I admitted this, I started to live where I actually lived.

Call it the Little Bang: since the day I discovered that my right hand could do more than scratch my ass and began drawing, my cozy little world suddenly became a universe. It started at five or six with crude airplanes and continued through adolescence. (So it's more a reverberation than a bang.) Drawing felt right. I drew and drew. Drawing expressed more than, say, farm animals.

Simcoe had as much to offer the young artist as it had flamenco dancers. What triggered my Little Bang can't be explained by genetics, environment, or neuroscience. Nothing in my childhood suggested a latent creative spark. Two siblings also drew, but without talent. Simcoe had as much to offer the young artist as it had to aspiring poets. Our parents, like all other Simconians, could be described as philistines. They neither handed down a love of art to their kids nor looked for signs of blazing talent. They wouldn't have much prized it if they'd found it.

So softly did this Little Bang go *bang!* that nobody heard it but me. It helped smother any vain ideas. McCall family doctrine, at least for us kids, dictated that you keep your mouth shut in triumph and suffer defeats in private.

The only humans I drew from the beginning were sad sacks, shysters, simpletons, bums, and unlovable orphaned boys. They lacked spirit; stuck in a stygian slum, hanging around tumbledown horsemeat shops, Greed's disgustingly dingy pool hall, Sid's Church (entry five cents), Floyd and Lannie's ptomaine-heavy bake shop, and Tunoblur Studios, home of films such as *Oh, That Mustard Gas!* and *Arnold in Madrid.*

I dreamed up these films, then invented a dyspeptic critic named Leeman Bonky to review them. His/my column, "See What I Mean?," mercilessly attacked Tunoblur's cheapskate rip-off style. He was more world-weary than angered by these stupid follies, yet kind to the morons and layabouts dragooned into "acting" in them for no money. These included Ancient Sid Malone, a sweet-natured rummy, and Rio Rita Jackson, the three-hundred-pound femme fatale. They and other cast members were drawn from the dregs of my imaginary slum city. I poured serious energy into Leeman Bonky's reviews. The screenplays made no sense. He loved wading through Bedlam-quality trash and confessed that he had abandoned any attempt to follow story lines. The impetus behind this weird little creative detour was my passion for B- and C-level Republic and Monogram pictures—usually westerns—that intrigued me because they were so awful compared with the output of the major studios. A stupid inspiration, admittedly. I invented Tunoblur, its movies and casts, then reviewed them so I could create posters and write hyperbolic self-praise for the shabby results, satirizing Hollywood's styles of the time.

The movies made a highly visible target. A similar satirical enthusiasm, running parallel to the movies, was baseball. I created teams and lineups, feeding in my rabid fandom for actual stumblebum big-league teams, focusing on the hapless St. Louis Browns and almost-as-hapless Washington Senators. I wrote game reports, profiled players, and illustrated them with drawings that imitated the crappy team photos of the times.

The focus of my ardor was the Sumach Browns—same uniforms as their St. Louis namesake. ("Sumach" was a place-name invented to set my fantasies in some identifiable location.) For reasons I can't quite fathom even now, a slummy Toronto neighborhood popularly known as Cabbagetown was transformed, in my version, into a permanently depressed and impoverished dump. My fond depiction had the advantage, for a fictional fantasy, of my having never set foot in Cabbagetown, thus freeing me to explore extremes of misery way beyond earthbound reality. Sumach Street—an actual thoroughfare—was chosen to be the epicenter, the real Sumach shoved down into a medieval-level hell. Sackville Street got a similar loving drubbing; their team, the Sackville Romans, I created specifically to let me use a familiar Roman fretwork pattern on their uniform sleeve trim.

I didn't bother inventing an equivalent to the American League for the Sumach Bowns to play in. My satirical zeal was satisfied by the Cabbagetown model. Silly names were too good a satirical subject to avoid. I did invent a few competing teams: the Chain City Gluemen, the New Huskard Barometerisers. I was flailing about and hoping to catch, and ridicule, actual organized-baseball team-naming styles.

The baseball part was enlivened (or burdened) by my awareness of postwar geopolitics. The Sumach Browns pioneered the signing of foreign players. Sensitive to these factors, I created Klein Nachburger, "the Hamburg Wheelhorse," the first German—and the first ex-Nazi—to pitch in a postwar North American game. I deposited Tang Onamuro, the first Japanese import, at shortstop. First base was occupied by Bruce McSunnyworth, a fictional version of myself and, naturally, a yappy incompetent.

A perennial Browns favorite was the ambidextrous pitcher Jasmun Chickerby, who lost thirty games throwing lefty and thirty games as a righty. He had last won a game in 1937, when the opposing team was disqualified for robbing the box office and the score was reversed. One must bear in mind that Jasmun was seventy-six years old in 1952 and had been the Browns' rubber-armed moundsman for forty-three years.

My movie and baseball activities were intensely personal and private. Maybe they were subliminal masturbatory fantasies or further examples of a thoroughly warped mind. In any case, it was vital to keep them secret. Not that anyone—not even the generally supportive Mike and Hugh—attempted to crash into my files, searching for movie and sports idiocies.

■ ■ ■

Scattershot inspiration began to feel insufficient after a thousand renderings of isolated events. My seedy tableaux, grotesque characters, and their unbroken record of failure after failure had about exhausted the genre. I tried enlarging the scope—e.g., the *Snider Lily*, a rusted hulk of a passenger vessel too broken-down ever to leave its berth. Not enough. Some overview was missing, some way of tying hundreds of disparate fragments together.

Now everything coalesced. I had been blundering in circles. I had been stringing together a narrative, but that narrative needed a setting and a protagonist. Thus was born the legend of Li'l Grubber. The name fits, with admirable aptness and clarity. Li'l Grubber was a little guy, and his life was grubbing—for food, for shelter, for survival. His backstory is blank; he simply appears in the Sumach setting one day and becomes a Robin Hood, leading a small band, the Tumblin' Rovers, on missions aimed at sticking it to the powers that be. Grubber is seen in his raw, early form, and he's shown as he's elevated to prosperity in the legitimate world. The inspiration for this mischievous, lovable hero was, of course, me. I created him as a surrogate for myself. My real self. Through his exploits, his pluck and bravery and unquenchable cheer, I gave myself the security, the pleasures, and the eminence I so ached for in real life and feared would remain forever beyond my reach.

I lavished my hours and days on chronicling Grubber's rise. His heartwarming apotheosis came not magically, overnight, but incrementally—a touch of realism. His circuitous route through Cabbagetown to the executive suite, from ballsy desperado to upper-middle-class dandy, was illustrated in a hundred drawings. Moving from gray pencil renderings of garbage-dump ambience to four-color magazine spreads erased sad times for both of us. I fitted out my diminutive alter ego in smart suits, posed him in front of his Tudor mansion, beside cars marking his ascent from a rusty 1940 Dodge to a gleaming new 1949 Nash Airflyte in his (well, actually, my) favorite two-tone brown-and-white paint scheme. Grubber's body and head matched his persona perfectly. The head and face were fixed with my first attempt and never needed to be changed. I didn't flatter myself that I had a gift for cartooning, but that simple physiognomy is still, in my opinion, one of the most successful drawings I've ever done.

Grubber and his life obsessed me for two years. So immersed

had I become in wish fulfillment that writing and drawing weren't enough to contain my enthusiasm: I worked up a low, croaking voice for him and ventriloquized stream-of-consciousness monologues from my bunk after lights-out to a captive, laughing audience of Mike and Hugh. Grubber was literally living in my head, somewhere between my brain, my eyes, and my vocal cords.

But after those intense two years, as I approached seventeen, I had to admit that the bromance with my sawed-off friend was about played out. I had brought Grubber from the slums to affluence and contentment; there was now no place to go. He had made it. As his real-life proxy, I felt as if I had, too.

Simultaneously living Grubber's life, tracing his upward climb from the depths to the heights, sweetened my existence in the sour real world. I had used his happy saga to buffer ugly reality. His presence—even if only in my head—gave me an optimism I doubt I could otherwise have sustained. He was, in no altogether imaginative way, a loyal friend. Li'l Grubber was so deeply, idiosyncratically, intimately bound up with my emotional life in that miserable period that I shirked from revealing his role. It seemed too embarrassing, too childlike, to share with the outside world. But I came to believe that withholding this episode and its positive effects on my creative life—on my life—would be so incomplete as to distort it.

And then came Punerania, a place that expanded my oeuvre to encompass not merely a crummy urban neighborhood but a whole nation. Once again the object of interest was a place no sane person would visit, much less reside in. I broke away from Cabbagetown and fashioned a fairy tale of despair. Punerania was depicted as a flat, wet nowhere, as stagnant and featureless as the East End of Toronto that inspired it. I relished this paradise of sloth. The Puneranians were a race of dumb, bulb-nosed runts wearing identical knitted toques, as passive as grass and unemployed to the last man.

Punerania was a hotbed of ennui. The populace stood around Bomsak, the muddy clearing called the capital, energized daily for a few minutes by alarms from the border: the dreaded Billywoshians were coming! Puneranians saw a vandal horde in what were actually hundreds of fuzzy powder-blue earmuffs spilled from a truck and windblown across the border toward Bomsak. The earmuffs/Billywoshians blew back and forth but never into Puneranian territory. Still the Puneranian army fled, escaping what they believed to be vandals bent on conquering their inert domain.

The Puneranian skies were either raining, just about to rain, or had just stopped raining. I worked to capture a late spring afternoon in Toronto: a faint violet, tinged with pale yellow. The puddled mudflats surrounding Bomsak stretched to the horizon at all points of the compass, littered with abandoned wrecks and crashed airplanes. Presiding over this do-nothing nation was do-nothing King Gus: torpid, meek, a dithering, indecisive cipher with nothing to do. His palace was a battered old house trailer, a busted wicker chair his throne.

Punerania was, of course, another romp in sublimated wishing. Barren and waterlogged, it stood for my experience of Toronto. Nothing happening transferred the tedium of Danforth Court to a neutral, in fact nonexistent, site. The Puneranians were stunted gnomes, unlike the thugs in school who bullied me. King Gus—you guessed it!—was Dad, redesigned to be harmless.

Punerania was short of females. All my work was. Women remained absent from my prepubescence, adolescence, juvenilia, and beyond. I wasn't a slow starter with the opposite sex, I was a nonstarter. The absolute lack of contact with females, plus an undersocialized home life and the conviction that my appeal was a laughable bad joke, kept me in trembling ignorance well past the normal evolution into maturity. I was a gutless sap, making do with hapless crushes on girls who wouldn't give me the time of day.

Spring of 1953 found a rejuvenated Bruce McCall. Maybe I'd found my stride. Maybe it was an aftershock from the Little Bang. Maybe the years of domestic wretchedness and the clammy taste of isolation would someday—sooner rather than later—do a U-turn and at least show me the first steps on the path to well-being. Maybe. Yet to feel so suddenly lifted out of the shadows and into the light—to sense everything shifting as easily as turning a page (wait a minute, cool down)—this couldn't be my life. And it couldn't be me, living it.

I had transferred to Danforth Tech (a slippery word for vocational school; it sounded less déclassé) in the fall of '52. My former school, Malvern Collegiate, with its excellent reputation and such alumni as Glenn Gould, Norman Jewison, and, later, Kiefer Sutherland, fit me like an iron maiden. I flopped scholastically, continued to go nowhere socially, and despised many of my classmates. Malvern's student body was full of kids from the affluent Balmy Beach neighborhood.

My fast-developing socialist sympathies were abraded by the crude snobbishness of certain female Balmy Beach classmates. One example still flits in memory like a bat. A girl from the wrong side of the tracks—I'll call her Dolly—wore cheap and ragged clothes. Lank hair hung off her head. She wasn't very nice. Before class one morning, noticing Dolly's unfashionable dress, the other girls lit into the poor thing. Teasing her, mocking her, mouthing nasty comments about every flaw they could find or invent, her tormentors kept up their barrage. Dolly fought back, forcing a smile, acting unbothered, until one insult too many broke her spirit and she collapsed in tears at her desk. Malvern supplied too many memories as painful as that.

As both an artist manqué and an aspiring writer, I had given up art at Malvern for a conventional academic education. A vocational school, Danforth Tech taught art classes, but its resources for an academic curriculum were slight. Wherever I went for my schooling, my education in art and my education in more intellectual pursuits couldn't both be served. When I began high school at age twelve, art beguiled me. But I failed ninth grade at Danforth Tech, and my art enthusiasm took a dive, so I transferred to Malvern to pursue the life of the mind. Three years of declining marks, the intellectual stimulation of a train schedule, and the resurfacing of my artistic interest reversed my course. Back to Danforth Tech.

Third time lucky. My art class at Danforth Tech irradiated my soul with the first firm sense of security since I'd left cozy Simcoe. I rushed to school every morning and lingered every afternoon. Life at last smiled. It wasn't even particularly annoying that half the curriculum of the art class was hilariously irrelevant to its ostensible goal of preparing students for commercial art careers. Heraldry. Stained glass. Leatherwork. Bas-relief sculpture. Commercial art must have been a very different trade back in the Victorian age, when Lewis Carroll or some other mystic designed that lunatic's holiday of a curriculum.

Within my first week in art class I'd made five or six friends, one of whom was a girl. Could my long and lonely period of friendlessness have been a simple matter of looking in the wrong places? Did this bounty mean that I'd been selling myself short, that I had never been the hangdog loser, devoid of personality and charm, who trailed through his life, unaware of a fulfilling destiny patiently waiting for him to finally discover it?

I was too engaged with my exciting new life to brood about what it meant. Admittedly, competition for artistic merit here fell short of beaux arts caliber. Perhaps half a dozen students had serious ambition; most of the rest showed no visible talent or interest. Pleasant and chummy as my classmates were, few had a sense of a calling. They'd enrolled in the art class only because it seemed an easy route through high school and was a way to kill time until the Voice in the Sky told them what they really ought to do with their lives. I'd call these skimmers of art dilettantes, but that describes someone light in the brainbox and easily distracted by novelty. My classmates took their assignments seriously. They toiled conscientiously. It didn't seem to rankle them that they weren't any good.

April wasn't girlfriend material, her life ruled by one of those off-brand religions that bans fun and wouldn't know joy if it drove up in a Cadillac and dropped a bag of money on the porch. But April offered something I needed more than God: a warm, sympathetic, mature female presence. A motherly figure, in brief. Maurice was my one serious rival for top dog, not only in his skill but in a passion for art that was unique in a high school student. It should be no surprise that Maurice would become a master of Canadian nature painting, much of it devoted to Arctic scenes.

It became clear by Christmas that Maurice and I were the two class members with fire in our bellies. My hundreds of hours spent drawing had given my hand a sensitivity that derives from constant practice.

I realized that my strange upbringing and the training gained from it put me far ahead of the class in sheer drawing skill. This had been my first opportunity to gauge my talent against the world—albeit a comically unthreatening world. I knew I'd be tested eventually by serious contenders, and that was no discouragement. Confirmation that I was actually above average at something that really mattered to me sparked a tingling sensation. Confidence, after eighteen years without it, can work wonders.

The end of my renaissance came swiftly and without warning.

The evening of March 23, 1953, began promisingly. I had arranged the first date of my life. The female, a redheaded classmate named Betty, was neither pretty nor fun to talk to. I hadn't stirred her, either. A romance could break out, but Betty was as lukewarm as I was. Neither of us would admit it, but our date was practice, a dry run. Still, it seemed a useful experience.

Dressed in the nearest thing to a not-entirely-clownish outfit I could scrounge from the bedroom closet, I garbed myself in a red corduroy smoking jacket discarded by Mike. My powder-blue gabardine trousers had hung so long on the hanger that a vivid horizontal crease and the standard vertical creases fought for supremacy. The horizontal crease won. My oxblood loafers were my favorite—and only—pair of shoes.

Betty lived in a small house on a pleasant little street with her mom, a freelance illustrator. We met up about halfway between her house and Danforth Court, a distance of perhaps a mile. Woodbine Avenue was our chosen route; a hill led us down half a mile or so until we'd hit the bright lights of Kingston Road. I mumbled something about our maybe getting a coffee (though I'd never sipped a cup of it, and wouldn't for eight more years). Betty was agreeable, but Kingston Road had closed for the night. Staring into shop windows, marveling at displays of plumbing supplies and kiddie clothes and a barber pole perpetually twirling, fascinated me, while Betty waited on the sidewalk. I had no ideas, so I suggested heading back up Woodbine, where Betty could turn off to walk the couple of blocks home. She hastily agreed. Had I valued her company more and foreseen a romance, I might have been offended, but we shook hands and went our separate ways. Relief flooded my heart. It had been a nothing outing, sure, but it wasn't the disaster it could have been.

I got home by nine. Mother wasn't tipsy. She was ironing clothes in the kitchen while Foster Hewitt on the radio called the playoff game between the Leafs and Bruins. The phone rang. Mother picked up; it was Dad. He was on a business trip and probably checking in for the night. I wandered into the living room. Then, hearing Mother put down the receiver, I sauntered back to the kitchen.

"What's new with Dad?" I asked, feigning interest.

Mother had already turned back to her ironing. She paused a moment. "Dad's taken a job at Chrysler," she said. "We're moving to Windsor in June."

Driving the Amphicar: It handled like a car in the water and a boat on the road.

Chapter 3

Chronicles of Wasted Time

The British man of letters Malcolm Muggeridge titled his autobiography *Chronicles of Wasted Time.* I succumbed to the temptation to swipe it for this chapter title.

I arrived in the industrial Ontario city of Windsor as an adolescent and left as an adult. Of the roughly 2,500 days I spent there, a couple of hundred felt good. I'd resisted moving to Windsor, where I proceeded to drop out of high school and squandered the next six and a half years in a futile attempt to achieve competence as a commercial artist. Within a span of fewer than two years of each other, both of my parents died. Nothing positive ever came from living in Windsor. I had to leave and start my life over again from scratch.

Moving to Windsor was never a choice. I was forced to accompany my family when we moved there from Toronto in June 1953. My dad had taken a new job, as Chrysler of Canada's director of public relations. I'd desperately wanted to remain in Toronto and continue in high school, then go on to an art career. No dice, Dad ruled. Like it or not, Windsor was now home.

Boy, did I not like it. I saw no upside to moving from big-city Toronto to a factory town where the only art we knew was the mayor, Art Reaume. I'd excelled in my high school art class; as I interpreted it, leaving Toronto for Windsor was akin to being demoted from the St. Louis Cardinals to the Class-A High Point–Thomasville HiToms. My idea of boarding somewhere and staying in Toronto never had a chance. Dad was no loosey-goosey liberal. What I proposed was unconventional. In his musty book, "unconventional" meant communism, free love, and drunk driving.

Our new home beat our hideously cramped Danforth Court apartment, by dint of its being a house with a basement. There was the smell of fresh paint, there were new hardwood parquet floors, new kitchen appliances, and the up-to-date 1903 convenience of a little pass-through cubby where the milkman left our daily orders until the refrigerator could be invented.

Our house sat cheek by jowl in a semicircle of virtually identical little homes. A development recently bulldozed out of empty fields, it was an artificial neighborhood. In 1953, as in Danforth Court, my parents were a generation older than the young veterans just starting out who surrounded us. So babies and tots constituted ninety-nine percent of the kids, and I found no contemporaries. No traffic, human or otherwise, stirred here, in a daylong silence that gave me the creeps. Sitting on the front steps of our house over long summer afternoons in a vain attempt to make contact with human life, I lived smack in the center of the world's first outdoor sensory-deprivation chamber.

On the brink of our move to Windsor, I attempted to find a reason to hope for some positivity to emerge from an otherwise unpromising new environment. Desperation conjured the idea that a change of circumstances, new surroundings, new experiences, new friends, would miraculously smash the dreariness of our domestic life. Perhaps the move would jolt new energies, transforming our lives—and Mother's. That hope was immediately dashed. Nothing changed. Mother stayed loyal to her own separate life. Alcohol was her friend, the only friend she needed. And she didn't want or need to share. The emotional letdown of living with a mother who declined to be a mother killed my hope. Meanwhile, Dad's role remained distant. He continued to almost belligerently maintain his hands-off relationship with us. Mike was the cherished firstborn, and Chris, as the last-born and a daughter, suffered Dad's brusqueness less than the rest of us.

The McCall family's economic situation had been precarious for years. Dad's income rose by a healthy increment with the move to Windsor, but there was still no money to replace our moth-eaten furniture, or to buy changes of outfits for Tom and Walt, or for vacations. We kids weren't materially coddled. Somehow we clung to the belief that the McCalls had something that lifted us above mere money: a pedigree. Dribs and drabs of miscellaneous lore, and the impulse to mythologize, bolstered the case. Our ancestry harked back to noble Highland Scots—a book, *The Scottish Clans and Their Tartans*, placed us in the powerful MacDonald clan. We kids got, or manufactured, the impression that our name ranked us among the quality. McCalls had their own tartan and escutcheon.

In reality, that book flattered virtually every Scots-related name, pioneering the fake-ancestry industry. Ninety-nine-point-nine percent of our claim to eminence was pure lowland bullshit, including the tartan and the escutcheon. But Dad and Mother did stand out ancestrally somewhat from most of their Simcoe forebears.

■ ■ ■

On my father's side of the family, the Scottish emigrant and family patriarch, Donald McCall, loyal to George III and a veteran of British army skirmishes before 1776, had been brutally ousted from his Philadelphia home by a Yankee mob at the Revolutionary War's end. He and a band of fellow refugees fetched up in British Nova Scotia. Awarded land grants in Upper Canada for their service to the king, Donald and a small party sailed from Nova Scotia and landed on the northern shore of Lake Erie. There they founded the Long Point Settlement (later Simcoe), more Scottish than bagpipes and haggis and Robbie Burns, and put down stakes not pulled up for a century and a half, when in 1947 Dad moved everyone and everything a hundred miles away to Toronto.

Patriotism distinguished my forebears, even if great fortune was elusive. McCalls helped fight the Americans in the War of 1812. Fears of an American invasion kept Canadians living near the U.S. border jittery for decades: out of that hostility came the United Empire Loyalists, a mildly paranoid body of superpatriots, a sort of male-led counterpart to the Daughters of the American Revolution. A McCall was a boatman on the River Nile when General Kitchener headed an army en route to Khartoum to avenge the murder of General Charles "Chinese" Gordon. Grandfather Walt, father of my father, volunteered in 1900 for the Canadian Army contingent supporting Great Britain in the Boer War. (Just like Winston Churchill, he was captured.) Perhaps the gaudiest patriotic gesture of any McCall came from my father. Dad was thirty when Britain declared war on Germany. Too old for combat duty, he waived the exemptions available to him as a family man and sole breadwinner, and pestered bureaucrat friends in Ottawa until they relented. He was forthwith commissioned as a pilot officer in the

Royal Canadian Air Force. His role would be that of a press liaison officer, writing propaganda for the home front and representing the air force as a PR man with various public events, including the filming and world premiere of morale-boosting Hollywood movie *Captains of the Clouds.* In 1943 he shipped overseas to join the Canadian Sixth Bomber Group, based in Yorkshire, where he wrote stories about air crews for home consumption. As time passed it became harder to bear the repeated tragedies of bright young men he had just interviewed taking off on bombing raids and never coming back, not to mention the passing of Chris Bartlett. Dad suffered a nervous collapse and by May 1944 was back home.

My sympathy is still muted. The father of five kids (soon to be six) ages three to ten left his wife alone in Simcoe to raise us on a financial shoestring, with no help in running a demanding daily workload, stuck in a lonely existence in a one-horse town. In the diary he kept during his RCAF period, Squadron Leader Thomas Cameron McCall frequently fulminates about the war and its horrors, his screeds rising to patriotic heights. He somehow never wrestles with the most profound issue of all: how he arrived at the decision to march off to war, in a job almost anyone could perform, knowing that he had left his wife and family to fend for themselves. It was Mother who had the worse war.

That first unbearably empty month in Windsor was ninety-eight percent content-free. Guilty about never having used my summers off from school to earn a little money, I found work in a shabby little side-street car wash. I was handed a hank of thin cloth and joined a gang of surly derelicts hosing down cars as they jerked along the line. The constant flow of freezing-cold water turned my hands red and numb. When the endless day was finally over I pocketed two dollars, enough to cover the cost of the bus ride home. I would end my summer's employment with as much money as I'd begun it. The ennobling experience of work—at least this work—proved degrading. That evening I plotted to end my durance vile in Windsor. The next day I borrowed twenty dollars from Mother, left a deftly unapologetic note to Dad, and beat it via Greyhound back to Toronto.

Six weeks of giddy independence awaited me. My friend Dave got me an usher's job in a run-down neighborhood fleabag of a movie theater, the Allenby, that was stuck in a time warp: its marquee still proclaimed "Dish Nite every Wed.," as it had since the Great Depression. The mixed aroma of stale popcorn and body odor clung to my skin for months, but I loved the Allenby. Twenty repeated viewings made me so familiar with the film *High Noon* that I could describe it, cut by cut, for years afterward. And I hung out with Dave, soaking up the joys of independence in the big city.

It was, of course, too good to last. I dreaded the oncoming Labor Day. In late August, Dad phoned to summon me home. My plea to be allowed to stay in Toronto was halfhearted, if only because I knew I couldn't convince Dad to let me stay. Perhaps he felt I was enjoying myself too much.

Nothing had changed in my six-week absence. The household was still wreathed in a miasma of gloom. Dad snored away in his frequent naps on the living room chesterfield* after lunch and after work every weekday. We kids shamed the Last Mohican as we silently moved across the minefield that was the living room without waking him. By six in the evening, Mother was wobbling

* Many otherwise intelligent Americans believe that "sofa" is the correct word to describe a chesterfield. They are wrong. "Chesterfield" is the correct word to describe a sofa.

half-drunk around the kitchen preparing dinner. Every evening I expected servings of gastronomic horror to land on the table, but perhaps some stubborn pride inspired her: amazingly, she surprised me every time.

Meanwhile, upstairs in our claustrophobic bedroom under precipitously slanting eaves, with space only for a tiny desk wedged between two single beds, Hugh and I transported ourselves to less troubled places. Books, drawing, and model-making, the time-honored pursuits of the isolated powerless, and tuning in to CBC Radio, supported the plunge into escape. Upstairs at 1793 Byng Road was a safe zone. Mother never visited. Dad rarely intruded, but whenever we heard his heavy tread on the stairs, Hugh and I knew we could expect no fun. His motives were invariably matters of gloomy necessity: to wearily explain that our monthly boarding payments were in arrears or that his recent—and sincere—memo "suggesting" that we chip in to buy a new TV for Grandfather Walt hadn't drawn contributions from either of us. In-person chats, however, were rare. His usual method of contact consisted of frosty memos, crisply typed, carbon copies left on our beds to be found when we got home from work.

Evenings downstairs presented the specter of Mother drunk and Dad evidently unaware of it. Certain television shows—Sid Caesar, Jackie Gleason, and Jack Benny—drew the whole family into the living room. This brief respite from censure and tension doubled the siblings' pleasure and left us wondering why it couldn't always be like this. The answer was that even attempting to raise the tragic issue of Mother's alcoholism, routinely ignored while the family spirit deteriorated, would have collided with Dad's edict that anything "serious" wasn't serious unless he judged it so. Either through self-delusion or cowardice—it would have ruined his life if he'd faced reality—he didn't treat Mother's problem as a matter of urgency. Any attempt to even hint at trouble would only have stiffened his policy of blunting bad news. Dad won. He never did talk about it, even after she was gone.

Back in Windsor and resigned to my dismal fate, I set out on the day after Labor Day to enroll myself in W. D. Lowe Vocational School. That sunny September day would deliver two interlocking dramas. Had I known what lay in store, I'd have stayed in bed; my fate was about to be sealed for years. I entered Lowe, a grim stone Tudor fortress in the style favored by school architects in every Canadian town, and sought out the guidance counselor. There would be paperwork and the usual formalities of transferring from one city's school system to another. I explained my case and handed him my academic history, plus my last report card. He sat there at his desk and I could tell that he didn't know whether to laugh or cry.

He finally spoke. "Lowe Vocational doesn't have an art class," he said. My heart sank. If I'd stopped to think, I'd have realized that the likelihood of an art class in that gritty little city was as realistic as finding a Rolls-Royce dealership in Coboconk. He continued. "Your high school record is . . . quite amazing. If you're allowed to enroll here, your only choice will be a grade-eleven commercial class," meaning I'd be primed for the life of a bank clerk. This represented another backward tumble into a den of scholastic lepers, the same limbo that had entrapped me years before, at Malvern Collegiate in Toronto. No thanks.

By lunchtime I had trudged back home, burning with humiliated indignation. I had been an A student in Simcoe, I had entered my high school life avid to learn, expecting success. Avid to learn, yet it had all gone miserably wrong. I encountered a late-Victorian educational system populated by bored, tired, half-there teachers. School wasn't the core reason, though: I was awash in the domestic turmoil of our household, guts churning with anxiety, a depressive genie on my shoulder, my self-regard in the dumpster. And no sign of hope. Cranked through the high school grinder, I was judged to be a dunce. Education's summary verdict: Bruce McCall, age eighteen, is hereby officially classified as a dolt and should not be allowed to waste his teachers' time for another school year. Out he goes. Period.

Back at home I braced myself for the ritual harangue. Dad was there, having driven from his Chrysler office a mile away for lunch and a short nap. He was by now inured to my chronic underachievement and had clearly lost any faint hope that my losing streak would be snapped. I had failed again—and this time the defeat would force a new life plan. I deserved his contempt. Excuses? Even I couldn't blame anyone but myself. I tried to suppress my anxiety at having to confess that my shot at formal education had just been euthanized. I had earned Dad's ill will by upstaging him one time too many, expressing views contrary to his. And, to be candid, by being an irreverent pain in the ass. I girded myself and sputtered a quick one-liner that derived from wisdom I didn't know was there until the words came out. I hadn't failed high school, I trumpeted. High school had failed me.

"That's rotten," Dad said, his voice relaxed, his demeanor calm. "Looks like you'll be needing a job. Why don't you call a fellow, Rudy, who runs a studio downtown. They're looking for an apprentice." Then, having discharged his paternal duty to guide his ne'er-do-well son toward gainful employment, he crushed the butt of another Lucky Strike and descended to napland. *What a guy*, I should have said. What I did say—to myself—was a baffled *What the hell was that?*

It was a flabbergasting moment. Dad's emotional temperament was a miracle of explosiveness, all the scarier for its unpredictability. Item: One day, Tambo, the family cat, leaped up with obvious hungry intent to the kitchen table where sat the Thanksgiving turkey. Dad happened to be nearby. His hysterical reaction registered a three out of ten on my mental Dad Dudgeon Meter. Item: One weekday afternoon a few months later, the entire family except for Dad clustered around the TV to watch Walt, invited as a guest on a local kids' afternoon show, display a dozen of the more than fifty scale-model fire engines he had built—accurate to the tiniest detail—without plans, using cardboard, shoelaces, and whatever household scraps he could find. Dad arrived home in the middle of the show, and one glance at the screen propelled him to the gates of apoplexy. Furious, he bolted out of the house, banging the door behind him, therewith scoring a record eleven out of a possible ten on the Dad Dudgeon Meter.

Walter had evidently committed some vile transgression, but he didn't know what it was. Dad's rage at what the rest of the family and the TV audience found praiseworthy still baffles me. Walt returned home to a reception better suited for a child molester than for a kid prodigy. With his father's lifelong blend of indifference and contempt ratcheted up a notch or two, he banished himself to the safety of the fetid little bedroom he shared with twin brother Tom, secure in the belief that neither parent would show enough interest to intrude.

Dad's venom failed to deter Walt, who thereafter toiled in secret, like a Stalag Luft prisoner forging a passport. He clandestinely built a hundred more fire trucks (they were secreted under his bed) until he'd exhausted vintages and types to model. Walt loved fire trucks the way other fourteen-year-olds loved Davy Crockett. He would ultimately write several books of fire engine history and lore, universal go-to references today. He also edits the official newsletter of the fire buffs of America. Walt's enthusiasm peaked, in 1971, when he bought his own fire engine: a 1927 Bickle-Seagrave pumper. He was driving the big red beast around town one day when the carburetor started belching fire. Quick-thinking Walter rolled his flaming Bickle-Seagrave into the nearest fire station (he knew the location of every fire hall in the county) to have the blaze extinguished.

▪ ▪ ▪

Pick up any magazine of the 1940s and '50s and you'll be seduced by lavish four-color ads. Ad budgets were ballooning, and commercial art and editorial illustration were on a roll. In Pompeii in AD 79 nobody noticed the ominous signs on the horizon until disaster struck, and so it was with commercial art. Television was a beast that was increasingly hoovering up the available advertising dollars.

In 1953, commercial illustration was ripe fruit ready to fall on another front, and on this one, all the money, all the talent in the world, couldn't prevail. American life in the postwar era was in upheaval. New ideas, new directions were changing the mainstream. The energy that had gone to war came back; established entities collapsed under the unstoppable surge of the new. The war had sobered popular taste, and sophistication was edging out fantasy. Commercial art was about to be undone by the very artificiality that had flourished in the previous age. Because a skeptical postwar world wanted fresh means of expression, the commercial illustrator would soon be shunted aside, his heretofore valuable skills now disparaged as corny, old-fashioned and, in the pejorative sense, unbelievable.

Windsor Advertising Artists was a small studio serving a single client, Chrysler of Canada, by handling Dodge and DeSoto advertising. Across the street, the Greenhow & Webster studio did likewise for the Chrysler and Plymouth brands. One key difference was that WAA delivered competent illustrations. The Dodge-DeSoto advertising agency, Ross Roy Inc., was located across the river in

Detroit; the only aspect of advertising it didn't handle was the artwork. This arrangement miffed both entities. Ross Roy people saw WAA as the undeserving beneficiaries of a political scheme: How could these hosers dare compare themselves with America's best automobile illustrators, a few blocks away in midtown Detroit? Windsor Advertising Artists reciprocated the disdain: taking orders from know-it-all Yanks was humiliating. This strange arrangement was Canadian politics, writ awkwardly. It was meant to showcase Chrysler of Canada's patriotism, allaying Canada Firsters' gripes that this nominally Canadian enterprise was the timid handmaiden of its giant American parent. Which, together with Canadian Ford and General Motors of Canada, it certainly was.

Switch the drawing boards for desks and Windsor Advertising Artists would be a modest insurance brokerage. (Although no insurance brokerage needed a back-room air compressor chugging all day to power the illustrators' airbrushes.) Radios droned in every artist's workspace. The pungent reek of benzine and rubber cement perfumed the atmosphere and probably corroded lungs, though six and a half years spent sitting five feet away from those benzine fumes did no physical damage to me.

Dad suggested I contact Rudy Suzana, who ran WAA. I slapped a portfolio together, raced downtown to the modest-size studio in a modest two-story building at the modest intersection of Pelissier Street and University Avenue. A dark, unmanned reception area finally disgorged the studio co-owner, senior illustrator, and boss. Rudy was swarthy, taciturn, and solemn. He didn't exactly invite intimacy; in fact, our relationship was no warmer on my last day in the studio than on my first. This was a major reason why the studio atmosphere never got relaxed or chummy.

Rudy's scan of my portfolio was cursory. I don't think he gave much of a damn about my talent or potential. He needed an apprentice who would earn his keep by running errands and performing humble tasks. One day, if I was diligent and patient, I would ascend to the brotherhood of commercial automobile artists. I was hired, for $39 a week.

I unreservedly admired Rudy's illustrative skill. He robotically generated immaculate painting after painting, neatly avoiding the flashy and the ordinary. He found, or devised, ways to caress the eye and excite the imagination: an extra tone of gold on a yellow car that would otherwise look gaudy. My deepest insight about Rudy came much later, and it explained why he mastered the craft, and the secret of success, for both commercial art studios and commercial illustrators. And why I could never succeed in the field. Rudy practiced art without being an artist. His was the perfect example of that approach. No other art form interested him. The richest artistic rewards—pride, satisfaction, a sense of achievement, the joy of creativity—were of zero interest to him. He didn't have to set aside his artistic nature because he didn't have one. Rudy was distanced from any emotional connection with his work, which liberated him from anxiety, second-guessing, and self-doubt. I envied this bastard relative of mental discipline, but not enough to emulate it.

That first month as part of the workforce propelled me into a whole new life. Learning a trade and finding my footing stimulated my senses. I'd expanded my understanding of the workings of the adult world. I busied myself assembling the tools every commercial artist needed. Little jars of gouache paint, differentiated from watercolor by its opacity. Sable brushes, expensive but necessary professional equipment that kept a point, didn't get as stiff as a broom after a few uses, and wore out slowly. Pencils. Erasers. Metal rulers. French curves. And an airbrush, the indispensable secret of rendering smooth, slippery automobiles.

Airbrushes were expensive. I made do with various hand-me-downs. I never met an airbrush I didn't loathe. That diabolical steel tube sucked its air supply from a hose that was connected to a compressor. The airbrush could spray large areas, such as the body of the car, or details—the highlighted curve of windshield glass or the tiny, sparkling sunbursts of highlights on chrome trim. The premixed body color was fed into the airbrush via a thimble-size metal cup on the side. Inside the tube, a fine steel needle sprayed a mixture of paint and air onto the illustration board where the drawing of the car awaited. In skilled hands the airbrush created a delicious illusion of paint so slick, so liquid-smooth, that fish could swim in it. In my hands the paint–water mix never worked. Either too much paint clogged the needle like mud, turning the intended light spray into a hiccup of spurts and blots, or too little paint and too much air created a pale, watery slick. My airbrush learning curve was a straight horizontal line. In the hours I spent disassembling that diabolical contraption—reaming out the tube and scraping incrustations of paint off the needle, trying hundreds of mixtures and failing to make the magic happen—I could have learned Urdu and Tagalog. Or graduated summa cum laude from the local taxidermy academy. Instead I sat there cursing the stupid, recalcitrant piece of shit.

I had felt out of place in this world at the outset, and that sense of apartness never changed. Most commercial artists I knew had brains and lively minds but were disinclined to exercise them. I don't think my fellow artists had ever read a book for pleasure. Books and reading had been baked into me early, growing into a habit and dictating a value system. I was no intellectual, but my natural interests skewed toward the life of the mind. Braggadocio wasn't justified—not by my embarrassing academic underperformance, capped by dropping out of high school. I stood awkwardly somewhere on the scale between very smart and very stupid. Which one was dependent on my environment of the moment. Reading was a big part of who I was. Without a constant intake, I'd starve. I never bonded with my studio workmates, but that was on me, not them, and I was too insecure to draw invidious comparisons. I simply aspired to ideas beyond "Hey, look at the tits on that one!" and "How's about those fuckin' Tigers, huh?"

Fantasy played a hefty role in my youthful thinking. It's no surprise that I had naively hoped Windsor Advertising Artists would be not only a workplace but also a refuge from the ongoing domestic psychodrama of the McCall household. I soon saw exposed an internecine strife that was a miniature version of what I had at home. Rudy's partner, Wilf Chauvin, was the gregarious client-contact man and handled the business side—most of the time from the cocktail lounge of the Norton Palmer Hotel down the block. The easygoing, soft-spoken, and reliably-plastered-by-dinnertime Wilf and no-nonsense Rudy were a match made in Bedlam. Meanwhile, the garishly talented, hotheaded second illustrator, Dick Miller, felt unappreciated and underpaid, and was both. Dick had been blessed with next-to-genius-level creative instincts, possibly a divine gift to offset a Snopesian upbringing on the wronger side of the wrong side of the tracks.

My instincts were creative: false starts, repeated failures, a messy way of working, all necessary parts of a process of discovery, the route to originality. Commercial art had no place for that process. Reliance on creative inspiration and its uncertainties was dangerous. In order to expend as little time as possible on a job, and thus to earn a profit and meet unyielding client deadlines, Rudy understood that painting almost anything—if properly approached—could be reduced from an ostensibly creative act to a series of specific steps. Without any grand plan, without conscious effort, he turned painting a car for advertising into a strict formula that made sound business sense. Rudy's rules were his personal code. He never called it a formula, but a formula it was. He figured out how to save time: a basic tenet was *Avoid creative innovation.* Having no other point of reference, total ignorance of this mysterious craft, and all of two weeks' commercial art experience, I naively embraced the formula, blissfully unaware that it was switching me onto a track that took me ever farther away from where my brains and proclivities wanted to go.

It wasn't a conscious rebellion against the prevailing Stalinist orthodoxy so much as a burst of my natural whimsy when, a couple of months in, I painted, obediently formulaic in every detail, a Studebaker Champion—except for its rectangular wheels and tires. Then, a follow-up jape: the sacred Rolls-Royce radiator shell fronting a Buick Roadmaster. Rudy happened by, spotted these idiocies on my drawing board, and withdrew without a laugh, smile, or even a comment. I've since reflected on that incident. I believe it cooked my goose with Rudy, there and then: smart-ass kid, his reverence for the mission of glorifying Dodge Royal Lancers and DeSoto Firedomes dubious, his open playfulness an ill omen, his future as a Car Man unpromising.

A few years ago I acquired a 1954 Buick sales brochure, my personal Rosebud, to deliberately induce a *nostalgie de la boue* reverie. Leafing through its pages brought on that wallowing masochism even more intensely than I'd expected. In my second week of apprenticeship, there being no school to teach and test my skills, I had followed Rudy's dictum: learn how to become an automobile illustrator by copying other car ads. After copying enough of them, I'd have absorbed gut truths. I'd meet tough standards. I'd eventually compound lessons from all my efforts to create my very own style. I chose a Buick brochure that featured every 1954 model. It looked so simple at first: duplicate that printed Buick. Trace the illustration line for line, with excruciating care. First, paint the tires and wheel wells lampblack, to establish contrast. Mix the perfect color match of the body and roof. Begin airbrushing the body, working light to dark. Paint in illusions of depth, reflections, and bright sunlight on the body. Then dote on every grille bar and door handle and glistening highlight. Capture the look and the feeling of power, the smoothness of those flanks. I captured zilch. Late in the day, I carried two or three Buick renderings to the garbage can.

That brochure, I later conjectured, must have been an early example—perhaps the first—illustrated by Fitz and Van, the brand name of Art Fitzpatrick and Van Kaufman, who would polish their craft and reign over the automobile illustration culture of the sixties with their impossibly flash Pontiac ads. Their Catalinas and Bonnevilles set the realism of dimensions aside. They resembled aircraft carriers on wheels. A Pontiac was described as "Wide-Track" in ad copy, which granted license to stretch the car's width to parodic extremes. Fitz and Van's Pontiacs didn't belong in the real world. Neither did their settings: ritzy European city squares, fantasy Mediterranean yacht clubs, big-shot conferences in some Potemkin village in France. The final touch consisted of the people admiring the Pontiac (always parked just so). Grace Kelly's double at the wheel. A brigade of George Hamiltons in tennis whites or golfing outfits, cracking clean jokes: Pontiacs weren't driven by yahoos.

My attempts to hang out in Fitz and Van Land fell short. An HB pencil fuzzed lines and ensured grille bars that were mangled and of various sizes. Oval tires here, rhomboidal tires there. The airbrush I wielded spat uneven blurts of color. Dote as I might, the juicy details required of an authentic Buick read as crooked, misshapen, dulled-down experiments. I hid my hideous renderings from prying—i.e., professional—eyes.

If I could have afforded to be honest with myself, the saga of the Buick brochure would have suggested that I try some other line of endeavor, move on to something—anything—less fraught. I was afraid to admit defeat. Also, in a postadolescent fever dream, I had drunk the Kool-Aid: my fluky advent at Windsor Advertising Artists—an ogre of a father tossing off a clue that led to a job in an art studio that same day—was the work of kismet, and you don't cross kismet. So, I felt, there I should remain. My decision was sealed by the belief that I was a wretch, fit for no other job, anywhere. *So bear down harder,* I counseled myself. *You were ordained by fate to be a commercial artist. Where was it written that work in the adult world was supposed to be fun?*

I consigned my instincts to a mental steamer trunk, buried it deep in my psyche under a pile of other failures, and halfheartedly persevered. Sealing my fate was the absence of a mentor, a critic, a relative, or a friend—anyone aware of my potential and honest or simply concerned enough to blow the whistle. Rudy seldom stopped by to evaluate my progress (and frankly, avoiding that downbeat critic was a strategy on my part). Rudy wouldn't care about my agonies. I was the messenger/errand boy/studio dogsbody. That job description fit his needs.

Meanwhile, Dick had finally made good on his threats and bolted across the border to hit the jackpot in a big Detroit studio. His replacement was Bill Windsor, as earnest and sweet-natured as Dick was rambunctious. Bill had labored at the semi-medieval practice of hand-lettering Johnnie Walker and Canadian Club labels. He had never drawn or painted a car, but six months and a stomach ulcer later, he was ready. Rudy then hired Louie, an amiable dolt of about my age. Within the year he was churning out professional-grade illustrations. I added another humiliation to my résumé. Louie soon left Windsor and its Advertising Artists for greener pastures. What did that amiable dolt have that I lacked? Good question!

The two people who might have offered advice—Rudy and my father—had no advice, no comment: Rudy because at $39 a week he could afford a dogsbody and couldn't care less whether I ever made the grade; my father because he seemed incurious about my personal crises. His sole concern was that I never shame myself or him with joblessness, which was a crime, a curse, worse than mere professional failure. His absolutism helped keep me shackled to the drawing board, trying to ignore the acrid taste of bile inching up my throat and lodging in my craw.

▪ ▪ ▪

Creating a new piece of artwork began across the river at the ad agency. A sketch artist drew a tight rendering of every ad or brochure page—the model and color of the car, the angle of its positioning in one idealized situation or another, the even more idealized people inside the car beaming out at the world or standing nearby, beaming in. No single illustrator was deemed versatile enough to paint an entire ad. The final art combined the individual skills of a car man, a background man, and a figure man. Their various contributions were cut out and glued in place on the car illustration, forming a single image.

Talent wasn't necessary to slice up a black-and-white photo of the car featured in the illustration, but nerve was. Stretching its length, width, and ground clearance demanded brutal surgery. It required keen judgment to decide where the eye could accept cheating and where rampant distortion was revealed. The camera doesn't lie, but those freakishly elongated, low-riding beasts were whoppers beyond the capacity of the widest wide-angle lens. It would eventually confound me that the Chrysler engineers who vetted every illustration—checking for the correct number of horizontal grille bars, pointing out deviations in intricate upholstery patterns—never quibbled with the grotesque deformations of the car.

The original photo of the car was cut into pieces, distorting its actual length, width, and height off the road with extra spacing, and then this assemblage was scotch-taped into an image bearing a passing resemblance to the photo. This was placed on a primitive magnifying device, the Lacey Lucy, cranked up to an image twice or three times its size, and traced on a transparent sheet of paper on a big glass screen. This was the master drawing, set down on a clean sheet of illustration board. The aim was near-blueprint clarity. A surgical exactitude obtained; the artist who rendered it was flying blind. He had to trust the accuracy of that drawing.

This marked the semifinal step before painting. A sheet of condom-thin, transparent frisket film was laid over the drawing. One side was slathered with a mixture of rubber cement and benzine thinner that quickly dried into a sticky glaze. The sheet was turned sticky-side down and smoothed over the drawing. (No bubbles or wrinkles could mar the glassy surface; if they did, someone—inevitably me—would be charged with tearing away the defective sheet and starting all over again.) A scalpel-sharp X-Acto blade was used to cut out and strip away all areas of the car's body to be airbrushed. The frisket paper masked the grille and all non-body-color parts until airbrushing was finished. The frisket paper was then lifted off and painting could begin.

There were stringent rules about the color spectrum. For example, the artist wasted no time deciding how to render chromed bumpers, grilles, or wheel covers.

For skyward-facing chrome it had to be cerulean blue. Earth-facing chrome—bumper undersides and concave hubcap areas—

reflected the road in yellow ochre. The horizon line separating the sky and road was always a thin line of lampblack. Wheel wells and tires were also black and were painted early to establish maximum contrast with the raw white of everything else.

The face of every car was its grille, conveying power and authority and a fifties idea of costly elegance. This often meant bullet-shaped bumper guards big enough to bunt a locomotive into the weeds, tucked under a gaping, chrome-framed mouth stuffed with horizontal bars, patterned mesh, fake heraldry, and other fancies, all sufficient to frighten Liberace.

▪ ▪ ▪

Windsor was where I learned to smoke, drive a car, and unhook a brassiere. It amazes me today to realize that these feats all occurred outside the studio. The studio devoured my time to an extent normally experienced only by lifers in San Quentin. Half of every weekend was often spent, or misspent, in the studio. Then came catalog season, a siege of nonstop labor stretching from early June through mid-September. It was assumed that my weekends belonged to the studio. Of the sixty-six weekends over six summers at Windsor Advertising Artists, I managed to be elsewhere only six or seven Saturdays and Sundays.

The workload was crushing: page after page after page of illustrations, principally cars but also virtually every detail of every model. From instrument panels, to close-ups of push-button automatic transmissions, to rear-seat views, to open trunks, to V-8 engines, to Milady's dainty gloved hand twirling the power-assisted steering wheel and her shoe tapping the brake pedal, it amounted to far more work than the studio could handle. Rudy brought in seasoned Detroit freelancers to manage the overflow. He was even forced to use me. I painted Milady's shoe gently pressing on a brake pedal. Next I rendered the face panel of the PowerFlite automatic push-button transmission.

I wasn't trusted to depict all-new Highway Hi-Fi, a 45 rpm extra-cost option to be trundled out of the glove box to play musical numbers—very briefly, given the inability of the 45 rpm player to play for longer than ninety-six seconds. Alas, bumpy roads and smooth music couldn't coexist. A year later, Highway Hi-Fi no longer existed. Likewise what we called the swing-away seat, swiveling outward on the front passenger side for graceful exits. That extra-cost option exited before the next model year. The push-button transmission was a novelty for novelty's sake, a superficial innovation meant to help differentiate Chrysler from its better-selling GM and Ford competitors. Pushing buttons contributed zilch to gear-shifting efficiency and captured zero praise and feeble attention. Chrysler Corporation's product planners were twenty years late with the drama of the push-button concept: by the mid-fifties it was as all-new as a 1937 Buck Rogers comic book.

Why I lived this shallow, meaningless existence and allowed this farrago to drag along, summer after summer, and went uncomplainingly along with it, is the single saddest legacy of my stunted commercial art career. Those long, long, empty summers cost me a normal, active, healthy life. It wasn't as if I were contributing valuable effort to the cause: I reported to work not because my presence was needed but because I was afraid not to. Many a July Saturday and August Sunday, there was next to no reason for me to languish in my cubicle.

But to have preferred lollygagging outdoors would have offended Rudy. He gave up his summers without complaint. His example shamed me into guilty panic. The only way to assuage it was to demonstrate my enthusiasm and loyalty by never going AWOL. I was grateful to make a few extra bucks of overtime every week. Rudy, after Wilf Chauvin had been keelhauled and was gone, was now the studio's key artist and also sole owner of Windsor Advertising Artists. He must have cleared hundreds of thousands of dollars' worth of extra income from our grueling catalog seasons.

■ ■ ■

A burst of candlepower suddenly exploded over the gray Windsor skies in the fall of 1956 when I met the first real friend in the emotionally barren life that started when we left Toronto. CBE was the Windsor outpost of the Canadian Broadcasting Corporation. I was a dedicated listener. There was one deep-voiced CBE announcer who studded an otherwise humdrum morning program of light classical music with irreverent, non-CBC fare: witty asides, jokes, cultural rants balanced by personal enthusiasms, recordings of Noël Coward, folk singers out of the mainstream, such as Jean Ritchie and Pete Seeger, and uncommercial international artists. He often read passages from highbrow authors. Host Alex Pavlini expressed a worldview that jibed with my own taste.

My satirical talents were marshaled to create a fictitious CBE "Listener Guide," lampooning CBC Radio's dowdy, sobersided, elitist programming. I concocted new iterations of existing programs. One example should suffice to lend a sense of this idiotic exercise: Alan Hamel (later famed as Mr. Suzanne Somers) would do a remote broadcast from the Windsor jail, interviewing convicted criminals in their cells. Hard-luck tales, tearful confessions, random death threats—all parts of a rare mix of news, weather, time checks, and terror. I titled it *Hamel & Yeggs*.

I mailed my handiwork c/o Alex Pavlini, CBE Windsor. A phone call two days later introduced that deep-voiced personality in the flesh, so to say. I overcame my shyness—and the fear that something hilarious to its author was a bag of shit to adult sensibilities—and agreed to meet. Alex was shorter than me, and better groomed. He didn't converse; he declaimed in a stentorian baritone. He was pompous by nature, ambitious for a CBC job in Toronto, and as self-absorbed as an Italian tenor. I paid these deficits scant attention. Our first exchange in our first get-together was a spontaneous survey of each other's idols and villains, in literature, movies, music, and anything else that meant something important to us.

That checklist more than implied a mutual affinity. It ended up in soul-mate territory. The two of us shared an uncanny similarity in taste, attitude, and worldviews. Alex was the son of Hungarian immigrants with blue-collar values and almost no English who sealed themselves off from their adopted country. From that unworldly background Alex created the persona of an erudite, confident man-about-town. As was said of the gossip columnist Walter Winchell, he could strut sitting down. Alex felt guilty, I surmised, for betraying his parents' values. Long after he'd established his own gaudy lifestyle, he still slept at home. His mother did his laundry and ironing.

It was by unspoken mutual agreement that I was never invited into his modest family home. Poor Alex, like so many second-generation kids of ethnic immigrant background, constantly balanced loyalty to his family and the culture they wouldn't abandon with a fierce ambition to fit into cosmopolitan life. Yet he evinced pride in his Hungarian roots. Once, when I gently ribbed him about the superiority of my Scots ancestry, he reared back and in that stentorian voice declaimed, "Hungarians were composing symphonies when your ancestors were painting their asses blue!"

We spent many a late night discussing the profound issues of the day. The emerging folk goddess Joan Baez, Alex insisted, was a phony: backstage during one of her Detroit concerts, he had discovered that she was no barefoot child of nature because the labels on her clothes were from Saks Fifth Avenue. Once, we got deeply into it: I'd just watched on TV as Billy Graham exhorted thousands of followers in one of his well-publicized Crusades. I'd come away shaken. The fiery reverend made sense. The debate that followed this disclosure was heated, furious, and fervent. Having God on my side eventually failed to nail the pro-Christian argument. My budding romance with religion was snuffed out.

Our nocturnal debates were mostly held in a lane of the Big Boy fast-food drive-thru. For our daytime dining we favored Cindy's, a strange, usually empty, latter-day Miss Havisham's parlor on Walker Road, a riot of execrable bad taste festooned with fake flowers, framed photos of dead movie stars, Manitoba and New Brunswick license plates, and other, unidentifiable gewgaws. We suppressed our giggles. It would have been cruel condescension to chat with cook, waitress, cashier, and proud proprietor Cindy.

Alex's nightlife (I lacked one) centered around the small bar in a fairly modern little hotel on the main drag. I'd order a rye and ginger ale and sit there assuming a sophisticated air. I soon mothballed my man-of-the-world pose. Even had I pulled the impersonation off, the question nagged: Was I supposed to be a habitué of a brothel in Cairo? Could be. An Argentine stud farm? Maybe. But why would a man of the world be hanging out in a tacky little bar in a small Canadian city?

We'd roam Essex County in Alex's comfy old Mercury on winter Sunday afternoons, pausing at the shore of Lake Erie to watch angry gray waves pound the rocks along the banks. Alex never missed a photo op. He drafted my brother Hugh to deploy his Rolleicord reflex camera to shoot him prancing on the rocks and capture Alex the Great staring at the horizon, looking profound. Afterward we'd drive to nearby Kingsville and the Diana Sweets Restaurant. Alcohol was for adults; I preferred sugary treats. I'd order a pastry puff stuffed with vanilla ice cream and drenched in chocolate sauce, and would fall on it like an Eskimo wolfing down a slab of warm blubber.

Alex bought himself a neat little motorboat, taking our fun to the Detroit River. Hubris damn near tripped him—and me—up. On a humid August evening we ventured out to the middle of Lake St. Clair. It was a long haul back to the Canadian side. Of course, in minutes the sky turned purple, the wind was rising, and the storm raged. Half an hour later, a half hour that felt like half a century, a motorboat nonchalantly docked at Windsor and its nonchalant crew stumbled ashore.

▪ ▪ ▪

A young man in his twenties, with all limbs intact and no criminal record, shouldn't want for foolish pleasures and the headlong pursuit of fun. I was keenly aware of my inability to find out how this was done. Before Alex's advent, my husk of a life revolved around the studio. I feared spare time because it was a blank. There were too many days and weeks and months to fill without at least trying to make all that time count for something, ideally something related in some way to art.

So it was that I enrolled in the Famous Artists School. It was the late fifties, and magazine illustration had been my inspiration all my life. The school advertisement had me instantly wrapped up and sold. It was a photographic take on *The Last Supper*: sitting there, relaxed and genial, were—as the school's name promised—the twelve most famous illustrators in America, my personal heroes, assembled to signal their personal recommendation of their eponymous school. I felt morally obliged to enroll.

Norman Rockwell, Robert Fawcett, Peter Helck, Austin Briggs, Albert Dorne, Fred Ludekens, Stevan Dohanos, Jon Whitcomb, and a few other stars had joined forces to pass on their secrets of success to eager acolytes with $350 to invest. My artistic dreams were revived overnight. The illustrators who had bewitched me as a kid were reaching out to help me realize that original dream. A fat three-ring binder packed with diagrams, photos, and texts soon arrived in the mail. I was on my way!

Well, actually, no, I wasn't. Illustration proved as effective a correspondence exercise as learning to drive by mail. The steady critical presence of a human teacher guiding your progress turned out not to be that of Norman Rockwell or another famous artist but a faceless "instructor," qualifications unlisted, who occupied a cubicle at the school's headquarters in Westport, Connecticut. I'd submit my monthly assignment and in a couple of weeks would get comments scrawled on a tissue overlay on my drawing. My first assignment was to draw a pastoral landscape, a farm with a large barn in the foreground. Grooming the next Rockwell, my instructor pointed out that barn doors open outward, not inward. Noted. Thanks!

It finally dawned on me that there was no way these guys could have a hands-on role in a correspondence course, that Norman and his elite fellow illustrators had traded their names for a share of the school's profits, and that this—plus that group photograph—was the extent of their involvement. Eager hopefuls who sent their steep enrollment fees to the Famous Artists School could have saved a bundle by enrolling in one of those matchbook-cover "Draw Me!" contests. I felt cheated and dropped out.

■ ■ ■

My youth ended abruptly one Sunday night in November 1957. I was upstairs in my room, working on a Famous Artists School lesson. Mother was sitting with Dad in the living room. Suddenly, something changed. I heard a different kind of background noise and clambered downstairs. Dad was gently walking Mother around and around. She was doubled over in pain. Dad was in command. I returned to my room and ran through every medical problem I'd heard of. An ambulance appeared and whisked Mother away. Dad was beside her.

He stayed at the hospital all night. It was a different father, a different man, who rounded up the four of us (Mike was by then in the navy and so was Tom) for a briefing. Mother had suffered a ruptured aorta. Her chances of survival were slim. He had been informed that a doctor, a specialist in such cases, was flying to Windsor to examine Mother.

Dad would lose most of his life if he lost his wife of twenty-seven years. This kind of thing happened to others, not to him. He had left it to Mother to raise their brood and made cameo appearances with Hugh, Tom, Walt, and me when the mood struck him. He knew little about our lives and showed no interest in any of us. Six kids and a wife who needed him, but for more than twenty years he had contrived to live like a bachelor.

Hugh and I visited Mother in the hospital that afternoon for ten minutes and found her relaxed and funny. We drove away in brightened spirits and went to bed that night relieved.

We woke the next morning to find that she had died in the night. Once again Dad assembled us in the living room. His voice broke. He was a defeated man. He had never thought about family structure. He didn't know that concern for Mother was the glue that had held everything together. With her death the whole rotten, dystopian structure that had masqueraded as a family finally collapsed. Helen Margaret (Peg) McCall was forty-nine.

The service, held in Simcoe in a funeral home by the Dickensian name of Marvyn Veale, was brief. A last look at Mother in her casket, then the slow parade to Oakwood Cemetery. The place was crowded with dead McCalls, but this was my first interment. The devastation reached its peak—or its nadir—when the casket slowly sank into the ground. My clearest memory of that awful afternoon was watching our stoic fourteen-year-old sister, Chris, standing straight-backed next to her father as sleet, wind, and rain took turns whipping through the bare black branches.

Aside from feeding us and handling our laundry, Mother did absolutely nothing for her kids. By the time of her death she had given up even pretending interest in Tom and Walter, and evinced only a grudging degree more in Hugh and me. Her withdrawal kept us from even touching her or her touching any of us except Chris, and Chris wasn't exactly swallowed up in maternal love. Yet the instinct of us all was to protect her. No words, no events, no overt affection linked us. We needed no psychiatrist to know the cruel, sad, hopeless life Mother had lived. She was intensely private. She suffered silently. She was small and thin and delicate. She'd gone completely gray at forty.

She lived most of those years loyally ensuring Dad's comfort. Meanwhile, she was condemned to live an empty life: A victim of her husband's arrogant self-centeredness. Of her Gilbertson family's almost genetic passivity, letting her absorb the pain and never fight back. Of circumstance. Of the age she lived in, consigning bright women to the margins where life lacked challenge. Of a berserk disregard of birth control that burdened her with six kids, a family she didn't want and couldn't handle. Of a husband too thick to understand her and who cheated his kids of a father for nearly a decade by spending the workweek a hundred miles away in Toronto, then joining the RCAF.

Much of my affection for her was more like sympathy. Even when she sat night after night alone in the living room, too drunk to read or talk, I hated her condition but not her. She had slid down and down until alcohol became her one dependable friend, her only means of escape from unbearable reality. She was gentle and soft-spoken, and subversively witty. Her common sense balanced many of Dad's impulsive notions. Whenever someone blows cigarette smoke my way, I see Mother in her living room armchair, a cat in her lap and a *New Yorker* in her hands, wisps of blue smoke from her Player's Navy Cut cigarette curling around her head. Nostalgic perfume.

The mourning lingered, seemingly without an end. But eventually the dark fog lifted. Everything I saw, everywhere I went, and everything I thought ceased being a stabbing reminder of Mother. I was finally ready to slip back into quotidian life. I was twenty-two.

■ ■ ■

Six months later Diane came into my life. Or, to be accurate, I came into hers. She moved with her parents into a mirror image of our place, the house directly across the street. A young girl was briefly visible looking after shrubs in front of the house. She was tall, thin, and from what I could discern from across the way through her veil of long brown hair, good looking. That was enough for me. One May evening I saw her doing something outside and strolled over to introduce myself. She was prettier than I'd surmised, healthy looking, well groomed, and friendly. She was twenty-one and a doctor's assistant. I was hooked.

Her mother was a sweet soul, her life dedicated to cleaning up the messes created by her scapegrace husband, Milt, a cheerful near idiot who did whatever he wanted, paying nothing for his childish irresponsibility. Diane's older sister had briefly married a man who turned out to be a homosexual, suffered a nervous breakdown, quit her menial office job, and at age thirty-four withdrew from the outside world by barricading herself in a back room. She watched TV all day and all night, grew bloated, and regressed to a state of petulant childishness.

Physical attraction is always needed to sustain a love affair, but for Diane and me, our mutually shitty family plights provided an extra bond. Each of us found in the other a relief from domestic strife and worry. Physically we were a pair of magnets. We had both craved intimacy and warmth, natural affection without tension, for most of our adolescent lives. In this, we McCall kids labored under a handicap. All our lives our parents had refused to express love to their offspring. In the absence of any gesture of intimacy, of the knowledge that you're loved, powerful forces boil and stew. Mine needed only Diane to surface and explode.

My lifelong dread of physical intimacy evaporated. Maybe a firm handshake wasn't the closest possible expression of affection. Every night the whole summer long, in my car in the driveway behind her family's house, the passion I had buried was uncorked. I wandered home to bed at dawn. I should have been exhausted, day after day, by my lack of sleep. I was energized instead.

In late June I took Diane to a suburban Detroit touring production of a forgettable English romantic comedy, *The Little Hut.* Neither of us had ever seen a professional theatrical production. We left that theater a couple of cosmopolites, Noël Coward and Gertrude Lawrence fresh from the opening night of *Private Lives* on the Great White Way. Food tasted better. Music sounded sweeter and fuller. A life with love in it was incalculably richer. I was no better off at the

Windsor Advertising Artists studio, but now I felt armored. The job receded into a distant second place in my world. Yet another catalog blitz arrived, and it rolled off my back.

By late 1958 Alex had ceded his dominant position—or, to be candid, I had demoted him in favor of spending time with Diane. Alex didn't take it well. I hadn't bothered to notice that the two most important figures in my life were at odds until he went on the attack. He insisted that Diane wasn't smart enough for me. She would become a bore and a drag over time. She hadn't read anything, had nothing to say about anything. He hammered away mercilessly—not just because of the rupture in our relationship, he said, but because, moonstruck as I was, I had failed to grasp the importance of common interests, the real pleasures of a true match of equals. If I didn't wise up to that simple truth, a bleak future awaited me.

My defenses were puny and my susceptibility to Alex's worldly experience went deep. I started judging Diane by his strict standards. Alex was right, I secretly concluded. She was happy to be the dependent member of our relationship, without ambition, lacking intellectual curiosity. I could learn nothing from her.

I broke the news to Diane one November night: We should cool it off. See other people. I wanted—needed—more mental stimulation than she knew how to provide. Diane was shattered. She'd never warmed up to Alex: he was cold, self-centered, his life devoted to his vanity. She withdrew into herself. We met a few times in the next few weeks by accident. She was drawn, depressed, and still didn't understand the abrupt cutting of the link between us. She was the injured party. I was the injurer. Our idyll had crashed, and it was my doing. Bitterness replaced a placid innocence in her life.

When I was home I didn't dare look across the street at Diane's house. Inside ours, it was clear that Dad had abandoned every interest he'd had. His beloved stamp album sat on the coffee table unopened. Unwashed dishes clogged the sink. Golf at the Beach Grove Country Club no longer filled his weekends. It was as if his electricity had been cut off.

Hugh and I had had no practice at reaching out to lend support and comfort and companionship. The shoe was now on the other foot. Our bitterness dribbled out: Dad had never made the effort to know us. He was content that his superficial understanding—of Hugh, Tom, Walter, and me—sufficed. I experienced more than a frisson of near pleasure now that relations were reversed. His regime had backfired and lay in pieces. (Including myself as a piece.)

A few years earlier Dad had hired Don Tucker, a friend from his RCAF days, as his PR second-in-command. Don, his English wife, Madeleine, and Tom and Peg McCall had become an inseparable social foursome. I was fascinated by Don's wartime career as an RCAF navigator over Europe. Madeleine was a cheerful, maternal soul. The Tuckers became pseudo parents to Hugh and me. We spent dozens of evenings dining and shooting the shit with them at their suburban home. After-dinner conversations soon swelled into harangues by Hugh and me. Dad was so damned unpredictable. A bully. A tyrant who made our lives intolerable. I blabbed myself hoarse, but nothing was achieved. Why Don and Madeleine put up with two overheated knuckleheads, I never understood. They never got sucked into bad-mouthing the villain, but that was okay. We didn't need an ally. Just someone to listen.

Then, not long after Mother's death, the Tuckers were no longer mentioned in our house. A short time later Don quit Chrysler, moved from Windsor back to Toronto, and joined the Ford PR department. Perhaps Dad's brooding following Mother's demise made working with him too demanding. I never found out what ruined that friendship. I never asked.

Dad's grief was total. Alas, he hadn't the foggiest idea of how to connect with the only people who might have helped him cope. Hugh and I felt bad but not guilty. In the natural way of fledglings leaving the nest, we judged it was time to remove ourselves from 1793 Byng Road and the man who had left us out of his life. Let him suffer what we'd suffered. We moved into a crummy apartment on the upper floor of a house a mile away on Chilver Road. Dad affected resignation, but he was heartbroken. We left him alone and overpowered by pain, in the lowest moment of his life. What amazes me in retrospect is how little guilt I harbored. It was not my finest hour.

▪ ▪ ▪

Catalog season came around again in June. The changes that had been brewing for years walloped Windsor Advertising Artists in a single blow: no painted illustrations would be used in the 1960 catalogs. Instead, we got a batch of dye transfers—chemically treated studio photographs of the new models—to be lightly retouched. The tasks were so simple that Rudy gave me a good share of the work. Retouching involves no complex processes; the entire studio workload left my evenings and weekends free. By the beginning of August, catalog season was over.

▪ ▪ ▪

Dad drove to Toronto in August with Chris en route to a two-week vacation at Mont-Tremblant, a deluxe resort north of Montreal. They dined with Dad's good friend Wendell and his wife on Saturday evening, then checked into the Benvenuto hotel. After assuring Chris that he would sleep on his side so his snoring wouldn't keep her awake, he instantly fell into a deep sleep, as was his habit. Shortly thereafter Chris heard a change in his breathing and saw him jerk into a sitting position and then fall back, his breathing ragged. Chris shook his shoulder, half-afraid of his ire if she were to wake him needlessly, but there was no response. She paced the room, tried to rouse him again, and then called the front desk for help. A night clerk arrived and told her to dress and pack, then took her to the lobby while they awaited the arrival of a doctor. The verdict was death by a massive heart attack. The clerk called Wendell, who took on the melancholy task of making the immediate arrangements. He drove Chris to his home and the next morning put her on a plane back to Windsor.

Back on Chilver Road, the ringing phone next to my bed woke me. It was three thirty a.m. In the instant before I picked up the receiver, I sensed that someone must have died; no other reason justified a call at that hour. I braced myself, mentally vetting candidates. Wendell's news blindsided me. How could a figure so dominant be taken away in an instant? Shock waves continued to rock me for days afterward. Dad's passing reverberated through everything. It changed everything. For Chris, for Hugh, for me. For the six of us.

Again, the funeral was in Simcoe. Dad was interred next to Mother on a hot, sunny August afternoon. The grief that cascaded down on me and my siblings was intertwined with guilt. Mingled with those black feelings was an undeniable sense of relief. The overwhelming force of Dad's presence had pinned us down. Now restraint after restraint snapped open. Charged for so long by Dad's aura, the Byng Road household tensions vanished. The place was neutralized. Now it was just a set of rooms. Life itself suddenly felt freer.

■ ■ ■

It all made me think of my father's own father, Walter Sydney McCall, who was something of a rogue in his younger days, when he had often strayed far from home in pursuit of betting of various kinds, including the Texas cockfighting circuit. Grandfather Walt, born in 1887, entertained no dreams of worldly success. His total lack of ambition and his chronic irresponsibility caused hardships for his wife, his daughter, and his son. Dad felt sympathy for his mother, for many of the same reasons in the next generation I felt it for mine. A gregarious storyteller brimming with anecdotes, Walt spun fascinating tales that enraptured Hugh and me.

They failed to enrapture Dad. His cool reaction to our excited reports on Grandfather Walt's autobiographical snippets was puzzling, until I'd matured enough to dope it out: Dad found these adventures infuriating. While Walt was larking about, his wife, stuck at home, paid the price for his childish shenanigans. His absence sabotaged family life. Nothing could be certain. Walt left his wife and kids to go off adventuring. Dad seemed to me to be curiously aloof from his father in their later years. This biographical story shared a truth so sad, so simple, so familiar, it belongs in the realm of cliché: like father, like son.

■ ■ ■

Dad's sister, Margaret, was an energetic socialist early in her life. She would eventually become secretary of the provincial Co-operative Commonwealth Federation, the CCF, a left-wing political party (known by nonmembers as the Convention of Crazy Farmers). On her rare visits to our home, a nervous restraint prevailed. By ten p.m., the way my bedroom floor reverberated told me that all restraint was off: brother and sister—as was inevitable—had got into politics. Aunt Margaret savaged the very foundation of Dad's beliefs. Dad saw communism in her fuzzy-minded liberal crap. His ideological anger could have powered Howard Hughes's monster "Spruce Goose" flying boat around the world sixteen times. Without stopping.

Any effort to classify Tom C. McCall involves questions, mysteries, and deep frustration. He keeps hopping in and out of categories. His honesty, his appetite for hard work, and a well-furnished mind made him a valued executive. He dropped out of high school at age eighteen, worked his way through newspaper reporting, and went to Queen's Park, the seat of Ontario's provincial government, ending up as a senior functionary, Deputy Minister of Travel and Publicity. He won photography prizes, was a catcher in semipro baseball and a badminton tournament winner.

This same man was an emotional isolationist. He hated Germans and despised Frenchmen, Italians, Eastern Europeans, Spaniards, Arabs—all foreigners, in fact, except Jews. He was sour on the British, a legacy of his wartime stint in England. He saw a Colonel Blimp in every Brit officer, dismissing the lot as a bunch of condescending snobs. He wasn't exactly crazy about Americans, either. This otherwise broad-minded sophisticate held a stubborn contempt for virtually everything European, an attitude unsullied by knowledge. Example: I once came close to disinheritance for the crime of excessive enthusiasm for a twenties-style French telephone.

There was a strange blind spot in Dad's essentially moral nature. This same man abused his twin sons by ignoring them from the moment of their birth. He never struck Tom or Walt; his brutal indifference, his distrust, a contempt he couldn't disguise, were enough torture. By ignoring his wife's long slide into alcoholism, he sanctioned it. He never invited his kids to share his hobbies: photography, woodworking, golf, stamp collecting. He fenced us off. A childish dread of dentists consigned him to a mouthful of rotted teeth. His kids obediently followed suit. His paranoia about medicine became a McCall family trait and no small factor in his physical condition.

But then, without forewarning, this serious fellow would suddenly lapse into an impersonation of a drunkenly belligerent Great

War vet, bawling, "Where was *you* at Vimy!" In the same satirical frame of mind he threw the dignity of every family member into the trash can with an annual calendar illustrated with detailed photos of a beaten-down, cretinous family of the lowest class in comical Kallikak poses. All of us volunteered. It was a hilarious project. Dad lavished care on his photographs. He must have had second thoughts, though. Satire wasn't in demand in Windsor, and I don't think this masterpiece of misery ever left our apartment.

Nobody could determine whether Dad was an angel or Satan. The ultimate consensus was that he alternated between them. I crashed a brand-new sports car on a snow-slick road en route to Toronto and a New Year's celebration. The car was a total wreck, but somehow I escaped unscathed. I phoned home to report my latest disaster. Dad, who regularly blew a fuse if somebody made off with the sports section of the daily paper, was neither upset nor angry, only concerned that I was physically intact. An angelic act.

On the other hand, Satan in the corporeal form of Dad tore away from a card game in somebody's Danforth Court apartment one night and rushed home, crashed into Walt's bedroom, and dragged him, half-awake, into the living room. One of the card players had accused Walt of beating up his six-year-old daughter for the fun of it. Dad ranted and raved at his evil brat of an eleven-year-old son. Walt protested, but it was futile. He was convicted on the spot by his own father, on the say-so of a six-year-old.

He, like Mother, died at the bizarre age of forty-nine. What a waste!

▪ ▪ ▪

The year spun on until the end of December and the beginning of a new decade, the sixties. Rudy foresaw that the WAA goose was cooked. In fact it was blowtorched. Talks had begun in October: Maybe we'd merge with another studio. Maybe some big Toronto outfit would buy the business—i.e., Rudy and Bill Windsor and me—and relocate us to Toronto. Two or three reps from Toronto studios visited our humble quarters. Their mission was to do, in that awkwardly meaningless phrase, "due diligence," attempting to winkle out any vital secrets, look over the books, get a feel for the quality of the studio's artwork in magazine, newspaper, and catalog form. Also to meet the artists, to decide how many they could use and how much they'd cost.

The final inspection came in mid-December. Rudy being Rudy, any information stayed in his pocket and/or his head. The portfolio of my favorite renderings was slim. Also thin, and also unimpressive, even—or especially—to me. *Here it comes*, I thought, when Rudy called the meeting that would reveal my fate. Rudy was the prize and Toronto-bound. Bill Windsor was a fine automobile artist, but two was more than they needed. I wasn't awarded a job. I wasn't even discussed. The next morning, Rudy came to my cubicle bearing a check for one month's pay. He had no ideas or suggestions about another job. It wasn't a sad moment for Rudy or for me. He didn't wish me luck because Rudy didn't believe in luck. After he left my cubicle I never saw him again.

An hour or so later, having left Windsor Advertising Artists for a final time, I sat down on the living room chesterfield to ponder my situation. The hellish fate that Dad had warned me would be the worst worst-case scenario had occurred. I was unemployed. I didn't feel scared or guilt-ridden or even very worried, although the end of the world was nigh.

Or was it?

With no experience and less money, a friend and I dreamed up our own Canadian car magazine.

Chapter 4

Canada Trash & Tragic

I was now twenty-four, freshly sprung from six years of learning how to suffocate my instincts, thereby making myself into the worst commercial artist and least evolved person in Canada, if not the world. Windsor Advertising Artists no longer existed. Hugh and I had moved back to 1793 Byng Road and lived rent-free; the mortgage was paid by my parents' estate. Chris was back home from Toronto after a year at Bishop Strachan, a joyless prison of a school for rich kids, where Dad had placed her after Mother's death. For her own good, he'd thought. He'd thought wrong.

A small, frightened black female dog was sitting at the curb one October morning when I went out to grab the newspaper. She seemed to want something. Probably wants food, Chris said, walking the fifteen feet between the house and the dog. Which, terrified by the near proximity of a human, backed away and slouched down, as if expecting a beating. Two cautious steps forward, one step back, the dog could be lured up to the front porch only haltingly. Chris and Hugh and I competed to pat, baby-talk, and reassure this poor mistreated creature until she calmed down and ceased trembling. She was sweet and friendly. She wouldn't or couldn't bark. Dad had hated pets; this dog was our revenge. We named her Sapphire, probably from the *Amos 'n' Andy* character. She stayed with us, the one family member everybody could—and did—unreservedly love.

Three months after the studio was shuttered, I was unemployed, flat broke, and happier than I'd been in years. The world not only failed to end when I went jobless: the relief from that pointless life liberated me from a paralysis that kept me frozen in place for almost the entire duration of the Eisenhower era.

Dad had been wrong—as wrong as Red Hill Jr., daredevil son of a daredevil son of a daredevil father. Junior rode a barrel-shaped roll of inner tubes over Niagara Falls in 1951 and didn't live to tell about it. A paycheck had brought me freedom from something worse than the breadline: fear. Now the bogeyman who had been muttering in my ear for years was exposed as a phantom and swiftly dispatched. I had twenty—count 'em, twenty—bucks in the bank. *Wooo!* Disaster! Not exactly. Unemployment insurance coughed up just enough cash every week to keep me in Rothmans cigarettes and Pepsis and a full tank of gas for the car.

I took off the first six months of 1960, a month for every year at the studio. I knew I'd eventually have to go in search of work, so halfheartedly plugged away at a freshened portfolio—illustrations of office furniture and other nonautomotive subjects. In my spare time (and my whole life was nothing but) I borrowed Alex's Triumph TR3 and blasted over the empty back roads of springtime Essex County, pretending the TR3 was a Ferrari Testarossa. Concurrently, Diane and I had a rapprochement. My anxiety about an uncertain future transformed itself into sexual energy. I bedded Diane as often as possible, which was often indeed.

My values were shifting every week. So was my motivation. The new perspective persuaded me that I could have contentedly remained on life's periphery and never rejoined the workaday world. What was the downside? I hadn't dared to allow myself the luxury of wanting a career. Losers like me didn't aim for careers. Commercial art had beaten out of me the schoolboy delusion of riding my great gifts to fame and fortune. I was a mediocre nobody. Why not relax and live like it? Constant failure to cope had deflated my dreams to a midget scale. If I were ever lucky enough to pull down a hundred and twenty bucks a week, I could rent a tract house and buy a car. If my wife worked, we could have color TV and other luxuries.

Alex was the only person I knew in Windsor who had ambition, and it wasn't exactly a raging one. He'd have been validated, his dreams fulfilled, if he were transferred to Toronto and landed a job with the CBC.

I remember idle afternoons staring out the living room window at Walker Road, the street a couple of blocks away that led to the new Highway 401 heading east. I fantasized images of one day coming back on Walker Road the other way, basking in worldly success. But, whenever forced back to the real plane of existence and the dreary truths of my life, I knew I had no option other than to perform a self-lobotomy, take a few deep breaths, and offer myself one more time to my wicked stepfather, commercial art.

Windsor, thank God, was not even a possibility. Sign-painting was left as the only commercial art business in town, and contrary to recent evidence, I still had standards. I had never ceased aching to be back in Toronto. Now I more or less *had* to go there and try peddling my wares to one or the other big studios, churning out artwork for major agencies and their weighty client rosters. With my portfolio assembled, I turned my back on Windsor for good.

■ ■ ■

The return to Toronto was anticlimactic. Most of my school friends were embarked on careers, few of them connected to art. The city had changed since my enforced departure, and cosmopolitanism was no longer suspect. The cultural constipation of decades, challenged by the postwar infusion of European and Asian immigrants, had ended. A gleaming new subway—a civic innovation that lifted Toronto to status as a player among North America's big-league cities—symbolized progress. The new city hall, a Scandinavian confection that barely looked like a building, symbolized the fact that Toronto had cut its ties with musty yesteryear.

All well and good for most people. But as might be expected of me when faced with positivism and opportunity, I was pissed off. This Toronto felt oddly alien at first, as if some swankier, more streamlined city had swiped the name. Once again, I'd have to start from scratch in a strange new environment.

To my surprise—no, astonishment—I barely had to pound the pavement before a leading commercial art studio took me in, and at a decent salary. The "studio" (the name escapes me, as do so many places you can't wait to forget) was one vast, low-ceilinged room, more amphitheater than atelier. I sat at a workstation among orderly rows of identical spaces. There must have been thirty artists, and, in commercial art custom, every one of them was male. Squint and the studio could have been a frat house with very lax rules: continuous horseplay, lobbing of missiles, much bawdy howling back and forth.

Despite my outsider status and a temperament at odds with those of my boisterous workmates, I willed myself into the pretense of feeling at home. New start! New city! New horizons! Then I was handed my first assignment. *Blam!* That ugly old sense of inadequacy knocked down my flimsy resolution, flooding back and drowning hopes that the six-year curse in Windsor had magically lifted.

That first assignment was also my last assignment. Two weeks and two dozen runny, blurry, hopelessly inept tries at airbrushing a can of motor oil into a Container of the Gods later, a flaw in my work was exposed to the world. I lacked the skills of even a mediocre commercial artist. To his genuine sorrow and my even more genuine relief, the kindly studio manager, using that softly self-serving euphemism for being fired, let me go. Oddly untroubled, I went.

The next day, a sunny summer Saturday, I was giving my friend's then-girlfriend, Susie, a ride home when my tiny motorized tin can (an Austin-Healey Sprite) met with a taxi in a head-on collision. I cut a gash in my forehead. My right knee banged into the dash; I limped for months. Susie was less fortunate: she went face-first into the windshield. While her injuries weren't as severe as they could have been (mostly cuts and scrapes), it took her the better part of a year to fully recover. The Sprite was totaled. Had I paused and taken it as an omen, I might have been spooked.

▪ ▪ ▪

Well, I had always liked to write, and I wrote smoothly, a unique gift found in few kids (and adults, but that would need a paragraph . . . maybe later). I was a sure-fingered touch-typist. I could spell like a literate grown-up, almost perfectly. I wrote fast. I read newspapers and magazines avidly. I loved books, was young and untutored enough to indiscriminately lap them up, learning while thinking it was fun—the good and the bad. I read the new novel reviewers called "a work of genius." The obscure biography of a forgotten hero. Travel books, with maps. Books of nineteenth-century European history. Autobiographies of the latest heroes. Books about exploration. Science books. Sports books. Books about war.

I had inhaled prose through osmosis. Learning to write by learning to read obviated the task of learning grammar. If I could write a single page as clear, rich, and honest as A. J. Liebling's prose, I'd have made the grade. Was there any such thing as a dull person who wrote like Liebling?

My strategy for getting hired as a writer was as follows: Compose an intelligent letter, restraining the temptation to shoot my cuffs but dropping in some wit. Write a *memorable* letter, differentiating me from the overearnest applicant with magnificent qualifications but no perceptible personality. Make it a single page. Write on paper that crackles when folded. Send versions to the editor of every Canadian magazine with a mailing address, proposing my candidacy for whatever position was or might be open, at whatever pittance he felt like paying. I must have written and sent a hundred such beseechments. The cost in postage about exhausted my funds. I sat back to await my fate.

Where I sat was on a couch in a crummy small room in a second-floor apartment that if it was fixed up would qualify as dreary, a sublet on a humdrum street. I stared at my typewriter.

▪ ▪ ▪

I'd never had any money and never expected to. My meager earnings couldn't hang around luxuriating in a savings account. Whatever I earned in any typical week was spent by Friday. Dad must have instinctively foreseen my financial future; years earlier, he'd bullied me into an insurance policy with a cash payout of a fraction of its worth in a crisis. I declared a crisis, cashed out, and now sat atop the world's tiniest nest egg. With such solid backup I could coast along indefinitely, indefinitude being close to a fuzzy-minded twenty-five-year-old's concept of time's forward march.

Waiting for bites from my postal broadside, like the hapless Robert Falcon Scott waiting in his Antarctic pup tent for a miracle, led to days of mingled tension and ennui. They'd have been dead days but for my similar trials invented ten years before, in the cauldron of 2377 Danforth. I hurled myself back into a frenzy of creative onanism, and kept on bashing the keys until something, I hoped, took me out of my head. A rented Royal portable and a ream of copy paper and off I went, stumbling back down into the subterranean wonderland of my subconscious.

This header into an insane cosmos, sculpted out of fear and anxiety, explored caves and crevasses where no healthy mind had gone before. I wasn't composing pulp fiction. These were fantasies, yanked from steamy far corners of my imagination where I'd hidden them away, an attic stuffed with mental chaff, signifying nothing meaningful to anyone but me.

What it *meant* came from the frustrated rage, growing like a tumor, felt in my gut ever since I first detected the rickety hypocrisy that pretended to, but couldn't, support our family life. Parents who hadn't wanted six kids but ignored birth control. Who played the roles of Dad and Mom while killing any possibility of a decent family life. Who abused their twin sons for the crime of existing. A father who did nothing to help his sad, lonely wife as she sank into terminal alcoholism. Parents who boycotted doctors and paid for their neglect by dying before the age of fifty.

This Grand Guignol of lovelessness and casual cruelty had stunted my life. I became skeptical, then cynical, too early. Yet when I hunched over the keyboard, free to rant and vent and cry out for understanding, I did no such thing. In retrospect, I believe this was the funniest stuff I'd ever written. From breakfast until dark, pausing only to refill the cigarettes and Pepsi stocks, I slammed out page after page as if there were a gun at my head.

The claim of priceless hilarity can be proven or disproven only by reading that work. Alas, no chance. It disappeared shortly after I finished it and sent it off to Hugh, the family archivist in Windsor, for safekeeping.

It was a dense phantasmagoria, its meager plot following a troupe of my usual characters. My first stories were of bums, psychopaths, certified idiots, and indescribables—moving purposelessly through a landscape that, though rural and vast, hadn't brightened since the swampy grotesqueries of Grubber's world. I created a fresh collection of lost souls: Blimpet, a star-crossed tramp, selling phony patents door-to-door, even though there were no doors in this empty region; Cheese, the stupidest mystic the world had ever seen, worshipped by some; a fat young orphan, Doby Frout ("I got one tooth left, and even that one's hurtin'"), forced to live in the swampside shack of an aunt, who continuously cooked meals of carp and demanded that Doby eat, whereupon the obese sad sack bolted and hid out in the swamp until caught.

I titled the pile of narratives *Caught in the Cracks.* I knew it wasn't a commercial product and feared exposure as a purveyor of idiocies who made Lewis Carroll look mundane by comparison.

Previous forays into nutland had been all tableaux. This latest effort *moved* its characters and locations, setting forth the rudiments of a narrative, a story. I seldom laughed; as I wrote I was dead serious—not about being funny, but about the craft of it. I invested weeks and months in these creative binges. I considered what I was doing to be practice. I was also teaching myself to write. For what, I hadn't a clue.

Alas, *Caught in the Cracks* was evidently caught in the cracks. Hugh never lost things, but my masterpiece disappeared. It was never found. My contention that it was the funniest work I ever wrote may be nostalgic bullshit. But when the perfect adjective flies out of nowhere and perfectly fits, when your story seems to tell itself to you as you write and you feel you're simply transcribing it, when some seventh sense leads you to a finish with a satisfying final phrase, you've hit the sweet spot. And you know it.

This is the moment when I must confess: I didn't write that masterwork alone. The artist craves the presence of life as he works, to warm and soften the lonely hours. A famished mouse was my boon companion. He let me keep working, never interfered, stayed as quiet as a small, tame rodent. We shared a package of decaying hot dogs day after day. One night, hearing no familiarly faint scratching sounds from the kitchen, I tiptoed in to investigate. The hot dogs sat there, mouse-free. Curiosity led me to pick up a nearby cardboard box of molasses, left by a previous tenant. The top had been nibbled or gnawed open. I pulled it all the way open. There was the mouse, drowned facedown in the sticky brown goo.

▪▪▪

This fit of creative excess finally burned out in mid-October. It was now November and my third month of involuntary freedom. I couldn't wait any longer for my letter-bombardment of Canada's print media to respond. A couple of months ought to be time enough for an editor to gamble on an interview. None did. One, a South African named Royd Beamish, who was editing a Maclean-Hunter service station trade journal, did reply. No openings, but if I was a son of his friend, the late Tom McCall, he'd try to help when he could. Well, best wishes and good luck.

▪▪▪

Cars had gripped my imagination almost since I had one. First, in the immediate postwar era, foggy reprints from British racing journals of prewar Grand Prix. A golden age of mighty giants and fierce competition: Auto Union, Mercedes-Benz, Alfa Romeo, and Delahaye. Immortal drivers: Nuvolari, Caracciola, Seaman. Spectacular events in spectacular venues.

America had the Indianapolis 500, dirt-track racing, world-speed attempts on the Utah Salt Flats. The so-called sports car revolution, sparked by U.S. servicemen bringing home spindly little MG TCs, mushrooming into a whole car culture that ignored Detroit. By the time I could legally drive, cars occupied my mind and much of my life. A Ford Anglia, a Morgan Plus Four, two Triumph TR3s, a Porsche 365 coupe. The upward climb that often ended only in bankruptcy or death.

By the time I repatriated to Toronto, a Volvo 444 was my car. It looked like a humpbacked prewar Ford; it was fast, unbreakable, and utterly ugly to most prospects, leaving Volvo to highway hotspurs and club racing drivers. My best friend at the time was Eric, a cyclist I met while hanging out with Hugh and Mike, who'd met him somewhere or other. He was smart, articulate, funny, and a fast, safe driver in his newer Volvo 544. Eric worked downtown for a trust company and lived twenty miles away in Mississauga. The two of us screeched around cloverleafs and blasted into town on the Queen Elizabeth highway. Eric had quick reflexes, a sense of balance, and willpower. I never beat him on our cloverleaf epics.

He and I were both intelligent, hardworking fellows: both readers, both politically aware, both liberals. We were curious about the wider world, capable of serious conversation on subjects arcane and obscure. It puzzles me, embarrasses me, and in some sense annoys me that whenever Eric and I talked—at lunch, dinner, while driving, hanging around his house and my apartment, on the telephone—it was exclusively, spiritually, excitedly, nostalgically, and amicably about cars.

We drove together in the Canadian Winter Rally, a thousand grueling miles of slogging through deep winter snow and ice over one weekend. On Saturday night, near the halfway point in North Bay, both of us groggy from sleeplessness, the car slewed off the road, bulldozed through a snowbank and, *crunch!*, slammed into a buried fence post. We escaped with only cosmetic damages. Powered by the adrenaline of a near miss, Eric and I kept jawing about cars on the way to the overnight stop in North Bay and through dinner.

My Volvo needed an oil change. Money was running low. My job hunt accelerated, dropping standards by a few degrees and fetching me up at the A.V. Roe company building near suburban Malton. The firm had recently developed Canada's first supersonic jet fighter, the Arrow; praised as it was by the aviation world, the plane and its program had been canceled by the Canadian government. A.V. Roe was devastated. To attempt survival, its mighty presses were converted to bang out metal canoes, vending machines, and other civilian goods. My humble task was to retouch black-and-white photos of these products for sales brochures.

I got a taste of what working life was like for millions of people: tedious, impersonal, empty. I sat along with scores of fellow drudges in a hall that must have once seen aircraft assembly. This was my first job in a union brotherhood, and my last. The work was loosey-goosey doable: it was the shop rules I found stifling. Lunch hour began the instant a bell rang. Bad form not to instantly stop work. Bad form, too, to restart working one minute before lunch hour officially ended. At five o'clock on the dot, it was tools down and rush to the exit. I was informed that I must pay union dues. And I had to cough up five bucks every Monday for the weekly office lottery, the one event that stirred any enthusiasm.

Wednesday night, the phone in my apartment rang. It was Royd Beamish. I had a job, starting next Monday. On Thursday morning I quit A.V. Roe's blacking factory. Friday would be my last day. Not only would I be out of that soul dump, but I found I had won the week's office lottery. I had been there just short of forty hours. I'm certain that I left as the most hated employee in the annals of A.V. Roe.

▪ ▪ ▪

The next job started first thing Monday morning. The Maclean-Hunter copy cub department consisted of a few desks in an unused space on the top floor of the firm's headquarters building on University Avenue. Being noiselessly whisked up to the top floor by an elevator heightened my self-esteem. "Writer" was now my actual, official identity. It hardly mattered *what* I wrote. Being paid to crank a blank sheet of paper into a typewriter and run a string of words across it felt, from the first crank, like what I'd been born to do.

Down to work. Cutting a two-page press release on the latest sensational advance in slurry control to 150 meaty words, to be featured in the New Products section of *Canadian Paint & Varnish*, sent infinitely more pleasure signals to my brain than all the spot illustrations I'd ever done for the Dodge Royal Lancer brochure. This drab, isolated little cell was the place for me. These were my people, my new colleagues: Terry and Clyde and Madeleine (no relation to the previous Terry and Madeleine). And they actually read books. It didn't exactly hurt, either, that I typed faster and generated more copy tonnage per hour than any of them.

My artistic proclivities were on indefinite hiatus. The new thrill of editorial work and attendant mental stimulation eclipsed the lifelong pastime, or pathological urge, of scrunching down in a metaphorical foxhole and creating images meaningless for a connoisseur, or even a normal individual. But crude, smudgy, indecipherable images to banish my demons. For the first time in a decade and a half, the trap door behind which mocking satire had hidden could be bolted shut. If it threatens no more, why run away from reality? The energy thus saved, and utilized in positive ways, could turn my life away from a cave of darkness and toward the sun.

▪ ▪ ▪

Grinding out fare for the back pages of trade journals thrilled me for a few months. Then the sense of standing still, of a flattened learning curve, led to the stirrings of an appetite for bigger things. Almost any kind of writing qualified as a better thing.

I had lucked into the romance of driving at its fervent peak. Driving under the proper conditions—the right kind of car, small, light, and responsive to the slightest touch of the steering wheel, the gearshift, and the brake pedal—made driving a sport and a pleasure, with a frisson of underlying danger to penalize a lack of skill. Automotive literature goosed enthusiasm by serving up racing, new-car road tests, and similar information. Driving tours around Europe and America added color and fresh air. Technical articles and diagrams enlightened spare-time mechanics. (Karl Ludvigsen, an American writer, former editor of *Car and Driver*, and arguably the foremost automobile intellectual of the day, doped out the arcane Mercedes-Benz desmodromic valve system used on their racing cars. He was feted in Bad Cannstatt for writing an article about it. It was *supposed* to be secret.)

Mine was close to the last generation of car nuts. Cars have morphed into emotionally neutered large appliances, competing more on entertainment than performance, dulling risk with technological interventions that replace the need for judgment. Good for safety, inarguably progressive—but heading into a tomorrow where we'll all be guests in our automated, self-driving blobs. The automobile is becoming too sobersided, too good a planet citizen, to spoil the mission with fun.

This is now, that was then. Back in the hot-blooded heyday of driving as a hobby, Canada supported, marginally, a single magazine: *Canada Track & Traffic*. No such census existed, but an educated guess put the likely national readership of car freaks at maybe three thousand. The goal of *Track & Traffic* was to augment respected American enthusiast publications, such as *Road & Track* and *Car and Driver*, by covering the Canadian sport and industry.

The objective critic might ask, "*What* Canadian sport and industry?" Touché. Canadian sports car racing amounted to a few amateur regional races on dreary abandoned airfield circuits in Ontario, Quebec, and British Columbia. The Canadian automotive industry was a bunch of factories in Windsor and Toronto bolting Detroit cars together, to embellish Motown's bottom line with sales proportionate to Canada's ninety percent smaller population.

There was a myopic visionary at this time, living in a basement in the north of England, who had the answer to raising RMS *Titanic* from its watery grave: he'd pump millions of ping-pong balls into the hull until the wreck floated up to the surface. Meanwhile, two even more myopic visionaries in Toronto talked themselves hoarse about starting a second Canadian car magazine, crushing *Track & Traffic* like a cockroach and gifting Canadian enthusiasts with the finest car magazine on the continent.

Looking back, how could a pair of reasonable men *not* convince each other that this was an errand of two fools, a hubristic brainstorm with tiny brains, off-line, destined to collapse in total failure, humiliation, and the loss of other people's money? Simple: Eric and I were enthusiasts.

Actually, more than enthusiasts. We had talked ourselves into such a pitch, a foaming lather, that mere conversation was no longer sufficient. We never stopped yapping, but the time had come when this mutual obsessiveness was forcing us into *action*, transferring our knowledge into the real world. We'd be doing something to bring us closer to the epicenter, something satisfying to both of us, harnessing our unique talents to start a new, exciting magazine for the Canadian enthusiast.

As Canada's foremost unpublished car writer (with, incidentally, zero editorial experience, zero experience or aptitude for reporting, and zero contacts in the sport or the industry), I would be the editor. Eric would bring his weighty financial knowledge to the publisher's suite, an expertise gleaned in his junior post at a major Toronto trust company, not to mention a mathematical acumen *and* the inborn gift of gab that would mesmerize Midas himself.

Eric did a quick projection of our profits and losses after the first year. Pegasus Publishing would be the corporate parent. *The Canadian Driver*, like Henry Luce and Briton Hadden's *Time*, was to be the first in an empire of other brilliant titles. Eric forecast that *The Canadian Driver* would land us in the black by the second issue. A deep forensic examination, in the form of nonstop bull sessions between ourselves, was rich in guesswork and unbountiful in hard facts. But, white-hot with the heat of ambition (or could it be the metric tons of hot air just expended?), we taught each other and told ourselves what we wanted and needed to believe.

Winter 1961 turned sluggishly to spring. Rain, day after day, impelled a fashion and health crisis: the soles of my worn-out shoes had almost detached, flapping with every footfall and scooping water onto my cold, wet feet. I was forced to compensate by altering my walk to a kind of sliding shuffle. The solution appeared in the form of a bottle of rubber cement. Every night, I'd sandwich the sole and shoe together, bind them tight with a necktie, and know that next morning—barring a monsoon—I was safe for another day.

I couldn't neglect my duties in the copy cub department and betray Royd Beamish's rare confidence in me. Meanwhile, Eric had rented a tiny space in a small building on King Street. Pegasus Publishing needed to start somewhere. I worked on designing the corporate logo. (The order of priorities, in the birthing phase of a new entity, was always fluid.) I'd be there evenings and weekends. Eric checked in often, to report on his search for financial backing, or to jaw.

The target launch date was late May. We were now in mid-February. We hadn't thought about an art director. Eric's search for a space salesman was equally critical. So far, we hadn't raised a cent. It began to dawn on us that starting up a magazine must sooner or later stop relying on daydreams and face the icy-cold, stone-hard facts. How could our lavish new publication do without an experienced, top-flight art director, if neither of us knew any, knew where to look, and hadn't the money to pay for a Help Wanted ad?

The unraveling of the dream began about this time. I managed to inveigle and beseech my high school art-class friend Maurice to design the magazine, on the promise of a fat payday down the road. Eric faced an identical quandary in hiring an experienced, media-savvy advertising salesman for no money (until that hazy day when we'd all be rich). Our self-congratulatory fantasies started decelerating even faster than they had accelerated.

Eric had found a pair of young brothers with a vague interest in investing, fellows who were car-minded and naive enough to see part ownership of a car magazine as their entrée into the inner circle of Canadian motorsports. It was taking candy from a couple of babies. But by now, the belt of reality was so tight it pinched. Out went four-color printing, including the cover. The price per issue doubled, then doubled again. The rented office was abandoned.

The first mad flush of excitement had made editorial content a rousing game of imagination; this magazine would put the reader in the cockpit. Give top drivers the third degree in interviews. Go behind the scenes to discover the technical secrets of the winning machines, the men who designed them and the boffins who kept them running. Thorough coverage of the stellar racing events.

Come April and those glowing concepts lay strewn about like so many cigarette butts. I had gushed and bloviated about this new magazine, its classy style and great writing. Then I sat down at the typewriter to lay out the editorial content of the inaugural issue. The difference between enthusiasm and knowledge plunged me into a chasm. Specifics hadn't been necessary in the heat of inspiration. I hadn't a clue about exactly what a magazine about the Canadian automotive scene should actually be about.

We'd cover the Canadian industry, we said, discovering, too late, that there was no Canadian car industry to cover. We envisioned a national editorial reach, discovering too late that if we had bothered to think it through, we would have realized that a handful of amateur club races held four thousand miles apart hardly justified the term "national." Nobody on the west coast gave a damn about who had won a race at Harewood Acres, Ontario, three months before, just as no Ontario racing fans cared about some club event near Vancouver.

Eric and I weren't terribly smart about basic facts. In fact, we were ambitious morons. How could we have committed to founding a serious consumer publication, not only on superficial understanding of all the factors, but preening ourselves on our own brilliance? The magazine's complete News section was a six-month-old press release about an improved Maserati "Birdcage" sports racing car that no Canadian racing venue would ever see. I was the reporter/correspondent/editor, not because I wanted all these responsibilities, but because I knew no other skilled car-minded writers who were willing to work for free.

Our magazine was destined, we honestly believed, to explode the printed page with amazing fare that would lure readers back every month, in numbers that advertisers couldn't ignore. But in fact Canada's one great automotive magazine had skidded off the track before the race began.

Eric and I still met, but neither of us had the guts to come out and say it: *The Canadian Driver* was a few feet shy of driving off a cliff. No comedy writer could equal the laugh-until-you-cry story of the final month. Eric had found an ad salesman! Our Irish-immigrant friend, Nat. No, Nat had never sold an ad or anything else. He was a mechanic by trade, and, lucky for us, an unemployed one, able to start immediately. Nat's command of English was sketchy, filtered through a thick Irish brogue. His pay would be handsome, once the magazine got going.

Nat borrowed a necktie and went out on his rounds on a Monday. By Friday, he had pitched every automobile company and its ad agency, and circulated through the tire and accessories shops, major car dealers, and gasoline retailers. Nat hadn't come back empty-handed to the office (read: the coffee shop until we could find suitable quarters). In his big Celtic mitt was a receipt signed by an actual advertiser. He'd plunged $150 on a quarter-page ad heralding not only his gas station but also his Borgward franchise.

Some people, cast by happenstance into cramped metaphorical corners but too proud or too optimistic to accept an ugly fate as the ruination of their plans, shut out reality by drinking. Not Eric. As the bad news cascaded over *The Canadian Driver* like a cloud raining down piss, Eric whistled. He couldn't talk with you, nor you with him. He whistled when the phone rang, he whistled when it didn't. And in the manner of all champion twenty-four-hours-a-day whistlers, his was a tuneless whistle.

The magazine debuted and folded minutes apart. So far as I could determine, newsstand sales ran neck and neck with our mail-order business, both racking up perfect goose eggs.

We had had enough of magazines, talk, and each other. I never saw Eric again. His trust company office didn't know where he was. Nobody did. Years passed. My wounds inflicted by this failure had healed. But apparently not for Eric. In the mid-seventies, he suddenly resurfaced, on the wrong side of the law. Eric was charged along with two others for fraud in a scheme involving gold bullion from Brazil and got four years in the pen.

I've often wondered if the fiasco of *The Canadian Driver* drove him to a life of crime. And if so, what I could have done to prevent it. We were a couple of conceited blockheads, equally guilty of hubris, persisting long after all evidence had warned us that our project was doomed to fail. Eric wasn't a sneaky criminal type. I think his problem was an inborn optimism so strong that sometimes it outran reality.

■ ■ ■

The good that quickly befell me thereafter turned out to be fifty-one percent bad. The editor of *Canada Track & Traffic*, Bill Wordham, had just quit to become a TV reporter for the ABC-TV network (which must have been the most dramatic job-hop in history). Eric and I had fomented *The Canadian Driver* by spluttering indignant contempt for *Track & Traffic*. Our close analysis exposed *CT&T*'s shoddy journalism, which we took as proof that the magazine was not only inept but also shamelessly corrupt. Its European correspondent, for example, was named M. T. Line, clearly a cynical pun disguising the obvious fact that no European correspondent existed.

Our disgust with *CT&T*'s failings slopped over to lambasting its criminally crummy management. We'd never met nor seen Jerry Polivka, the Czech immigrant cofounder/publisher, but he must have been pure evil to brazenly sell such junk. Owing to the small world of Canadian auto journalism, Jerry knew I'd be interested and solicited me to replace Bill Wordham as editor.

Jerry had grown up dodging Nazis in occupied Prague: maybe distrust had become a trait. He should have been forced to wear a mask in any business deal. I took the editor's job. I *pounced* on the editor's job.

No one else on earth was clamoring to ride my editorial genius to the stars. I could no longer go back to huddle in the bosom of Maclean-Hunter, and my pay would crack the $100-a-week barrier. This represented an overnight leap, in my naive idea of affluence, to the respectable class of regular haircuts, new shoes every year, and the sheer *prestige* of lofting myself from hole-plugger for obscure trade journals to the pinnacle (or the nadir, it was too early to ascertain) of Canadian automotive journalism, barely six months after sitting jobless in a run-down dump of an apartment, my one steady companion a starving rodent.

Track & Traffic faced the same pitfalls we had at *Canadian Driver.* The magazine was editorially uninspired. Advertising was feeble. Nothing on the horizon augured for any improvements. Yet *CT&T* had somehow limped through a year of monthly issues, had its own printing press on the premises, and showed no signs of bucking the bailiff for nonpayment of bills.

Editorial independence would symbolize the trust between management (i.e., Jerry) and me. He had promised me a free hand, both in writing most of the magazine and "interacting" with potential advertisers (a face-saving way of offering a road test in exchange for an ad). Jerry proved as good as his word, which was meaningless. Editorial freedom, as he interpreted it, meant that if he won an argument, I was free to quit. I argued about awarding a cover photo and a glowing "road test" to a shitbox Škoda Octavia for a full-page ad, the same deal for lunatic junk like the Amphicar (which handled on the road like a boat and in the water like a car), and choice auto marginalia of all varieties.

A *CT&T* Xmas Gift List, maybe the sorriest of space fillers, was a golden opportunity to trade unromantic merchandise for quarter-page ads. Thus, what the gift list recommended to be placed under the tree were tire jacks, twelve-volt batteries, and perpetual wax for every kind of car.

No detail escaped Jerry's attempt to slash outgo—he paid five dollars per photo, and the photographer had to buy his own film. On the few out-of-town assignments I wangled, Jerry's Law applied: Why should he pay the bills, when I'd have to eat and sleep anyway?

I hammered out every article in every issue. That wasn't necessarily to satisfy my itch to write: asking a reputable journalist to bend his work to play favorites, while offering less money than he could earn mowing lawns, offended my pride before it offended his. I played at being the art director, to ensure that the caption under a Škoda interior photo wasn't misplaced to run under a photo of Ludwig Heimrath winning another race in his Porsche RS. Proofing the magazine was my job, too: nobody else on the six-person staff was good at spelling.

By the end of my first six months as editor of *Track & Traffic*, I had moved from thinking of my career thus far as one failure in commercial art and two failures at trying to turn out a decent car magazine. Jerry, aided by his girlfriend, Diana, had spent every hour of every year since 1958 struggling to keep it afloat, month to month. Then, in 1961, an angel showed up, willing to contribute significant funds.

A wealthy Montrealer of early middle age, Norm was a Corvette racing driver and a warm, intelligent balance to Jerry's brooding, almost paranoid assumptions that everybody was plotting to rob, cheat, and lie to him about everything. He came in from Montreal every month or so to get Jerry's reports on the balance sheet and any looming issues. He knew no more about magazines than Jerry, whose assurances that *CT&T* was as good as it could get, considering the odds against success, he swallowed whole. In any case, Norm's pockets were too shallow to fund a tremendous upward editorial push.

I'd slump through the door of my apartment on Eglinton Avenue most evenings, heartsick, pissed off, and cursing Jerry. Sister Chris, who was living with me while attending high school, patiently heard out my complaints. She was, like her mother, no critic of others' lives, and an ideal flatmate. Her even temperament, wit, and self-sufficiency allowed me to leave her home alone for two weeks, with no concerns, while I followed the Shell 4000 Trans-Canada Rally.

I realized that, as with Windsor Advertising Artists, I had once again managed to position myself in an almost hermetically sealed environment. Rudy had simply not cared about friends; Jerry's paranoia and probable sense of guilt about having suckered, hornswoggled, and generally dismissed most people he did business with made him someone with few friends except for Boris, a fellow Czech, and his girlfriend/secretary, Diana, whom he kept on a short leash.*

* Diana raced cars, as did Jerry. She was the fastest female driver in Canada, probably faster than Jerry, who took the sport very seriously and was quite quick himself; but running second to a female—particularly a girlfriend—surely nettled his macho Czechoslovakian soul.

Bailing out sinking scows does tone the arms, shoulders, and upper body. The magazine did, perforce, build up a few of my skills. I wrote, or in the cases of correspondents rewrote, every word of every issue. Designed the page layouts. Cadged photos from Avedons like my brother Hugh, the only adult I could find willing to pay for the film. I let Jerry exercise his droit du seigneur and pick the shots to be printed. Jerry had a Helen Keller eye for visual excellence. In another swindle, Hugh had painted a Lola sports racing car for an advertiser's two-page spread; it was maybe his best painting ever. When I presented it to Jerry, he hauled out a crude piece of shit, pronounced it obviously superior to my brother's crappy daub, and left Hugh insulted and unpaid. The fix was transparently in: Jerry had found some hack to portray the Lola, collected the fee from the advertiser, and pocketed at least half for himself.

There was no other way to survive in this one-lung operation than to write fast, composing "road tests." Every issue had at least one, because a three-page product puff—a single-page ad—from the three-hour ride most car companies trusted us with was not possible, especially if you consider my other incidental labors: improvising fixes under one-hour deadline pressure, begging contributors to take demeaning payments, and scrambling all the time to get everything finished on time, on a short, shredded shoestring.

But operating where things can't get worse is not necessarily the worst education for a neophyte. *Canada Track & Traffic* was a sorry magazine by any measure. So leprous was it in the Canadian car community that when Jerry and I trooped out to Ford of Canada's head office in suburban Oakville to present *CT&T*'s Car of the Year award for the new Capri, every executive in the building was otherwise engaged. A bewildered secretary eventually accepted our Scroll of Honor in their stead. Humiliation is sometimes justified, but God, does it sting.

My triumphal entry into New York fell flat the moment I arrived.
I was here. Now what?

Chapter 5

An Upgrade Called America

The American advertising industry had provided my ticket out: a mentor and friend persuaded me to leave my crummy journalism post, relocate to Detroit, and write car ads.

Canada jiggled in the rearview mirror, receded, and disappeared as I drove into the tunnel conveying me from Windsor, Ontario, to Detroit on a gray, snow-swirled afternoon in December 1962. I was trading a life in Toronto, in my home and native land, for a fresh start and a new chapter in the USA.

The decision to take Uncle Sam's coin wasn't exactly painful. The suspicion that I wasn't cut out for a contented Canadian life had become a conviction. I was temperamentally too antsy for that conspiracy of calm, phlegmatism, and compulsive self-effacement. Canada was a nation of nice that wouldn't say "poutine" if it had a mouthful. I shouldn't blame a country for my ten years of futility in commercial art and the lower forms of journalism. But it increasingly irked me that Canada shunned extremes of every kind, breeding what I saw as a wallflower mentality and a bland tolerance for mediocrity. Canada had settled itself without violence. The United States was founded on musketry and wars and dead Indians, a dynamism that depended on extremes—a natural breeding ground for violence. It bragged as if the world agreed with its tedious narcissism. The average Canadian keenly felt a dismal combination of ignorance and condescension in the American attitude. Ever average, I felt the same way.

But optimism defeated wariness. Long before I crossed the border, the prospect of America's energy busting my potential wide open infused me with a shot of American bullishness and optimism. Sorry, Canada; you wouldn't understand.

■ ■ ■

With the stodgy Eisenhower era finally over and JFK set to cheer up the White House and the nation, it felt like a propitious moment to immigrate. My mild qualms about switching national allegiances were just that. For me it was a win-win proposition. I was about to become a permanent alien resident of the USA, but remained a Canadian citizen and would still travel on my Canadian passport, albeit I'd pay my annual taxes to the IRS. If I could just avoid conspiring to foment a revolution and topple the government, I was home free. And, should I ever be hounded for a crime, I could skedaddle beyond the reach of my pursuers with impunity. In strict legal terms I had only loaned myself out to Uncle Sam. Yet there was a hint of profundity as I eased my car into the line approaching U.S. Customs.

I would exit the tunnel in my unglamorous Volvo to find no welcoming committee, nor be handed the key to the city. My advent was low-key, so no key. But so what if my entry to the United States of America fell short of the Emma Lazarus scenario: an immigrant standing queasily in line on the dock, having barely survived four grinding weeks confined in the airless twilight of steerage, roughly checked for signs of tuberculosis and lice, speaking not a word of English, with everything he owned in the world in the knapsack strapped on his back? But hey, that hadn't been my fault. Just like those Balts, Slavs, Pomeranians, and Ukrainians, I too was starting anew in a new country, in a new career.

The cheerful customs officer waved me through, and the most significant act of my life passed with all the drama of paying last month's water bill. The journey that had begun years ago, when as a five-year-old I fondled a Bakelite model of the Empire State Building in the family dentist's office, had actually transpired. That building stood for all the opportunity and excitement of America, aspirations I was only tacitly aware that I had. Twenty-three years later, I was now officially a landed immigrant.

Late-afternoon winter darkness was cloaking the city and the snow still swirled. I accelerated into the midwestern heart of America. Meanwhile, deep in my psyche, the lifelong fear of failure and the closely linked suspicion that the will, the guts, and the talents inside me would be exposed as fraudulent were suddenly defanged. I had told my mental tormentors to back off and shut the hell up. And they had, at least for a while.

I hadn't even started the search for someplace to live when Betty Skelton solved it for me. For my first three months I lived beyond my station, in a swanky apartment furnished like a *Playboy* pad. Diminutive and perky, Betty was a star aviatrix, skydiver, and speed junkie. We crossed paths at the perfect moment: I needed a place, she was off on some three-month mission and wanted to sublet her apartment. (I'd met her through David E. Davis Jr.—but more about him later.)

Some sublet! A glass-walled aerie in the deluxe Lafayette Pavilion, a new building in a moribund neighborhood, near downtown and a five-minute stroll to the Detroit River. The living room, carpeted wall-to-wall in off-white moon dust, featured a bar and a cabinet as big as a small apartment containing a color TV. An Ericofon advanced telephony so far I couldn't decipher how it functioned. A wall featuring a bas-relief solar system overlooked the vast sectional sofa. The bedroom was eighty percent bed with the approximate dimensions of a boxing ring. Once I'd lived down my sense of fraudulence and decided that living this high was just another element in my profile as a rising young adman, I felt myself slipping into a fresh new state of being. I felt supremely cool.

Detroit in 1962 hadn't yet virtually vanished into a sinkhole so deep that half of its two million residents would eventually vamoose. This proud, culturally, and financially rich midwestern city would soon suffer a mighty fall, tumbling so far, so fast, that once-regnant "Detroit" became a worldwide synonym for urban squalor.

Step back to the Motor City of fifty-eight years ago. Grosse Pointe, a mansions-only suburb stretched along the shoreline of Lake St. Clair seven miles east of the city, was the poshest neighborhood west of Greenwich, Connecticut, and east of Malibu. Estates of a gaggle of Ford heirs and other panjandrums drew rubbernecking weekend sightseers and disappointed them all; vast lawns lay between these modern palaces, while far in the distance were tennis courts and polo fields and swimming pools. The stupendously rich and their circles congregated in these Xanadus.

More recently minted grandees founded exclusive new suburbs in gently rolling golf club country a few miles north of the city, Bloomfield Hills and Birmingham among them, accommodating the overflow of millionaires. The old money (huge fortunes had been amassed before the automobile existed, from logging and Great

Lakes commerce and shipping) remained all but invisible. These conservative elders dwelt in less flashy neighborhoods under towering elm trees dotted about the city. By 1962, wealth had sprawled in every direction. To the tourist casually cruising around the city, Detroit must have seemed one giant upscale ad featuring naught but porte cocheres fronting handsome brick houses.

In the postwar flush of prosperity circa 1960, it would have been unthinkable, indeed laughable, to connect these manicured symbols of American wealth and security to nasty fates like, say, disaster, depression, and bankruptcy. Go ahead, the boosters' chorus piped: Detroit's sunny well-being was built on the burgeoning, ever-growing, inexhaustible appeal of the automobile. Compared to Detroit's blithe sense of permanence, ancient Rome was a tent city. Downtown glittered with places to spend money. Woodward Avenue ran arrow-straight northwest from the Detroit River to Pontiac, twenty-four miles away, splitting the city into east and west sides. Downtown shopping had been anchored for generations by J. L. Hudson, a vast Bloomingdalian department store. Grand Circus Park, a few blocks north and west, linked Detroit's theatrical and financial districts in a necklace of hotels, restaurants, high-end stores, movie palaces, and cultural fixtures such as the Detroit Opera House. Farther north, just off Woodward, the New Center complex lined West Grand Boulevard with upscale apartment residences cheek by jowl with the elegant Fisher Theatre, the mighty General Motors Building, and merchants stamped with New York prestige such as Saks Fifth Avenue.

Detroit was hardly a strange new environment for me. The McCall family had moved from Toronto to Windsor in 1953. That gritty little Canadian industrial city's meager supply of entertainment, shopping, and related distractions lured Windsorites, including my parents, across the river on balmy summer evenings to window-shop the haberdashers' and ladies' shops on Grand Circus Park. There were birthday dinners in restaurants with napery on the tables and wine menus. Tigers night baseball at Briggs Stadium. Red Wings hockey at Olympia Stadium. No McCall even knew where the Lions football team played, or cared.

Sunday runs out to suburban Dearborn let us marvel at the Henry Ford Museum's staggeringly rich collection of historic self-propulsion technology. What a treat. You could see and touch giant Rocky Mountain locomotives and swanky transcontinental trains. A Pitcairn autogiro dangled above. So did a big passenger plane built by a Ford-owned company and renamed the Ford Trimotor, the first reliable commercial airliner.

My brother Hugh and I had morphed into serious car consciousness years earlier, and our thirst for knowledge became insatiable. Magazines weren't enough anymore. So imagine our joy at being let loose to paw over a hundred automobiles lined up in neat rows like soldiers in review, from spidery black Ford Model Ts to the Brobdingnagian Bugatti Royale, the largest production car ever built. And every other kind of car from every era—extraordinary and wacky, civilian and racing machines, cars ordinary and iconic alike, brought here from Europe and Great Britain and Asia, dating from the self-propelled automobile's 1886 birthday to landmark cars covering every decade since, with every car cosmetically and mechanically perfect. The entire frozen parade of automobile history stood there, glowing. So did Hugh and I.

A cultural gem of a different stripe was the internationally famed Detroit Institute of Arts on Woodward, greeting visitors with Diego Rivera's huge murals, damning the automobile factory as a stygian hell of backbreaking labor and ceaseless mechanical violence, right under old Henry's nose.

■ ■ ■

That I no longer labored in the mire of a crummy little journal in a dead part of Toronto was powerfully confirmed when I first laid eyes on the General Motors Building, a stately limestone and granite pile on West Grand Boulevard. Albert Kahn had been commissioned to design a working monument to the vision and business wizardry of the corporation's founder, William C. Durant. Modesty wasn't in the GM genes; if this hard-edged Ozymandias of commerce seemed to shout that GM was the once and future monarch of the automobile world, nobody inside it would disagree.

The marbled, high-ceilinged lobby blended the gravity of a large banking institution with the majesty of a cathedral. Raising your voice seemed almost sacrilegious. Nearing Christmastime, GM automobiles of the season sat dotted about the lobby. A live organist favored the assembled with sacred music, instilling a reverent mood in a temple of mammon.

On my first day as a copywriter on the Chevrolet account at Campbell-Ewald, I stopped by the newsstand—and blinked: there was an early edition of that day's *New York Times*. Stacked next to it, that morning's *New York Herald Tribune*. Daily New York papers! Right here in Detroit! An inspiring omen: if Detroit was so plugged in to the biggest, most important city in the country, and daily interaction with it was normal and necessary, this wasn't the isolated midwestern burg I'd feared.

Campbell-Ewald had been Chevrolet's sole advertising agency since 1928. So tightly bound were the two entities that visitors and newcomers often confronted a puzzle: Where did the Chevrolet Division of General Motors begin and Campbell-Ewald end, and vice versa? A legitimate question. Advertising history tells us—well, at least me—that no agency has ever ridden an account through depression, management change, and new ownership and escaped the ax. Chevrolet and Campbell-Ewald, however, formed a relationship almost destined to stick. Should Chevrolet management ever reach a point where Campbell-Ewald just had to go—for reasons of lame creativity or chemistry issues at the top—it would be easier for the agency to fire everybody and start over again. The account was so huge, so many-faceted and just plain busy, that transitioning to a new advertising partner would take a year or more. And no car company could afford to stand down from advertising for that long.

Uniformed operators controlled the elevators that whisked VIPs up to the top two floors and offices in the carpeted hush of Mahogany Row and the Chevrolet executive suites. The rest of us piloted our own elevators up and down. As I prepared to elevate myself up to Campbell-Ewald, I worked on trying to flatten my cowlick, now that the gluing effect of my morning half-quart of Vitalis had faded. The same couldn't be said about that pungent Vitalis scent preceding me.

I finally blundered onto the fourth floor and into the agency. My advertising career could begin.

▪ ▪ ▪

My preparation for this job had dictated that my first priority be a mental showdown to rationalize my casual contempt for the advertising industry. Was it simply the ubiquitous cliché, shared by almost everyone not in it, that advertising was as sincere as a mortician's handshake, a manipulating con job run by hucksters dedicated mostly to boozing, lunchtime sex, and obscenely bloated salaries? The mid- to late fifties storm of exposés—bestselling books like *The Hidden Persuaders* and *The Man in the Gray Flannel Suit*—whomped the industry for its sins. It had been a big, unruly business before the twentieth century began. And compared with the almost gleeful, unregulated chicanery back then, the current standard of truth and product effectiveness was unimpeachable.

Now I was standing in the reception area, waiting to be christened as a copywriter, making more money than anything I'd ever earned before, lofted to a prestigious role in a big-time advertising agency linked to a giant of commerce.

What in hell had brought this about? Two weeks ago I had been sitting in the less-than-plush offices of *Canada Track & Traffic*, which was itself less than a magazine. I was the "Editor," a grandiose title for ads traded for articles. Canada didn't need a car magazine, and this one would ultimately strangle on its own financial shoestrings. That ignominious period of my career was soon to be forgotten. Having never been dubbed Mr. Success at anything, and with zero experience in that legendarily fierce arena, I was being elevated to a role in Chevrolet advertising that made sense to nobody.

Except perhaps to David E. Davis Jr. It was David E. (nobody called him "Dave," for the same reason nobody called Charles de Gaulle "Charlie") who plucked me from anonymity at that legendarily crummy Canadian car magazine and hauled me across the ice floes to Detroit and Campbell-Ewald, where he wrote enthusiast ads and swanned around the executive suite, a Cardinal Richelieu to top agency management.

We'd casually met one April night in Saskatoon, Saskatchewan, in the spring of 1961. I was covering the Shell 4000 Rally, a trans-Canada slog important enough to draw entries from Renault, Volvo, and Saab. In the overnight-impound section of a parking lot I noticed a big, rangy guy with a tomato-red face and a handlebar mustache. He was holding forth with a gaggle of Shell Rally drivers and mechanics, following the event for the agency on the sketchy rationale that there was ad potential if a Chevrolet pulled off something heroic and photogenic. Laughter exploded whenever he said something. Later that evening, he held court in his hotel room. I'd never encountered such a combination of wit, intelligence, and charm before. And never would again.

I learned from close association with racing people of the early sixties that David E. deployed certain natural gifts that abetted his ambition. He was fast on his feet. He seemed to remember everything he'd ever read or heard. His manner of speech was graced with a natural fluency, laced with a wicked wit. Anecdotes flowed from some mental library. His passion for good books, well-chosen classics and strange historical episodes, and every magazine he found interesting got woven into his quotidian conversations. He knew what he was talking about, aided by an IQ substantial enough to kindle jealousy at a Mensa convention. He knew everybody.

I mightn't have been so gobsmacked by David E. Davis if he hadn't been the first sophisticate I'd ever met. His example illuminated what I had dimly suspected: life meant more when you were deeply involved in what truly mattered; curiosity sparked an engagement with learning for its own sake; the precious treasure of a well-furnished mind; interesting company, usually smarter than you; the pleasure of mastering a craft, an art, or a skill, and pride in the accomplishment. David E. awakened in me an awareness of the richness of life almost celestially beyond my previous twenty-eight years' experience. Yet I freely admit that David E. was less than universally admired.

His oversized ego deserved to be studied by the National Science Foundation. Unsurprisingly, his critics focused on his predilection for showboating. He delighted in making a spectacle of himself. Clad in white linen suits, wrapped in an Inverness cape, he shut down ridicule with confidence. I never saw him sweat. Far from hiding his light under a bushel, he took a match to it and kindled a bonfire. His faults weren't secret. He was as vain as a matador, and could be almost capriciously cruel to the innocent undeserving. He harbored an inner rage and started feuds with longtime friends and his own staff. He was never known to apologize. And to my baffled dismay, David E. made no secret of his party-line sympathy for the NRA and the wild-eyed defenders of the paranoid right against their ubiquitous, illusory tormentors. Confronting this intellectual zigzag was akin to discovering the Reverend Al Sharpton to be a King Kleagle of the Ku Klux Klan. I painstakingly averted flocks of subjects that might set him off on a wild-eyed tirade about anything that threatened the fragile conversational peace.

It was almost Christmas 1962 when I was struck by the thunderclap of the announcement of David E.'s departure from Campbell-Ewald. He was to take over a New York–based car magazine. I was anointed as his successor, the agency's performance-car ad writer. David E. owned every particle of my admiration and trust. No adult had ever spotted unusual promise in me; he had instantly caught on to my eccentric written and illustrated satirical humor, valued it, and pulled me out of the shadows to do something with it. And now, the one hero in my life, by far a better father figure than my father ever even tried to be, was taking a powder before our residencies at Campbell-Ewald could overlap for a single goddamn day. It was now too late to back out. I ransacked my brain for reasons to do what I'd always done when unjustly treated: quit, then sink further into an even darker depression than the state of hopeless inertia that had smothered my days.

Depression was staved off, and my decision was simple. If the august David E. Davis had publicly pronounced me as the best writer to continue glorifying the Chevrolet performance story—well, who was I to argue otherwise? Of course I didn't believe him.

But I had a good ear and an affinity for mimicry, so until practice produced the necessary volts, I was in.

▪ ▪ ▪

My arrival in Detroit coincided with another epic change: the accumulated cobwebs of the fifties were being broomed away, even here. The nation's mood was shifting. The era of the befinned, bechromed behemoth as the ideal car for American buyers couldn't be sustained. The luxury of extravagance was collapsing from terminal fatuousness, speeded by a shove from smaller, cheaper, infinitely more practical European, then Japanese, cars.

The big V-8 had been all but a birthright to most Americans, who deplored the drop in status of a downsized car. Now the Roadblaster El Supremo Limited's tailfins were losing their novelty: they looked stupid. Chrome bumpers, trim, medallions, and such were becoming gauche. Detroit awoke one day in the early sixties to find the American car buyers' tastes were changing fast. And so began Detroit's evolutionary move to safer, sanely sized, fuel-efficient cars styled to look as sober as a judge compared with the blimps of yesteryear. Chevrolet spent big on full-page newspaper ads as fine as any competitor's. But newsprint can blotch the sexiest car photo, so Jim Hastings, Campbell-Ewald's art director, skirted this problem. Jim commissioned great pen-and-ink illustrators like Bruce Bomberger to provide big, gorgeous, black-and-white renderings—starring a Chevrolet or two—that filled almost a whole newspaper page, without the blemishes common to photo reproductions.

I knew I would be committing seppuku if I tried passing off my Corvette copy as David E. Davis–style prose. It read the way he talked: breezily laid-back, tossing off casual insights, never heavy-breathing or macho. All four hundred words unrushed and mellow as a summer's day. A Davis Corvette ad was a feast of delicious word-pictures. What a way to sell a sports car. I swore off imitating the master; I was neither old enough nor worldly enough to ape that voice. Finding my own would require a delicate balancing of confidence and amiability. No chest thumping: not even a car nut would stand braggadocio. And in the end it all had to sound Corvettish.

Campbell-Ewald was too big, its layers of command too complex and individual tasks too varied, to allow an intimate atmosphere. We creative drones seldom even saw our ostensible partners, the account executives. A fragmented organizational system kept Chevrolet car and truck creative groups physically separate. The TV creative department was a ten-minute walk from that of its print coevals. Print copywriters and art directors, the creative infantry, worked in rectangular cubicles no bigger than they had to be to hold a copywriter, his typewriter, and a small wooden credenza. Drawing boards replaced the typewriters in the cubicles where art directors sat. I wish I'd pilfered, or even paid for out of my pocket, the big old Underwood that came as standard equipment in my cubicle. You could drop one of those machines to the street from the tenth floor and it might bounce but it wouldn't break. What most endeared it to me was its elegant typeface. It transformed banalities into profundity and ad copy into deathless prose. I'd type nonsense just to marvel at the crisp authority it bestowed on everything it typed.

Modernity hadn't interfered with practicality since Campbell-Ewald had taken up residence in GM's kingdom: dark wood, frosted glass, and a stiff sense of order lent an aura of solidity and security—and a kind of charm reminiscent of a stuffy bank. It certainly didn't feel, on first impression, like the ad agency of sleazy song and raucous story. The Chevrolet print creative group functioned in a quiet, organized, friction-free environment. Where were all the prima donnas and assholes of legend? These were amiable, intelligent people.

None of my new colleagues invited me along for lunch in my first week or so. I was relieved; the process of acclimation made the midday break a chance to digest my new experience. I ate at a saloon across the street from the GM building, getting back within an hour to a largely empty fourth floor. The break-in period ended when a grizzled, middle-aged fellow copywriter named Bart took me to lunch. Bart's enthusiasm, if he ever had any, was buried under a thick layer of cynicism. I proved just the audience he preferred: naive, impressionable, and clueless.

Bart would have fit perfectly in *Mad Men*. Drinking was his hobby. Work didn't interest him. He introduced me to the two-hour, three-martini lunch. It wasn't Bart's invention, but nobody ever did more to honor it. My experience was bereft of lunches in places above the Three Guys from Athens greasy-spoon level. Red-leather banquettes and linen tablecloths charged those luncheons with shots of glamour and booze. Bart had mastered his three martinis through years of dedicated practice; with scant exposure to brown goods, I never drank beyond two Rob Roys. Only two? That seems a modest intake only to the non–Rob Roy drinker; two would adorn your neck with one of the descendants of the Albatross from "The Rime of the Ancient Mariner." Three Rob Roys, downed by a rookie, jabbed the skull with ice picks for about a week.

Bart, with his toilet humor and alcoholic passion, would eventually wear me down. What had at first appeared to be stylish and glamorous revealed itself as pathetic. I had been in Bart's thrall out of ignorance. Time to grow up and move on. No sooner did I accept this than the first friend I made at Campbell-Ewald, the art director on the Corvette ads, swooped in and made lunchtimes useful. His name was Roy. He was an insouciant boulevardier with a gigolo's looks and perfect taste in clothes. His every waking hour furthered an avid quest for fun and pleasure, with not a thought in the world to deter it. I'd grown eager to shed my sad-sack Canadian identity. We clicked.

Roy persuaded me to put Saks Fifth Avenue suits on my back and taught me, a sophisticate-in-training, the right drinks to order, how to approach a woman you don't know, how to feel socially poised. Roy affected a homburg and pretended he was just in for a visit from London or New York. He didn't have moods; his temperament was stuck on Happy. He wore his suavity like a pricey cologne. I trailed in his wake, an apprentice flaneur, until my imitation of his style and amiability had to end. Maturity was always a tardy arrival in my life. But I eventually conceded to myself that I wasn't Roy and shouldn't try to be; better to be your real self, imperfect as you may be, than to pretend to be someone you're not. And suffocate under the mask.

▪ ▪ ▪

In my romantic solo Detroit life I never entered a bar or lived it up at a wild party of louche young hedonists. Wild parties of louche young hedonists must have been banned in Canada. Or my mousy existence had kept me far from such noisy, hectic, thrillingly seductive venues. Naw, that couldn't be! Yet I felt that a wholly new social environment, in a city of two million, must be absolutely writhing with attractive young women fond of fun and men who could spell and had never contracted a social disease. Detroit presented a rare opportunity to adjust my personality and meet female partners. They didn't need to know about my crappy life, played out against a drab background. That me was in the rubbish pile. I was starting over: the new, Americanized Bruce McCall, worldly, charming, wittier than six Oscar Wildes, was about to hang out his shingle.

I thought I'd achieved a splendid makeover to qualify. Gone was the socially awkward gink in shabby outfits of zero style. The surly loner who never smiled. Who didn't play football or show up at dances or run with the fast crowd. Now he was recast as an interesting guy, a dynamic catch, fresh from the home of the Mounties and the high-steel Mohawks.

By my sixth month in Detroit, Ms. Skelton had reclaimed her apartment and I had clambered back down to my usual level. I had rented the mini-loft above a carriage house that was tucked behind a redbrick manse on Iroquois Avenue in Indian Village, a stable old East Side neighborhood of fine homes and leafy elms. In the former stable downstairs sat the successor to my Volvo, my cute silver 135-horsepower 1963 Corvair Monza coupe. What was wrong with this picture?

What was wrong was that I was the guy who wrote the Corvette ads, a guy who had a mandate to immortalize the most powerful production sports car in American annals, yet was driving, as his personal choice, the weakest entity in the Chevrolet performance fleet. Bolder driving ambitions rumbled in the hothouse culture I was paid to stimulate and perpetuate. Unmarried young rakehells bound for the open road didn't need four-place cars. I'd belatedly seen the car I drove as a key—indeed the basic—element in stamping my identity (now that I had the general outline of one) on the world.

For the first time in my life I had some money in the bank. If anybody had less reason to avoid the joys of driving a Corvette, it was the guy who wrote the ads for them. Fate once again elbowed its way in and took over the project. Once again it was Betty Skelton who delivered a solution. She offered to sell me her Corvette.

I didn't buy just any old Corvette. This was astronaut Alan Shepard's 1960 Corvette, acquired by his good friend Betty after being custom-modified and "breathed upon" by Shepard's pals in the Chevy skunkworks. More than mere hot-rodding was his aim: Shepard and several cohorts in the Manned Flight program loved racing up and down the access roads near the Cape Canaveral launch sites in their free time, coming as close to escaping velocity as an earthbound internal-combustion engine could achieve. These were among the most competitive guys extant.

I now owned a sizzling chunk of the Right Stuff. The Corvette had evolved since its 1953 introduction as a sheep in wolf's clothing, a fake sports car that was underpowered and flaccid. By 1960 it was a muscular kind of sports car, as American as a cowboy, if also about as crude. Gobs of V-8 power forgave a multitude of sins. And with a driver strong enough across the shoulders, it could be hogged through corners surprisingly fast. A retrograde solid rear axle and drum brakes kept the Corvette something of a techno-laggard, but it outperformed while underpricing everything near its cost level by thousands of dollars. Grudging acceptance of America's only sports car morphed into a sneaking affection. It became the Vette.

My responsibility to obey the Corvette way of driving weighed lightly: Corvettes weren't exactly outlaws, but all that power, and the term "sports car," meant something other than gentility. You were expected to be crude: mash the gas pedal and burn rubber accelerating from every stoplight, treat highway speed limits as suggestions, let out the loudest exhaust belch possible with every upshift. And get all Conan the Barbarian whenever you and your Vette came near another car with performance pretensions. Living up to the Code of the Corvette could be fatiguing. Top-down driving raised the stakes by fifty percent: no open-air car would dare to duck a challenge.

■ ■ ■

Our boss in the Chevrolet creative group was Jim Bernardin, and a nicer person didn't exist. Jim smoked a corncob pipe symbolic of his West Virginia roots. He was soft-voiced and patient and the least cynical advertising man who ever lived. Part of his creative director role was to present finished layouts of upcoming Chevrolet campaign ads to the client. His copy and art staff writers started work after a session of informal interpretation of the client's needs from Jim. The presentations that ensued once the ads were conceived were where great creative ideas went to die. Only out of respect for Jim and sympathy for his plight did the Chevrolet creative team attempt one more time to roll the boulder up the hill.

It's the very definition of the creative advertising man or woman to get famous and rich by making magic—to make a name, build a reputation. That dreamy ambition can succeed only if the client wants boldly innovative work. Most agencies, and most creative types, are worn down and worn out by unimaginative or gutless responses. Smart, bold creative work usually terrified the average client's advertising manager, who was inevitably a corporate second-rater less impelled to demand greatness than to cover his ass. His insecurities made him fearful of risk.

Some clients, desperate for attention and squeezing smallish budgets, can't afford not to go for broke. Volkswagen of America ranks as the all-time champ of this approach. The cheap, ugly, dismally underpowered Beetle, via madly unorthodox advertising, earned a niche in American folklore as a plucky, beloved underdog on the one hand, and on the other earned a sales success that would ultimately shake up Detroit and euthanize the insolent chariot.

Chevrolet's advertising was powered by almost diametrically opposite factors. Every ad is part of a strategy, and this strategy didn't call for VW-like surprise. A lack of surprise was in fact considered smart. Chevrolet sold one of every ten new cars in America in 1962. That success was nerve-racking on executive row, treated as much as a burden as a plus. Once you've reached first place, how do you stay there? In bare terms, you run scared all the time. And you never take risks, either in designing Chevrolets or in selling them.

▪ ▪ ▪

David E. had slipped me into the least-square job in the Chevrolet copy department: writing the so-called buff book ads (buff books being the monthly car magazines beamed at America's thousands of enthusiasts of performance, racing, and sports cars). Every American manufacturer eager to be credible among the competition-savvy cognoscenti searched for somebody—not necessarily an adman—who could talk the talk, walk the walk, knew the industry from the inside, and could write comprehensible "enthusiast" ads.

Chevrolet's sister GM division Pontiac, flailed by wunderkind general manager (and future carmaker) John Z. DeLorean, had sneaked its way into a lethal one-two combination of performance-car lab and maker of sexy sedans and coupes. This pissed off Chevrolet. Goaded by a client spending millions to support a largely sub rosa racing program and itching as well to inject performance fever into the blandly white-bread Chevrolet brand, Campbell-Ewald had tapped David E. Davis Jr. to do the job. And now it was my turn.

I had a lot to work with: indeed, a pack of saliva-inducing road thugs led into the arena by the flashy, sensationally capable 1963 Corvette Sting Ray. These included a line of big, special-option "Super Sport" sedans and coupes transformed into fire-belching V-8 roadblasters no normal family should ever be allowed to sit in;

a second phalanx of compact Chevy IIs also fitted with brawny V-8s; and the star-crossed Corvair. Chevrolet general manager Ed Cole's attempt to raise Corvair's power output by clamping on a turbocharger lifted performance, but not enough, alas, to come close to competitive levels.

Total ignorance of advertising wisdom was my starting point in writing ads. In the performance sphere, writing talent and advertising savvy were all well and good, but they were useless if the ad didn't talk the talk and exude authentic cool. I performed my writing tasks as if there were no rules. There weren't. And I had nothing like a philosophy of advertising to guide me. Copy needs could easily be summarized: just concoct four-hundred-word paeans of praise and we'll slap them into an ad. What a sandbox to play in! My Underwood coughed up a dozen versions of every such copy block, packing in the peppiest four hundred words, with the most adjectives and least reader breathing room ever achieved in English. These were overheated, overwritten imitations of how an amateur thought a performance-car ad should sound: slick and superficial and insincere.

I got that part exquisitely right. Cowed by the glimmering halo of authority shining down on the Performance Car Expert, nobody dared question anything I wrote. It was a mysterious language that bound writer and reader, and I was immune from criticism. Nobody stopped me. Nobody even edited me. Those initial efforts must have been some of the most wretchedly inept car ads ever printed. But the paychecks kept on coming. Have another Rob Roy! I learned nothing about writing ad copy, or the more general craft of advertising, in my time at Campbell-Ewald. I didn't even know there was anything I needed to know. What more could there be to it than spinning aerated fluff? It turns my ears hot pink today to recall the Corvette headlines I perpetrated, then passed all checkpoints to get in front of the performance-oriented magazine reader.

A startlingly original design, capable on looks alone of making people want to buy it without even knowing what it was, the 1963 Corvette Sting Ray was the most technically advanced and arguably the least criticized car in General Motors history. And yet "Clip Along the Dotted Line" was the headline on one Corvette ad. A lame pun; the photograph above it showed a Corvette clipping along the dotted line on a rural highway. Another inanity of stupendous irrelevance: "We Took a Little off the Top": borrowing a barbering phrase to prattle about the doors of this hot new sports car from Mars slightly cutting into the roof was devised to spotlight a virtually meaningless feature. I can plead a newcomer's ignorance, but that idea was seen and green-lighted by the chain of command. That nobody said anything tells you a lot about Campbell-Ewald's advertising prowess.

Not that Chevrolet advertising in general set a standard for innovation. Corporate advertising clung to "Jet-Smooth Ride" as the slogan for the entire model line for years. Even when new, this slogan conjured an image with all the panache of a Don't Walk sign. Jets no longer implied superlatives. "Jet-Smooth Ride" typified the retrograde thinking that plagued Chevrolet advertising year after year. By sheer coincidence, this gem had come from the pen of Campbell-Ewald's chairman, a Buddha-size man of a certain age whose name, ironically, was Mr. Little. Nobody knew his first name, and he was apparently too busy to set foot outside his Mahogany Row office and certainly too engaged to tour his agency's creative cave. I never actually glimpsed our monarchical leader in my time at Campbell-Ewald.

This feudal culture of the all-powerful authority figure personally in charge of everything, remote from his lieutenants and answerable to nobody, was not the key to advertising greatness. Happily for Mr. Little and Campbell-Ewald, greatness wasn't required. Chevrolet preferred to maintain the status quo ante. Its advertising was risk-averse: if it ain't broke, don't fix it.

Someone at Chevrolet decided that the failing Corvair could be repositioned as an ideal runabout for Milady: rear-engined and thus light-steering, gutless enough not to frighten a spinster, cute as a button in feminine pastel colors. Into the breach lunged Mr. Little, an unchallenged copywriting tyro such as only an agency chairman could be. His Corvair headline: "She flirts with you, that's what she does." The creative troops cringed.

■ ■ ■

My girlfriend for a year and a half was a secretary in another ad agency in the GM building. She was petite and pretty, divorced, with a seven-year-old son. I spent summer afternoons and evenings with her at her parents' house in Royal Oak, Michigan, verbally fencing with her resolutely far-right father, a highly successful building contractor. Mom was a chatterbox, firing off opinions that were devised, I quickly saw, to needle and occasionally draw blood from her hubby. Although the domestic atmosphere teetered on the brink of explosion, for me, having nursed a lifelong ache for warmth and security in family life, even that fractured household provided a sense of comfort.

We took advantage of the city's offerings: Nichols and May, the Weavers, Joan Baez, all live. Dinners in the London Chop House and a swanky little restaurant, Jimmy's. Drinks at a bar on Woodward, listening to the cool, jazzy duet Jackie and Roy. Our mutual appetites for top-notch entertainment were sated. Our sex was also plentiful. My carriage house served as our den of iniquity.

Sometimes—seldom conveniently—the copulation urge surged past all physical obstacles. My advice: Don't even try doing it on the passenger well of a '60 Corvette. It can be done. It was done. I walked with a limp for a week afterward. Her back hurt for a month.

The Corvette was more car than I'd dreamed of. Driving it broadcast the pleasures of self-indulgent excess. But in the mid-sixties, attention in the enthusiast world beyond Detroit was shifting to the other end of the spectrum. The age of the overachieving runt had dawned, led by a wacky little English box-on-wheels called the Mini. Front-wheel drive and an engine mounted crosswise meant a 1,400-pound car less than twelve feet long with plentiful space for four adults, a flyweight running circles around everything else. Tuning the small engine to the gills generated a shockingly potent seventy-one horsepower and a sublime power-to-weight ratio. This undersized brat ascended overnight to superiority in rally and racing competition. I had to have one.

And I got it: the hottest available version, a British Racing Green Mini Cooper S. Its Corvette stablemate gathered dust as I giggled at the Mini's freakish agility, making geniuses of stupid drivers. The English Disease—outdated design, hilariously careless assembly, and cheapjack components—dogged the Mini. But even if things fell off it as you drove, its phenomenal talents earned it forgiveness.

■ ■ ■

After two and a half years, my euphoria at having been given a professional home and the early makings of an advertising career had tapered off. I had learned just enough to start feeling restless. With an increased understanding of the creative side of the business, my work felt more and more like treading water.

Fueling my growing discontent were the recent defections of a couple of disenchanted copywriting friends to New York. Not only New York, but the hottest agency in New York and arguably the world: Doyle Dane Bernbach. DDB's Volkswagen work alone, studied and envied by creative people everywhere, heralded a brash new dogma that suddenly made big, conventional agencies seem constipated. John Noble's and Marv Honig's ambitions couldn't be slaked by annual predictions of an imminent Campbell-Ewald creative renaissance, so they decamped, and when they got to DDB they thrived there.

America's profound cultural shifts of the sixties were beginning to discombobulate every institution. Doyle Dane and a handful of boutique agencies smelled something in the air. They aligned themselves with the fresh new cultural norms, mocking the mastodons' research departments, mission statements, focus groups, and "safe" advertising: the intended target was a "consumer," hidden amid demographic charts and age levels, ad nauseam. Instead there arose a blasphemous sidestepping of social science, a practice of going straight for the jugular. The ads thus produced were ones that copy and art admirers tacked up on their walls.

My impatience to be one of Doyle Dane's stars forced me to join the throngs of job applicants before I was ready. I did up sample ideas that mimicked DDB style: fake Queens accent, clever puns, short copy ending with a funny kicker. The kindly rejection letter was not unexpected, and it failed to break my heart. It did strengthen my resolve—the first resolution being to get out of Sleepy Hollow, i.e., the Chevrolet copy group and Campbell-Ewald and Detroit—before the comfort and the lack of challenge permanently dulled my mind.

A murky Toronto character who claimed a role in the Canadian industry phoned me one day in August 1964: Would I go to Japan and tour the factories of all the big players in the domestic automobile industry, all expenses paid, and write a report to be published in an automotive magazine I'd never heard of? My knowledge of and interest in Asia and Japan wasn't deficient, it was nonexistent. Curiosity, and the certainty that another chance would never come, won out, and I flew to Tokyo on a two-week vacation. My research was a scholarly history of Japan by the late Nipponophile Lafcadio Hearn, who wrote in English but thought in Japanese. By the time my flight reached Honolulu, still stuck in the misty Japanese past, Lafcadio was likewise.

As it was, the Japanese present was confounding enough. Tokyo heat in August soaked me in near-liquid humidity. I'd arrived late on Saturday. Sunday morning I took a stroll and the exertion of walking a block plastered me to the pavement: I was the frying egg, the sidewalk the skillet. Japan on my first encounter left me feeling upside down, overwhelmed by the dizzying cultural difference; not even the men's rooms felt familiar.

A driver conducted me every morning to another car factory and another stilted talk in a gloomy reception hall, my hosts and I sitting in plump easy chairs covered by loose white cloth as smiling girls served tea and pastries. The factory host then handed me a gift and a guide-man led me through the obligatory assembly-line walking tour, a march-through of more or less identical sights. A Toyota shunted into a booth to be robotically spray-painted and blow-dried. Flat sheets of metal fed into mighty stamping presses and emerging seconds later bent into Nissan doors and roofs. My notepad recorded a blizzard of boring factoids and statistics that would serve me well back home to stud my report with meaningful-sounding details.

Home, when I finally got there, felt sweetly welcoming and soothingly familiar. I later dutifully tapped out an article about my visit, probably the first and only story that found Japanese car factories funny. It may have been the last condescending pat on the head that that industry had to suffer: Japan at the time of my visit was about to scare the piss out of carmakers everywhere. I was chauffeured from Tokyo to Yokohama in an Isuzu Bellel, a diesel-powered copy of the British Austin Westminster. It had almost made it to our destination when it conked out. My guide called for a replacement. As we stood waiting by the roadside I noticed that our driver had vanished. The guide was unsurprised: the driver had lost face, he explained. At the Toyota test track in Nagoya, I watched a toylike, two-stroke Toyota Crown slog around on a test track, making loud noises disproportionate to its rate of speed.

Travel expands perspective. Back in the GM building, I was even more bullishly ready to move on. Chevrolet, and thus Campbell-Ewald, was a poor educational choice for an advertising neophyte. Chevrolet advertising might be okay in Detroit. In the eyes of New York admen it was dull and corny. The truth was that Chevrolet, too big to fail and too rich to take chances, had never been a hotbed of creative innovation and never would be.

I wasn't mad at my employer or unhappy in Detroit. It was simply my time to charge the barricades, to test my brains and talents in the big leagues, in the most competitive arena extant. In New York. Such ringing phrases, and such clear ambition, lacked one thing: a job in New York to put them to the test.

■ ■ ■

One gorgeous red-and-gold October afternoon in 1964 I was hanging around the paddock at the Watkins Glen racing course in the Finger Lakes region of upstate New York. A major event, featuring the cream of international racing stars, had drawn everybody who was anybody in automotive affairs. David E., who'd since decamped to New York, was in the midst of it, of course. He wasn't in the least perturbed by my impending desertion from Campbell-Ewald. For a different set of reasons he'd made the same trip; I think he understood that Detroit wasn't a goal but a stop on the way. He promptly introduced me to his former mentor, Barney Clark, now a creative elder on the Ford account at the J. Walter Thompson agency in New York.

Clark was a craggy-faced, avuncular older guy. He'd been the very first Chevrolet enthusiast writer, and a great one. As it turned out, nothing about my chance encounter with him involved chance: David E. had organized it. He had seen to it that Barney got a pit pass that allowed him to rub shoulders with the American motor racing elite and a respectable number of the great racing drivers of the day. I had the same open sesame. Denny Hulme, Bruce McLaren, and Ricardo Rodriguez stood around the pit area after the race, trading reports on their various drives. A gaggle of insiders, including David E., kibitzed. Barney Clark showed up and David E. introduced us.

Barney never got an opportunity to dissuade me from leaving Detroit, even if he'd wanted to. As the original Campbell-Ewald enthusiast writer, he hardly needed my sweaty entreaties. J. Walter Thompson ran the Ford account out of its New York headquarters. Any copywriting job would do. Barney was taciturn by nature. The usual adman blather about a brilliant creative team, a great client, and such froth never escaped Barney's lips. Had there been any negative murmurs, my lust for a place in New York blotted them out. If J. Walter Thompson was sacrificing virgins, spying for the USSR, and paying its people in Canadian quarters, I didn't care. My mind had frozen on the idea of me as an official New Yorker.

Once again, the fix was in. Once again, a mentor exercised a personal connection on my behalf. Thus, no interviews with Human

Resources. No tear sheets in a portfolio. No sparring about money. A week after our chat at Watkins Glen, Barney called from New York. I was hired.

▪ ▪ ▪

Leaving Campbell-Ewald and Detroit tinged the palpitations felt on the verge of new adventure with a familiar sense of melancholy. I'd passed my first test in advertising, although I felt I still hadn't had the chance to truly prove myself as a copywriter. The life I'd carved out for myself as a young bachelor hadn't brought anything close to my expectations; my lifelong social timidity and awkwardness stifled initiative.

There was a bar at the foot of my street full of people my age milling around on languid summer evenings. I could never quite overcome the nameless, pointless fear of . . . what? . . . and join the crowd. Relations with my girlfriend had cooled. She'd begun talking about marriage, which provided a rationale for my refusal, and anyway, I realized I didn't love her. I wasn't even sure I liked her.

A more naggingly painful issue in leaving concerned Hugh. He and I had grown up as close as two brothers could be. Same bedrooms. Same jobs (Windsor Advertising Artists). Same interests (cars). Same friends (Alex). Except that they were all my friends, my interests, my life. Hugh was missing an ego, an identity, a sense of himself as a freestanding personality. I was indeed my brother's keeper.

Leaving Hugh behind in his empty life in Windsor, alone, felt like leaving a puppy at a shelter. To assuage my guilt I passed the last evening before my departure in Hugh's depressing apartment in a woebegone corner of town. He had taken up cooking—for something to do, I surmised—and cooked a decent beef Stroganoff for dinner. I sat on the living room couch, deliberately intent on drinking way beyond excess for the first time in my life. I guzzled enough straight-up Manhattans to float RMS *Berengaria*, blabbing my head off to avoid the impending issue, staying as late as I could.

I drove far too fast and carelessly back to Iroquois Avenue at two a.m. in a fit of drunken recklessness, a berserk attempt to blot out the pain I knew was going to descend on Hugh from the moment I stumbled downstairs that night and left him to his crummy fate.

By rights I should have crashed my Mini into the tiled wall of the Windsor–Detroit tunnel. Or gotten grabbed by the neck and yanked from behind the wheel, reeking of booze, at U.S. Customs. Or been pursued by cops until luck finally abandoned me. By rights I should have pushed the Mini just beyond the laws of physics into a flip, a somersault, and a barrel roll. The car should have come to rest and caught fire. The conflagration could have been seen from across the Detroit River, in parts of Windsor.

My brother Hugh would have gone to bed and missed the show. But then, he'd missed out on so much in life.

Bristol "Balaclava" Mk 1 Medium Bomber

The Balaclava was laid down to meet the need of Her Majesty's (then His) Royal Air Force for a sturdy, short-range medium bomber. It came within a whisker of doing so. Three years behind schedule and some 4,000 lbs. overweight owing to "fixes" needed to cure the problem of an unconscionable number of wings tearing off in flight, the Balaclava finally joined the 12th Bomber and Reconaissance Wing at Cantering Goony on 1 July, 1942 and served faithfully for several uninterrupted months, particularly excelling first as a morale-building exhibit during "Visitors' Days" at the aerodrome, then later as a target drone, then finally as a target. Power for this bristling behemoth of the air was supplied by two twin-screw 188_hp Bristol "Bosphorus" radial water-cooled motors; and although the opportunity to find out never quite precisely materialized, it was always assumed that a bomb load of something in excess of about 2,000 lbs. could have been carried against the Hun. Following cessation of hostilities in 1945, six squadrons of Balaclavas in virtually "as-new" condition were vended to the Portuguese Air Force. But the notorious Angolan uprising, known as "The Blow-Gun War," put paid to the career of this redoubtable soldier of the clouds. Today, if one will prowl about the Angolan fens, one may stumble upon the wreckage of a Balaclava: mute reminder of the treachery of the sharp-shooting Hottentot, and of a legend that almost, but not quite, might have been.

(Picture courtesy of Rt. Hon T.D. Guffin, FOB, Her Majesty's Custodian of the Heavier-than-Air Archive.)

The planes I'd drawn as a kid led to a career in satire, starting with this piece in *Playboy*.

Chapter 6

Scared by Success

My triumphal entry into New York fell flat the moment I flopped down on my bed in the Lexington Hotel. The antic saga of getting there, of losing myself in preparation, was finally ended. I was here. Now what?

Good question! I knew as much about living in Constantinople as I did about coping with New York. I lay there on my bed, cursing myself for cruising into the biggest city on the North American continent as if it were Ottawa, capital city of Canada and home of somnambulance. One belated question after another tumbled out of the mental closet where I'd stashed and promptly forgotten them: Where should I live? How do I begin looking? What about furniture? Do the even-numbered streets run east or west? What's the Avenue of the Americas? Where, exactly, is Staten Island?

My postcard visions had overlooked matters of substance, as in, I didn't know even one of my seven million new neighbors. I faced the evaporation of my gossamer fantasies, which were already fading in reality's harsh light. The excitement of the move swiftly transformed itself into a less gung ho challenge. I'd have to turn in my Mr. Magoo spectacles. The idea of New York as a cheery Disney metropolis had to be put on indefinite hold.

I couldn't miss the un-Disney-like indifference, inseparable from hostility, radiating from my cabdriver and the sourpuss faces in the lunch-hour streams of pedestrians on the sidewalks. Maybe it was my hypersensitive temperament acting up during the overnight transition from nowhere to the center of the universe. Some years before, back in my teens, the barber's shifting of the part in my hair from one side of my head to the other triggered a woozy discombobulation that lasted days. I interpreted this as a miniature example of a profound larger truth: Change jangled your life. Avoid it when you can.

All that was required for my recently acquired Detroit savoir faire to wither faster than Dorian Gray's face was an overbearing deskman at the hotel check-in counter. He was tall and he loomed. Blue suit and brown shoes, a Junior Teen necktie, and a manner that expected a "No!" before I asked a question betrayed my origins. An identity formed in a land where spices would ruin a meatloaf and a pair of neatly creased trousers drew a muttered "Clotheshorse" singled me out as a Canadian.

Yet the simple knowledge that I had made it to New York would soon fortify me. Granted, I might have come from the wrong side of the forty-ninth parallel, but I was entitled to be and act like a New Yorker: cool and tough, taking no shit from anybody (such as snotty hotel clerks). Until I found an apartment, my room in the Lexington Hotel would be a temporary home. I hadn't expected much and got less than that: a gloomy chamber that was dark even in daylight, as is often the case when the room's only window faces an air shaft. I paid for it with my total fortune, which was not enough to warrant a TV set or more than a single bath towel.

My first Sunday in New York, a spanking-bright early November afternoon, I decided to amble around the city. Five blocks later, I surrendered to a force greater than my spirits could deal with and returned to my cheerless room. The scale was too large, the buildings too high, and the streets too narrow. There was no relief for the eyes from the overwhelming busyness. I felt squashed, insignificant, ignorant, and stupid. Holed up back in my room, I lay on the bed reading a Mordecai Richler article about emboldened French-Canadian Montrealers sticking it to the snobby Anglophones who had ruled the city forever and now had to take their lumps. Boning up on Quebec politics failed to accord with my bold program to take Manhattan by force of personality. Solitary exile was the direct opposite of the likeliest means of achieving it.

Alas, solitary exile was the sole option. The bullish optimism that had launched me on this decisive quest was gurgling down the drain. Nobody was around to stiffen my spine, deliver a pep talk, kick me in the pants, and banish the mystery of how to belong. Fear was seeping back into my soul. Pretending otherwise, lying to myself, denying the core knowledge that wimpiness had been sabotaging my hopes of normalcy for much of my life, I'd never have the guts to change.

David E. Davis, my mentor and life guide, lived over in Brooklyn Heights. If I rushed there with my tale of woe and admitted to having fumbled my fresh start so soon, confessing that I'd left a big chunk of my ambition cooling down back in Detroit, David E. might find my conundrum not the cri de coeur of a tortured soul, but a whiny bleat. He'd been known to inflate into high dudgeon when disappointed with people, and could take my panicky dilemma as a sign that I might not be the front-runner he'd imagined—and that, as a result, I was as worthy of his friendship as a truck full of chickenshit. A classic nightmare scenario.

No, no more frigging self-pity. I made a trip to Brooklyn Heights (after some coaxing from David E.), where, in the living room of the Davis home on Henry Street, Sunday salons were held. Cocktail parties, I guess you could call them, but less formal. Here David E. was in his element: genial host to every famous European racing driver passing through town, American heads of imported car brands, automotive writers and photographers, and most of the staff of his booming magazine, *Car and Driver.* The salon wasn't a salon without the louche characters David E. had collected here and there. One was a blond gamine, dance-crazy and the wife or girlfriend of a slippery Brit, a professional hanger-on who was always about to take a job too secret to talk about. Pookie was her name. She did the Twist amid a forest of moving legs. Norma, David E.'s wife, served hors d'oeuvres. The Beatles, the Mamas & the Papas, and the Lovin' Spoonful warbled distantly, behind the conversational hubbub. I didn't yet belong there.

▪ ▪ ▪

The J. Walter Thompson agency ranked at the time as one of the biggest ad agencies in the world and was also America's oldest. Ford Motor Company aside, its list of clients included Pan American World Airways, Kodak, and a slew of category leaders with big ad budgets. Joining J. Walter felt similar to enlisting in the army: an entity so big and decentralized and balkanized that nobody really knew its direction and purpose; a hierarchy of ranks and layers and the inevitable bureaucracy; senior brass you never saw, running a machine so complex it left them no time for the foot soldiers.

Morale didn't often thrive in an agency this busy and this big. If J. Walter had a point of view and a value system about its mission, defining itself to potential clients and uniting employees behind a single and singular philosophy, I never saw or heard about it. I got no sense that this bothered the brass. The sole gesture of team spirit I ever experienced at Thompson was the day every employee got a brass medallion the size of an oatmeal cookie commemorating the agency's hundredth year. Before the end of the day I'd, er, misplaced it.

As with every big agency of the day, JWT's creative department roughly consisted of three component parts: a few killer talents, then journeyman writers and art directors below them, and at the bottom, drones, hacks, and juniors. The stars generated a goodly portion of the agency's multimillion-dollar campaigns, and bidding wars to land these creative talents were fierce. There were never enough of them to meet demand: job-hopping was worse than in the current NBA. Meantime, journeyman agency writers, art directors, and TV producers handled the bulk of the creative work. Most stayed in place for long periods, assigned to two or three accounts and juggling the workload. Longevity on an account assured continuity and made certain creative people indispensable. The most effective of these solid performers earned positions of responsibility as copy chiefs, art supervisors, and group heads. Drones and hacks served as permanent spear-carriers. Some hovered on the border of competence. Few were happy about their futureless futures, working on a diet of drudgework that kept them unsung. But most of them realized that their talents were modest, recognized that they were never destined for big bucks in big jobs, and remained at their humble stations because they couldn't earn the same money anywhere else.

Standards of advertising quality are elusive, but that they exist can be easily proven: give a drone or a hack the chance to make an ad for the current campaign for his or her account. The result is guaranteed to be off-strategy, and either stupefyingly dull or incomprehensible. Drones and hacks don't have what it takes to be journeyman creative contributors. That's why they're drones and hacks.

▪ ▪ ▪

My work experience at Thompson forced odious comparisons to Campbell-Ewald. I had no complaints that my reception lacked fanfare; no ceremony was involved. A brief encounter with a graying fussbudget nominally in charge of staffing gained me a health-insurance booklet and other spellbinding paperwork, whereupon the fussbudget's secretary marched me through a bewildering series of halls. Finally I was ushered into a grotto of an office for two and left to my fate. My roomie, a mystery man on the Ford account whom I barely saw, devoted most of his day to loud, prolonged, profane telephonic tiffs with his missus, quacking in his Brooklyn-accented Donald Duck voice. The office doorway stayed open to the jabber, hallway disputes, and foot traffic passing by.

At least twenty-five people—of whom I met maybe ten—swarmed around the Ford creative room. An island in the middle of the space provided office cubicles for a few toilers.

Organization of the Ford creative group was evidently inspired by Charlie Chaplin on that assembly line in *Modern Times.* This proved inimical to creative inspiration, or at least to my creative inspiration. Individual brilliance was rendered pointless by the fact that the group functioned on the monkeys-and-typewriters principle: every writer in that glorified boiler room was commanded to churn out headlines and body copy for the same Mustang or Galaxie or Falcon newspaper ad. Every writer's efforts were tendered to Bert, the copy supervisor. There ensued the briefest of pauses while he speed-read the few dozen candidate pages. Then, minutes later, came individual summonses to Bert's preposterously cluttered little cubbyhole for his feedback.

Bert was the first workaholic I ever met or worked under. He would have dismissed the work ethic of Ebenezer Scrooge as featherbedding. He could scan two days' worth of headlines in two minutes flat and zero in on their flaws. His critiques were muttered in a rapid-fire monotone out of the side of his mouth. Bert wasn't lavish in his praise or anything else. He was all business, all the time. He approached making ads as a grim, joyless exercise: boiling the fat out of every line of copy, driving his writers to the wall with orders to go back and whip up more, more, more headlines and text.

Bert favored—insisted on—sugar-free copy. His unsubtle approach was to grab readers by the scruff of the neck and rush them through a volley of bullet points to the bottom of the page. He begrudged a wasted word. The resulting ads were as hardworking and unsentimental as Bert himself. The romance of language, the allure of the automobile, gooey emotion of any kind, diluted the hard sell and earned Bert's quick dismissal. As the self-declared poet laureate of driving's pleasures, I chafed and fumed at the diminishing of copy to brisk word clusters cleansed of every space-wasting adjective and adverb.

After the rich banquet of Corvette, writing on the Ford account was lukewarm gruel. The environment was boot camp. The pressure never let up. I perforce got to be adept at the art of compression. I learned to clip, chop, tighten, push away the sludge to shape a selling argument to the buyer's needs. It felt good to be good at it, but it wasn't enough. Gloomy Bert, taciturn, ever-preoccupied Bert, had no time to be lovable or even likable. He and I had zilch in common. It didn't surprise me when, a few years later, Bert, all energy and edgy perfectionism, rose to CEO of J. Walter Thompson.

Fellow Ford copywriter Art Odell was the one close friend I made at J. Walter. He and I shared a penchant for satire and fed off each other's subversive glee. The dreary routine in a corner of that impersonal place was relieved by our frequent cross-office exchanges: lovingly detailed drawings of spectacularly idiotic airplanes, parodies of our own Ford advertising ("Ford Fever Strikes—Whole Town Doomed!"), or whatever else struck us as worthy of ridicule. Art was gentle, pixieish, pathologically insecure, and a terrible fit in the advertising trade.

Six months in Bert's blacking factory was all the learning I could absorb. I was feeling familiar pangs of restlessness. And with the statute of limitations on gratitude close to its expiration date, it was time to find a place more amenable than Ford, Bert, and J. Walter Thompson could ever provide.

Whereupon Kismet, a.k.a. the Good Fairy, enters from the wings and plants a big wet one on my kisser. Once more, all I needed to do in order to escalate to a better job and a richer life was to sit on my prat, twiddling my thumbs, until the telephone rang. And ring it did. My good friend Roger Proulx, a colleague from the *Track & Traffic* days (he wrote some pieces for the magazine), had just heard from a friend that Mercedes-Benz was starting over in the United States and had hired Ogilvy & Mather as its advertising agency.

▪ ▪ ▪

A week later I was head copywriter on Mercedes-Benz at Ogilvy & Mather. The best cars in the world, linked with the best advertising agency in the world. A job that hundreds of copywriters would gladly walk through fire to attain had dropped into my lap. With luck like this, who needed initiative or savvy?

The Ogilvy in Ogilvy & Mather, David, had elucidated a radical advertising philosophy in his 1963 bestseller, *Confessions of an Advertising Man*. His confessions mostly concerned his success. From first page to last, D.O., as he was known by everyone in his agency, hammered home the doctrine of rationality. He extolled it as the long-forgotten and neglected principle of advertising all goods and services. He had studied advertising as a researcher and had measured its effectiveness. Real-world advertising clobbered trendy "creative inspiration." He wrote copy that flirted with the outrageous. He spun adages that stuck in the mind as inarguably true: The more you tell, the more you sell . . . People don't buy from clowns . . . The consumer isn't a moron, she's your wife. David Ogilvy codified advertising relentlessly, persuasively. He compiled his findings on every tiny detail and rained hellfire on lazy writers and art directors who ignored them. He elegantly railed against advertising creativity untethered to a selling proposition. This enraged adland's liberals and made him a pariah to most of them. Understandably, it also began to attract clients. The reassurance Ogilvy's doctrine offered—stern, objectively proven facts versus creative hot air and guesswork—clicked. Relief at last for CEOs' constant agonizing that the millions they'd invested in advertising had essentially always been a form of gambling. His axioms sided with their contempt for know-nothings. Ogilvy's philosophy refuted the shibboleth so many clients subscribed to: "Half of our millions of advertising dollars are wasted every year—but damned if I know which half!" David Ogilvy knew.

David himself was a major part of Ogilvy & Mather's attraction: a tweedy, pipe-puffing, deep-voiced British aristocrat. He was the best public speaker, the wisest pundit, the most fearless critic of humbug and smarm and self-indulgence. No one had written and spoken more frankly and persuasively about advertising in the history of the genre. His prose was bone-clean and unaffected, E. B. White on speed, not a comma wasted, pompous Englishisms shunned. As in all fine writing, his was crystalline. The reader of an Ogilvy ad entered a deluxe selling machine, was royally entertained, and on exiting was punch-drunk on the merits of the product. And grateful for the ride.

Accomplished individuals can be major pains in the ass, so it was lucky for D.O. that most of his flaws actually burnished his image. He had the ego of a Shakespearean actor. He was a ham who loved the spotlight. His quick temper frightened people. For D.O., arguments were a kind of exercise: should he lose, he wouldn't admit it. Log enough time around him and you'd discover that deep behind the charm of that upper-class British persona lurked Willy Loman in a Bond Street suit and red suspenders. He aimed his keen intellect, writing talent, and passion for truth at selling, and nothing but. Scorning those ambitious to write books, he huffed that their very presence was a bloody waste of space.

I had read *Confessions* a couple of years before joining O&M. Detroit taught me nothing about making successful advertising. His book threw me a lifeline. As it did to would-be experts everywhere with a lust to know the inner secrets of selling. Within this modestly smallish volume was a virtual step-by-step tutorial on how to make not only effective but distinguished advertising. David Ogilvy became my hero. Single-handedly and almost overnight, he levered advertising—at least, his advertising—out of the clichéd demiworld of lowbrow hucksterism. Advertising didn't have to be a near-criminal conspiracy. It could be tasteful, honest, and useful. People of intelligence and high cultural standards, like—well, for instance, like me—rallied to the Ogilvy cause. A certain snobbery inevitably attached itself to the agency's image, a faint trace and no more. (Americans profess contempt for snobbery while secretly enjoying the hints of class superiority that define it.)

The O&M offices at Forty-Eighth Street and Fifth Avenue felt on first acquaintance like those of a prosperous London legal firm. Prosperous indeed: advertising growth was exploding, and Ogilvy & Mather was just beginning an overseas expansion. In New York, creative people occupied not cubicles but offices. Ubiquitous crimson carpeting suggested the House of Lords more than the tackiness typical of much ad agency decor. I was flattered and proud just to walk into the building every morning before eight and work until six or seven in the evening.

David Ogilvy himself stomped through the halls, ten times more formidable in person than in prose, the ultimate headmaster. It wasn't in him to waste time or words. His physical presence scared people when, as was his frequent habit, he dropped into your office with no warning. Today he's carrying a proof of the ad you've just written.

"Tell me what you think that headline is actually saying," he barks. You assume he's being critical, but your defense is waved off. He's already moved on to some other topic.

"How do you talk to a millionaire?" He is serious. You blurt out some bromide. He talks through and over it. He hasn't heard you because he's answering his own question:

"I'm a millionaire," he says, "and what difference does it make when you're selling me this gadget, or that car? I want the same information as anybody else!"

He turns to leave. Over his shoulder, he snaps: "Copywriters use the most unctuous, ornate, silly language when they're selling to millionaires. They think they have to suck up to the rich and they end up sounding like butlers. Fools!"

And as suddenly as he barged in, he barges out. Such impromptu visits, after the Great Man had exited (without a goodbye, as was his wont; not rudeness but shyness, because he didn't know his quarry's name and felt bad about having to ask), were sometimes embarrassing to the unready and the dull-witted. For the rest, they were bracing enough to cancel the visitee's panicky initial impulse to soil his pants.

Wealth and breeding defined David Ogilvy. He'd be at ease in 10 Downing Street or the White House. He never condescended to his agency staff or his audience. He was allergic to pandering. This reversed the reflexive cynicism of advertising tradition so that most O&M employees forgot the dogface's ritual resentment and jealousy of the big boss. They admired, respected, and were awed by him.

In presentations he cast an almost hypnotic spell. He dealt with captains of industry as an equal and wasn't afraid to bluntly tell them unpalatable truths about their products and reputations. He once harangued a convention of American automobile dealers because research had found that the public rated them dead last in trustworthiness and related virtues. When he finished his hiding of the audience, they treated him to booming applause.

A David Ogilvy new-business pitch was brilliant theater, featuring his inimitable self. The crux of his talk (sans notes, *naturellement*) was a parade of charts that incorporated the fruits of deep, imaginative, and meaningful research. These charts steamrollered tired and dated beliefs. It was difficult to quibble with such clear proofs, but somebody always did. Watching this poor fool's challenge get politely smitten by David's verbal broadsword was an entertaining moment before the lights flickered back on and the meeting ended.

Imaginary headlines swirled around in my head as I commenced settling into life at Ogilvy & Mather: "High School Dropout Makes

Good" . . . "'Comeback Kid' Proves Doubters Wrong" . . . "McCall Earns Huge Raise on First Day." Alas, McCall was never able to sunder the copywriter–art director division. No writer, by an ancient tradition that was frequently reinforced, was ever allowed to so much as suggest a layout or fiddle with any graphic element. The custom also held that no art director should presume to tinker with a copywriter's words. That rule was almost never tested, because the average a/d read as little as possible. Unfortunately this applied to ads for which he was responsible. "Functional illiteracy" is too strong a term, but some a/d's came close. My art background cut no ice with them. I could draw better than any a/d I ever worked with (a fact, not a boast), but any suggestion I made was rejected out of hand. My heart was scalded when a stoneheaded a/d botched a graphic element in favor of a second-rate solution.

Mercedes-Benz had been slow to plant itself in the postwar American car market. The three-pointed star hadn't exactly been a household name in prewar America, either. The brand was associated with fading images of something German, stuffy, well made, and expensive. With that to work with, O&M had to position Mercedes-Benz against the "luxury" segment of the U.S. market. A Mercedes-Benz was expensive, and that ended its similarity to the American concept of luxury—literally, more than is needed. In the American vernacular, luxury meant more trim, more padding, more weight, more size, more gadgetry. These "luxuries" didn't make a car better, just gaudier. The price of a Mercedes-Benz bought no superficialities, only superior technical solutions and the superior performance they guaranteed.

A car designed for German conditions and a different automotive culture had to compete with the longer, lower, roomier, sexier, higher-powered American luxury sedan, like Cadillac or Lincoln. Mercedes-Benz simply outflanked the entire U.S. luxury car precept and positioned its automobiles as an almost grimly rational alternative to the traditional American luxury car. The benefits could be seen and felt. Like a cold shower, the range and value of these benefits shocked the prospective buyer into seeing a Mercedes-Benz not as a status symbol but as a superior machine. And made that buyer wonder why such machines weren't American. The Monroney sticker (government-required manufacturer's specs and price details) on a Mercedes window delineated a sound investment in driving efficiency, practicality, quality, and longevity.

This appeal to common sense could hardly have hit the American luxury-car market at a more vulnerable moment. Postwar prosperity had created a binge mentality. Detroit luxury cars had gradually departed from the notion of automotive excellence. At their zenith they sported tail fins, became bloated and heavy, and morphed into status symbols that celebrated affluence. By the late fifties, styling was the selling point. Technology had stagnated. Innovation had all but disappeared. The novelty of the American road yacht was fading fast. Just in time for a visit to your local authorized Mercedes-Benz dealer.

■ ■ ■

Meanwhile, in faraway Stuttgart, the pace of technical progress hadn't slackened since 1886, when the company's founder, Gottlieb Daimler, unveiled the world's first practical automobile, twenty-one years before the Model T. That lead helped ensure that most important innovations in passenger car technology would appear first in the cars of Mercedes-Benz. The risk that American car buyers, allergic to technology, might blink and turn the page was real. The advertising challenge was to convert this Swabian book of Genesis into all the benefits of owning and driving a Mercedes-Benz that could fit on one page.

David Ogilvy had created a prototype with his now-legendary Rolls-Royce ads. He pioneered the counterintuitive technique of long copy—not for one or two ads but an entire campaign that limned the product's benefits in such vivid prose that the reader was left in a daze of admiration. The long-copy format looked like important news and dramatically introduced Mercedes-Benz to America. Only long copy could do justice to the story of one engineering landmark after another and their benefits. Moreover, it sharply differentiated Mercedes-Benz at a glance from all American car ads. And all American cars. It was expected that not everyone who saw these ads read through to the end. The impression told a story in itself. Even casual notice paid dividends, i.e., "If they have that much to say, it must be a damn good car."

I wrote and rewrote Mercedes-Benz copy night and day, seven days a week, and it hardly mattered if it was a small-space dealer ad or a two-page magazine ad or a full-page ad to run in *The New York Times* and *The Wall Street Journal*. I suspect that my deficient formal education and my viscerally insecure place in the world goaded me. I also craved the approval of my mentors, Messrs. Davis and the soon-to-be-introduced Hank Bernhard, who could validate me. And David Ogilvy, who only had to be David Ogilvy.

I thought and worked myself into an Ogilvist, while also serving as the moral guardian of the oldest and most respected manufacturer of automobiles on earth. There were the names on the list of owners of the Grand Mercedes 600 limousine, including Mao Tse-tung, Marshal Tito, and His Holiness the Pope. Not to mention Elvis Presley. I saw my job as more than a prestigious slot in adbiz; it was a higher calling. I concentrated on following D.O.'s inimitable copywriting style, achieving a result somewhere between imitation and plagiarism.

This was an absorbing mission, the focus of every hour I spent at the agency. Nobody else seemed as zealous about it. So, more or less by default, I was soon not only the seniormost Mercedes-Benz writer but also the creative head. I proceeded to blunt or starve the career of every writer under me by doing all the writing myself and keeping the poor bastards at a distance. Had any of them shown the potential to grow, or given a damn about cars or advertising, I'd have groomed them. But then and later, in similar situations, I couldn't trust any other copywriter to think like D.O. or generate perfect forgeries of that singular, sublime style. I freely admit to being probably the worst copywriting teacher who ever lived.

I was proud of the fact that the Ogilvy & Mather philosophy disdained the gaudy ritual of annual creative awards. These curious galas celebrate creativity for its own sake. The winning ads are brilliantly imaginative and beautiful and often witty as hell, but these awards have no connection to what advertising is for: to sell things. Selling is irrelevant to the major awards shows. They substitute for the personal fame so many advertising practitioners lust after but are denied by advertising's tradition of creative anonymity. A gold medal from the One Show trumps a sales leap traceable to sound but unflashy advertising. The annual Effie Awards, honoring sales success in various categories, enjoy scant success or meaning within the industry. Sic transit gloria bullshit.

■ ■ ■

Into my office and my life one August afternoon charged my next mentor/father figure/hero—a big, blond bull in a china shop, a passionate workaholic supercharged with a kind of dynamism that frightened the meek and lazy. Hank Bernhard was titularly the Mercedes-Benz account director. Account executives were the suits, business school grads who liaised with the client, looked after the budget, and coordinated the media, research, and creative departments. An unofficial cordon sanitaire traditionally barred the account types from meddling in creative work; their job was selling our work to the client and never presuming to dictate how it looked or read. Hank blithely ignored this tradition, infuriating—among many others—my group copy supervisor. However, it failed to piss me off. Hank's ear was more acutely tuned to copy—to the rhythms, wordplay, and power of written language—than that of nine out of ten copywriters. He cared and often knew more about typography, photography, media, the science of advertising, Mercedes-Benz, the company and its cars, than anybody.

Strong polymathic tendencies were evident in him, and sometimes exhausting. You either loved Hank's blend of passion, brains, compulsive work habits, and fierce loyalty to the client or you hated his guts. He lacked, shall we say, communication skills: he bored audiences, who nodded off after the first half hour of his stiff, clunky style of speaking, a style punctuated by spontaneous segues into lengthy anecdotes sans punch lines. Hank was frequently impatient, a tyrant and a bully. Withal, he was that rare creature who changed a room simply by entering it. Maybe it was his almost visible energy flow charging the air.

Hank and I bonded within our first hour of meeting. I was as eager as he was to alert America to Mercedes-Benz and its cars. He trusted my dedication to David Ogilvy's advertising crusade and my familiarity with the automobile world. We functioned in tandem: I'd hand in the pages of the next ad and wait. Before the end of the day my phone rang, a memo came in the office mail, or Hank in person thundered into my office with my typed ad, heavily splattered with notations in pencil and ink. The two of us—well, Hank—edited, moved lines and paragraphs around, changed a flat-sounding word to an active one. I transcribed his handiwork and added gems of my own. Far from resenting Hank's intrusion, I welcomed it. He couldn't abide sloppiness or carelessness, and he drove me to think deeper, work harder, and do it better in the fourth revision and better yet in the fifth.

Henry Paul Bernhard never relaxed. I learned from him that brutally hard work is the secret of great writing, that if you're patient, there is always a better way to say it. I also learned the importance—so true of Mercedes-Benz—of learning everything you can about a car or a lawn mower or a pair of shoes, because buried in those mountains of tedious facts could be diamonds that become extra selling points.

Those first six months on Mercedes-Benz at O&M would be my happiest, most fulfilling time in advertising. I was made a vice president. No corner office, no more money, no say in agency affairs, yet it did look good on a business card, and it let me sit back and savor having further escaped my dismal past. (The world didn't really need to know that an advertising agency vice president was the equivalent of rear admiral of the Swiss navy.) Our little gang of zealots, abetted by a typographic angel, the Danish freelancer Ingeborg Baton, stayed late on many nights. Lavishing half-insane care on every line of type, removing ugly "widows" to gain extra lines. Rewriting a caption to delete nine characters so it would fit on a single line. Hunting down typos at the very last minute. Having the fun, feeling the fizz known only to people in love with their work. Our introductory campaign was financed by a modest budget, but it sparked a sales jump that surprised even Hank and had our U.S. client dancing with joy.

▪ ▪ ▪

Outside of the office, the stubborn hobgoblins that had made me more an observer than a participant in life kept me isolated from wherever I should have been. I dated girls, but lost interest before anything happened. Work was my number one priority, and a bulletproof alibi for limited social activities. Maybe my job did leave nothing in the tank . . . but come on. My social life stank because my social skills remained stagnant. It would take a lot more than a mere resolve to change.

I finally abandoned a squat I had rented on the East Side, dragged the crummy furniture brought with me from Detroit downtown to Greenwich Village, and settled into a space below street level in a brownstone in an effort to feel the vibes and get groovy. A feeble hiccup of rebelliousness had drawn me to that gloriously seedy area, long a bohemian capital and now the epicenter of East Coast mid-sixties upheavals. The deepest I dared probe into what was now officially known as the counterculture was to wear a macho work shirt and clomp about in L.L. Bean boots on weekends.

It was the Summer of Love, 1967, young America churning and burning with a sometimes violent antiestablishment energy, wallowing in a spontaneously messy new subculture. The social and sexual freedoms—it was about freedoms of every kind—both lured me and scared me. Viewing it all from a fourth-floor window in an office building on Fifth Avenue at Forty-Eighth Street, a straight-arrow conformist with a brush cut in a three-piece suit, I brooded on which fork in the road I should take. I lacked the confidence born of self-knowledge that could furnish an unambiguous answer. I wasn't ready to make such a critical decision. So here I was, at thirty-two, still a guy without a fucking clue.

Steve Smith was my one close friend. Like most people I knew, he worked for David E. 's car magazine as a kind of utility man. His unpredictable mood swings terrified me at times, but mood swings didn't account for everything; even when coasting along in normal range, Steve could be a hostile prick. The attraction was his blazing intelligence. I don't think he believed in anything, which left him free to argue both sides of any subject. He'd read everything I'd read, and more. He sharpened my wits, caught me out on my sophistries. He kept me honest. An exhausting, annoying, off-putting, worthwhile friend.

By this time Hank Bernhard was no longer my mentor and partner in making Mercedes-Benz an American success story. In early 1968, as the first acquisition of an advertising agency that would ultimately see Ogilvy & Mather buy, merge, and otherwise grow into an international giant with offices worldwide, the William Heumann agency became Ogilvy & Mather in Frankfurt. Hank was sent over to run it.

He had his hands full. Advertising—*Reklame* in German—was still in its early stages. Prewar advertising hadn't gone beyond the poster stage, and politics had blocked the importation of American know-how. Postwar Germany, still reeling from complete ruin and not at all eager to be a clone of Madison Avenue, fostered its own advertising culture. American luxuries such as consumer research were unknown. Heumann rated no better or worse than other agencies, but its client roster serendipitously matched up with important ones on O&M's list, including Mercedes-Benz and Shell Oil, so Heumann it was.

Hank's advertising savvy, herculean energy, and the fact that he spoke passable German commended him to the task of turning Heumann around and making of it a solid O&M agency. Meanwhile, I was pondering how to give *life* to my life. Whereupon I stumbled straight into the ursine embrace of Hank Bernhard. On one of his frequent trips back to the New York office, he descended on me like a famished grizzly. The Bernhardian barrage of flattery, persuasion, and the limning of vast, exciting new horizons was music—loud, stirring, brassy march music—to my ears. A couple of hours of it and I had agreed to join Hank in Frankfurt, in a nebulously defined creative role. This was my opportunity to live abroad, to work in a congenial environment, to get back to feeling again those hectic, heady days working with Hank.

I wasn't a shrewd bargainer, for lack of experience and, truth to tell, because I was a born patsy. I couldn't even think of conditions to set. What, me worry? Hank had arranged my Frankfurt life on the most cushiony possible terms. From a salary bump, to a company Mercedes, to a rent-free flat, to the *Putzfrau* who'd clean up after me and do the laundry. The exchange rate was pegged at four deutsche marks to the dollar, which rendered it difficult not to live hedonistically.

On a gray day in mid-November, I took a cab to Kennedy Airport and forsook New York for an indefinite time. Ahead waited the adventure of living and working in the heart of Europe. Pushed aside, for the nonce, was the matter of how to solve the life I was running away from.

A Mercedes-Benz copywriter job dropped into my lap.
With luck like this, who needed initiative or savvy? I'm on the far right.

Chapter 7

A Thousand Moods, All of Them Somber

Growing up during the Second World War had ingrained in me an image of Germany as an ugly land, dark, harsh, and sullen. What the country had been before it stumbled into the totalitarian Third Reich interested me. History had always fascinated me. Now, in 1968, German history focused my attention on the Weimar Republic and the bumpy downhill slide into war and horror. The hackneyed question, asked but never satisfactorily answered—How could this cradle of culture and science have stooped so morally low, so fast?—was for wise men to determine. My curiosity focused on what the war had blotted out. A non-martial Germany must have existed, but I in my ignorance had made it a mystery. To explore its history seemed akin to breaking into a sealed room.

My interest evolved as I followed this history through the centuries. I was shocked that the state known as Germany had existed only since 1871. The Great War divided its history into Before and After. Under Kaiser Wilhelm, the nation had achieved wealth and power, all of it blasted to smithereens in the 1914–18 conflict. The crippled country was forced to try reinventing itself, a process thwarted by the culture's scant familiarity with democracy and the vengeful terms dictated by the Versailles peace treaty of 1919 that gutted Germany's already wobbly economy with monstrous debt repayments, spectacular inflation, and worldwide depression. Aggravated by bitter political turmoil and the myth that Germany had been "stabbed in the back" by domestic sabotage that cost it the war, serial crises ultimately ushered National Socialism, like the fox in the henhouse, into position to wreck all hopes for a decent national polity.

The Weimar Republic fascinated me as no political or cultural entity ever had. From 1919 to its collapse in 1933, Weimar—so called in reference to the small city serving as the seat of a feckless series of weak governments—burns in memory as the symbolic, frantic last binge of interwar freedom. Weimar's dancing on the edge of the abyss brought forth the bitter, haunting music of Kurt Weill, in "Mack the Knife" and *Mahagonny*, piercing my imagination as Gershwin, Piaf, and Noël Coward could not. A quasi-symphonic piece of that time, composed for radio by the now-forgotten Eduard Künneke, was the Weimar Zeitgeist captured in music. It had lain in the back of my mind since I heard it on CBC radio in the mid-fifties. The *Tänzerische Suite* sounded exactly like the Weimar of my imaginings: alternately desperately jolly and carefree, sagging into melancholy, then suddenly wailing with what was—to me—the despair of lost hope. It seemed to have trapped the soul of Weimar in the very ether, sensing tragedy in the wings.

Marlene Dietrich in *The Blue Angel* did on film for Weimar what the *Tänzerische Suite* did for music. The stage production of *Cabaret*, borrowed from the play *I Am a Camera* by John Van Druten after Christopher Isherwood's book *The Berlin Stories*, lifted

Weimar into the imaginations of a new generation.* *Tänzerische Suite* sank my emotional intensity so deeply into the grooves of the record that I felt myself transported to Weimar circa 1929. It dramatically demonstrated the power of music to convey atmosphere. Result: Germany, from the moment I first stepped on its soil, looked, smelled, sounded, and moved exactly as I'd imagined. It was déjà vu in a place I'd never been.

▪ ▪ ▪

My first week in Germany, I stood shivering in the November chill in a pastoral Swabian landscape near Waldorf, supervising the photo shoot for the 1968 American Mercedes-Benz brochure. The image was burnished by posing new '68 models with classics from the rich Mercedes-Benz past, each pristine machine fetched from the Daimler-Benz Museum in Bad Cannstatt: the big, hulking 1936 260D, the world's first diesel sedan, backgrounding the 1968 200D; the immortal 300SL "Gullwing" racing sports car supporting the new 230SL roadster. By the time I arrived in Frankfurt I was more beguiled than ever by the glory of Mercedes-Benz.

Glory didn't characterize Frankfurt am Main, city of a thousand moods, all of them somber. In 1967 it was a banking and business center that shut down by six every evening, its executives having returned to their suburban homes, leaving downtown to clusters of

* A new twenty-eight-episode TV series, *Babylon Berlin*, a German production from 2017, re-creates Weimar, its panicky energy, corruption, and tangled politics, with dramatic power, uncannily capturing the atmosphere—and music—of that tragic historical moment. It lifts Weimar into the imaginations of a whole new generation. It is also the best twenty-eight hours of television you'll ever see.

homesick Poles and Turks and Serbians, *Gastarbeiters* hanging out in cheap ethnic cafés. The few "decent" restaurants were stuffy old hives with waiters in tailcoats serving stuffy old couples traditional, stuffy German food. Frankfurt's once prominent Jewish population had all but vanished. There also went much of its cultural impetus.

The Frankfurt that greeted me was a gray place exuding a gray spirit. The aircraft of the RCAF, RAF, and USAAF had left the city a smoking pyre. A huge chunk of its character was lost when the lovingly curated medieval Sachsenhausen section of the city fell victim to British bombs. Aesthetics had subsequently been sacrificed to the pressure for immediate covered space. Frankfurt had been hastily rebuilt with low-lying structures ready to be torn down when commercial prosperity returned. The once celebrated opera house in the middle of the city had been left a broken ruin, an unsubtle reminder of the recent past. It would be another twenty years before Germany's postwar *Wirtschaftswunder*, the economic boom, bathed Frankfurt in money and caused a glut of silvery office towers to rise: thereafter and probably forever, Frankfurt am Main functioned under the sobriquet of Mainhattan.

My command of the German language, despite a crash Berlitz course before I arrived there, grew haltingly and never approached the far suburbs of fluency. This should have doomed my Heumann, Ogilvy & Mather career. It didn't; as with air traffic, the universal language of advertising had become and remained English. In the Frankfurt agency, the barrier worked both ways: if you couldn't speak German, too bad for you; if you couldn't speak English, tsk-tsk, too bad for you, too.

My social life suffered before I managed to secure a flimsy foothold, distancing me from the culture that had so beguiled me from four thousand miles away. Naiveté, despite having given myself a cram course in German customs and manners, initially led me into Ugly American gaffes. Item: making a beeline for a nearby watering hole was an almost reflexive activity in every New York agency for a band of after-hours cronies (myself included; if I had nothing planned, an evening sometimes seemed to stretch out to infinity). I needed only a couple of weeks to establish my Ugly American credentials. An effort to reproduce the Manhattan bar cruise in a Frankfurt setting quickly revealed itself to be the pathetic mistake of a parvenu.

Three times I invited my German office friend Heidi to join me for a drink or two at some nearby bar. We strolled after work a few times to a seedy-looking nightclub called Old Daddy. (This was far from the strangest loan from English: my favorite was Drugstore Up to Date, apparently an attempt to promise hungry visiting Americans a homelike eatery. The name turned out to be the only American reference in the joint: the menu was strictly schnitzel.) Poor Heidi must have wondered, *What's this clown doing?* as we sat inhaling the glamour of a gloomy room empty of life save for two twits. I ordered a bourbon, assuming bourbon was an international refreshment. The waiter-bartender repeated the word as if I'd asked for calves' brains in anise with a rum chaser. I hazarded a dainty test sip. *Blaaaaargh!* This bourbon must have been distilled from shoe polish, rat fur, and his own urine by a desperate Devil's Island escapee. I needed three Cokes to wash the aftertaste out of my mouth. The bill for that puddle of orange liquid was seven American dollars. If that was the cost of never seeing Old Daddy or any other nitespot for the rest of my tenure in Frankfurt, it was a bargain.

Maybe because it was so seldom heard or seen in North America, the German language seemed exotic to me as a kid. Its special quality was a kind of DIY factor: you manipulated it like a box of metal pieces, a verbal Meccano set that could be bolted together into sentence-long words, the sentence concluding with a loud thud where the key word came. Mark Twain wrote that spoken German sounded like a man in a suit of armor falling downstairs, and the language does strike many foreigners as blunt and guttural. I came to suspect that too many spittle-spraying German characters in World War II Hollywood movies, barking like hounds, taught English speakers a vaudevillian sense of the language. As Ute Lemper proves every time she sings, German can also be soft, romantic, and seductive.

Fluency wasn't even an ambition once I was plunged into the fast-moving language stream. I had thought my fine ear would earn me respect for speaking in clear German: then I heard a recorded snatch of my voice. My spoken German proved to be a twangy joke. In addition to everything else, I sounded funny. After that it got doubly difficult to drag myself into the language.

Few speakers of English could penetrate the idiomatic argot very deeply. Nor the slang and verbal dexterity of a native German. Nor solve the complex, fiendishly constructed crossword puzzle cum Rubik's Cube of proper German grammar. Copy written in colloquial English and translated into German transmogrified into nonsense. Translation, as I painfully learned, isn't a simple exchange of words you know into foreign words you don't. Language is ideas, idioms, expressing different cultural values and constantly in flux. English phrases can be translated into literal German and vice versa, but words alone don't cut it. They're the planks that need to be assembled into a house.

I was the agency creative director, in name only. My relationship to the copy and art people mirrored relations between a U.S. advisor and the South Vietnamese military. I had the same lack of faith in my troops. The agency's creative corps was young and green, and they were expected to learn the Ogilvy credo, its thickets of dos and don'ts, by osmosis. A spectacularly naive assumption. None of them had ever been taught the rudiments of advertising. Most didn't care: they relied on their linguistic genius to master complex strategies, the yield of expensive research, to pass muster with American standards and Ogilvy dicta.

None of these dozen writers ever came close to solving a creative problem in a logical way. Heinz Blattner, a middle-aged writer and the only one to earn Hank's trust, served as the informal creative chief and a kind of benign Henry Kissinger, advising him on client attitudes, and a generally useful employee without portfolio. I lunched with Heinz often, to talk about the world beyond the agency. A dyed-in-the-wool liberal, he recounted being drafted into the Hitler-Jugend movement as a fourteen-year-old. He screwed up so badly so often that he got kicked out.

The late sixties were close enough in time to the war that many of the senior HOM employees were veterans. Kurt Meier, the company treasurer, had slogged through the desert in the African campaign. Rommel's army fell, and Kurt, along with a few thousand other Afrika Corps troops, spent the remainder of the war as a British POW, emerging when peace came with the uniform on his back and perfect English delivered in a plummy British accent.

Herr Rumpler, an account executive, was barely eighteen when the Luftwaffe chose him to train as a fighter pilot. Germany in early 1944 was on the ropes. Aviation gasoline was stingily rationed. Fighter-plane production was at a crawl. Herr Rumpler's "training" regimen consisted of taxiing a beat-up Me-109 down a short runway, getting airborne, circling the airfield, and landing. The Me-109's knock-kneed, tall and narrow landing gear, combined with poor forward vision, made it a treacherous aircraft even for veterans of hundreds of takeoffs and landings. It made literal mincemeat of pilot trainees. Certain innocent mistakes led to accidents that meant court-martials for a number of candidates. A few were arrested while clambering out of a smoking wreck and taken away to be shot for the crime of willfully destroying der Fuehrer's property.

Germans are more intelligent, harder working, and more sophisticated than their advertising counterparts in a flock of other nations. Yet these same people can be arrogant, conceited, narrow-minded, and hostile to suggestions for improving their skills. Molding a competent advertising professional out of such stock is difficult; creating an advertising star is well nigh impossible. The copywriter uneducated in basic advertising theory and practice either learns and develops over time, or quits, or is canned for not trying. That's true in New York, Brazil, Kuala Lumpur, and modern Germany.

HOM's Frankfurt office faced another, unique problem. It drew from a small, shallow pool. Talented creative people spurned the place, as did their juniors and every kind of advertising pro in between. Munich, Hamburg, Cologne, Düsseldorf—these cities excited the creatively inclined. Culture flourished. Youthful energy led the way. Excitement got into the bloodstream. And there sat Frankfurt. Money was its reigning industry, and it lent the city a dull, orderly image. What gifted writer, artist, musician, or advertising practitioner would be inspired by huge banks, insurers, and other financial enterprises? Frankfurt had a fine zoo and several elegant neighborhoods. But one thing was missing, and it made for the ultimate downer: search the city north and south, west and east, and you'd find that Frankfurt didn't have a single drop of craziness.

▪ ▪ ▪

The writers who had to work with me ranged from surly Hagen Bertram to thoughtful Manfred Klein, sweet-natured Frau Meyer-Rothe, talkative Winfred Lauer, demi-hippie Boris Haneke, the Taciturn Twins Volker Ammon and Hans Schnapka, amiable and evidently talented Jochen Vollbach, hardworking and fast Fred Boos, and Robert Kroeber, stiff as a board and forcing me to stifle a belly laugh whenever he cleared his throat, snapped to attention, and barked another declaration. Kroeber was difficult to understand, since his compliments, complaints, and criticisms all sounded exactly the same: loud, earnest, and long-winded.*

A Rabelaisian Brit renegade, Ben Nash, was brought aboard by Hank Bernhard, the managing director and six-foot-tall spark plug of the agency. This accorded with the fact that every few years a supremely bright, lavishly gifted eccentric lands in an advertising agency and rattles the windows, but never stays. Ben typified the breed. An erudite Oxonian who spoke German better than most Germans did, he was a witty, irreverent, Oscar Wilde–quoting social companion. His office resounded with laughter and good times. It didn't hurt Ben's standing that he ate and drank to excess and helped teach a few creative types the rudiments of going too far.

I explained Ben's advertising career to myself as not so unusual for a certain type of Brit. Oxford and Cambridge seem to produce scores of brilliant young men who can't find their groove and wander the world having fun until their destiny arrives. Ben was of that

* Tragedy stalked the creative ranks: Heidi Meyer-Rothe killed herself shortly after I left Frankfurt. A year or so later, one of the agency's account executives went berserk in a meeting and shot senior copywriter Manfred Klein and art director Franz-Josef Walter to death.

ilk: intellectually far superior to the art of selling common things to the common man. I observed a man who despised himself for ducking the career he could and should have carved for himself back in Blighty. A surfeit of wine and beer loosened his tongue: he ridiculed the Ogilvy credo and Hank's diligence behind his back. Ben generated gales of hot wind but little outstanding work. I admired his brains and bonhomie, but he disappointed my expectations. Heumann, Ogilvy & Mather, starved for talent, couldn't afford morons. Neither could it afford overeducated footdraggers who hitched a ride and used an agency as a place to hide from their own talents.

Creative turnover was brisk—and financially costly to the agency. Germany had been the leader, early in the century, in legislating social services and worker protection against the power of employers, and this protection continued in the post-Nazi world. By law a union representative sat on the board of every company. Firings conferred liberal benefits on the firee—including payment of half a year's salary regardless of the reason for his or her having been bounced. Plus, if he or she so chose, there would be a hearing on the whys and wherefores of the dismissal, with the ultimate decision rendered by a regional government official. These arbitrators were seldom able to distinguish between the work performed by a truck driver and that expected of an advertising copywriter. Thus it was easier, and cheaper, to get by with mediocre talents; the shortfall would be repaired—by me.

▪ ▪ ▪

Hank's blind spot was his wretched performance in human relations. He was a sender, not a receiver, and was so focused on end results that he wasn't aware that morale in his creative department sucked. Nor would he have cared. People as people didn't interest him. His few efforts at personal diplomacy scraped my senses like fingernails on a blackboard: he talked too much and listened too little. He couldn't read minds. Or facial expressions. It never occurred to him that writers and art directors differed from one another, in temperament, in brainpower, in motivation, and in their pursuit of David Ogilvy's philosophy of advertising. Hank didn't discuss, he lectured. His victim wasn't expected to talk. Nodding would do. Hank used these occasions to ventilate, until the poor bastard on the receiving end stumbled away in confusion. Our boss's body was a pressurized tank. If it wasn't vented every so often, it would explode.

I was no Mr. Chips as a teacher. Some copywriters appeared to have a humble interest in at least trying to expand their advertising savvy but were foiled by my lack of empathy, zero patience for slowpokes, and misunderstandings in the endless skirmish between my German and their English, and their German and my English. Yet my linguistic ineptitude actually did little to weaken my value. Hank needed me, to spot and fix headlines and text, but far more urgently to act as strategist, conceptualist, sounding board, and creative cleanup man. He'd define the issues to be dealt with in an ad—"separating the fly shit from the pepper," as he put it. Their value was to cleave through the bafflegab, identify the real problems, and aim straight at the target. A well-written memo requires a supple brain. In this, Hank is tied with David Ogilvy for first place. Reading the clear, spare, inarguable conclusions in their memos was one of the keener pleasures of my advertising career.

▪ ▪ ▪

In my three years of living and working in Frankfurt, only twice did I earn an invitation to a German home. My social leprosy was probably not the main reason: by hoary tradition, wives and children were kept invisible to auslanders. German high schools stick to the idea that education means learning: no proms, no basketball teams. The American horror of being seen dining alone in a restaurant and the implied pathos of the lone social outcast doesn't fly in Germany.

Although this culture may seem cold to the casual observer, it isn't; German life is more formal than the American style, but it's just as human. (Consider the "*du*" ceremony, held when two friends acknowledge that this particular relationship has matured into a more intimate, meaningful bond. The standard German word for "you" goes from the formal *sie* to the informal *du*. And it does so for life.)

One Saturday morning in 1969 I watched from my apartment balcony on Schillerstrasse as the cops shot water cannons at Red Rudi Dutschke and a ragtag mob of followers. That was as close as I got to involvement with the scary, tumultuous, wacky sixties unfolding in the States. This estrangement from my times and contemporary life began to gnaw at me. Here I was, in a three-piece brown tweed suit and fifties haircut, grappling with the destiny of Rolf dog food and Frisch und Frei spray deodorant while America was convulsing.

My appetite for the news and the feel of American life forced me to the only English-speaking radio available: the American Forces Network, or AFN (formerly the Armed Forces Network, but changed on the theory of Let's Not Alarm the Natives). A five-minute newscast, mainly dependent on generic wire-service fragments, kicked off every hour. The AFN held the rare distinction of being broadcast from a time warp—the late fifties. Rock and roll barely existed. Stale radio dramas of the fifties abounded. Art Baker hosted a late-night program—a feat indeed: Art had been dead for years.

Yet isolation can sometimes be productive. Advertising has its limitations for the creatively inclined: self-expression plays no role, because it's never about you. It's a blunt tool, impersonal and anonymous, for broadcasting effusions inspired by marketing strategies. My one creative and intellectual outlet in Frankfurt was letter writing. I composed long messages from *Mitteleuropa* for a circle of friends and relatives—Chris, Mike, Hugh—venting and japing and unloading on pet subjects (like the above tirade). These were the days before faxes, the Internet, and the cell phone obliterated the personal letter. My curmudgeonly nature leads me to persist in letter writing, except that today it's not via the U.S. Postal Service.

▪ ▪ ▪

The Daimler-Benz offices in Stuttgart were the Vatican to serious devotees of automotive excellence. There, hundreds of engineers labored to advance automotive technology in every aspect of performance. Safety was a priority due to conscience, not government prodding. These were serious people doing important work, yet HOM's requests for information almost always elicited a response. Our team was small and serious. We met with various engineers for briefings on specific subjects; circled the test track and the stomach-turning "high wall"; toured casting foundries and the huge assembly works in Sindelfingen; and were ushered into a nearby domed room for presentations of new models by the chief stylist, Bruno Sacco. Data was gleaned, not necessarily for use in advertising but to give us insight into the philosophy behind the product. The founder of the automobile in 1886, and the company he formed to build new models, was Gottlieb Daimler. His motto was *Das Beste oder Nichts*—The Best or Nothing. He believed it. His successors still do.

Driving a Mercedes-Benz on the Autobahn was at first a fright, then a thrill, and ultimately a serenely smooth means of travel. Since Germany has historically hesitated to impose artificial speed limits, Mercedes-Benz has long recognized the need to build cars capable of sustained Autobahn performance. The firm demands engineering standards of total integrity, along the way earning numerous key patents and countless advances in safety and stability. Germans take their cars and their driving seriously. Tough annual inspections keep junkers off the road. Drunk drivers go to jail, period. The cars around you are clean and driven with pride. (The automatic car wash has been laggard in catching on; allowing machines to do that job is seen by German car owners as akin to paying some stranger to wash your wife.) Road safety ranks high on the government's priority list. Leave the Autobahn and drive the smooth back roads, and if you have an accident the road was probably not to blame. Weather may be, though. Northern Europe dwells in a meteorological sewer: rain and fog cover the land year-round. (My Mercedes roadster, a convertible, had its top folded down on exactly one weekend in the summer of 1968.)

Autobahn rest stops were spotless oases. For sale was damn near anything you needed and some things you craved—including beer, wine, and liquor. Every time I stopped I wondered why these places reduced the U.S. counterpart to black comedy: fatty fast food, sugary candy, grotty bathrooms, and vending machines for everything else. Yet Americans spend more time in their cars and rack up more miles than any other nationalities. Contrasts with back home were invidious enough to make expatriation seem a sane and sensible alternative.

That soon passed. I met many American expats in Germany. None seemed to be centered in their lives. Expatriation does relieve you of all the responsibilities of citizenship; you don't belong anywhere. For some, that grants the pleasure of relief. Many have been estranged from their homeland long enough to fear they wouldn't fit in stateside anymore. Severed for years from the fast-moving American culture, how could anybody function back home when it all feels so strange? The expat's place in German life has no appeal to me. An expat may speak the language, know that most stores close by six p.m. and all but one Saturday per month, and myriad other customs. Some may even marry a German. But the expat knows that he or she is dangling between worlds, in a nowhere universe, doomed only to spectate in a society and culture that can never admit them.

▪ ▪ ▪

By the end of my second year my energies were often sapped by certain realities: navigating through a different language with no time to grasp a new word or explain an old one; forever under the gun to get everything finished by yesterday; going into the office on Saturday to bang out headlines for a new Mercedes-Benz truck campaign; using body language and charm to persuade Herr Bertram to read a strategy memo before he started writing an ad; jawing with art directors about how magazine layouts need to share a visual identity in order to foster the sense of a campaign.

I'd drive down to Stuttgart on Sundays to meet my friend Dirk Strassl, then a Mercedes-Benz PR man and the best nonracing driver I ever quailed beside on twisty roads. Weekends in Amsterdam were movable feasts with my part-lunatic friend Peter Verstappen in command. Peter ran O&M's Amsterdam office. He could drink anybody not only under the table, but under the floor. Peter found fun and pleasure in everything he did, exhausting me in the process.

You could travel through five European countries in the time it took to cross Texas. I drove from Frankfurt to Geneva one weekend (how the Germans ended up calling it Genf still bewilders me) with a photographer friend on an assignment. Another time we motored from Frankfurt to Belgium to England to the northwestern Scottish Highlands in golden September sunshine. Then drove hard, through the foul English weather, to catch the ferry to Calais. Driving would never again feel so pleasurable.

With my German friend Klaus Lamm I did the American tourist thing and ventured through Checkpoint Charlie into East Berlin. Hollywood wouldn't have dared build an East Berlin movie set this decrepit. We walked along a wide, empty, dead Strasse until we spotted a restaurant—well, more like an intention to one day be a restaurant—on the mezzanine floor of the building on that street that seemed least likely to collapse. Sunday afternoons are family time in Germany. We were seated amid groups of sallow kids and bored parents in a large former auditorium. No dishes listed on the *Speisekarte* were available. Russian vodka outdid water as the GDR's favorite drink. We ordered coffee; I heard from Oskar Homolka, or his double pretending to be a waiter, what I'd learned to expect. There was a surplus of Russian vodka and Havana cigars, but the espresso machine was broken, apparently forever.

I noticed other customers staring at us and whispering behind their hands. Various lurid scenarios later—Did they take us for CIA agents? Was there a spy-spotter in the house, set to pounce?—came the bland realization that they were envying our clothes. Neither Klaus nor I was a popinjay. God knows what hung in their closets.

One sweet moment touched me: the house pianist, an octogenarian in a tailcoat, had sat grinding out the popular music approved by the cultural guardians of the German Democratic Republic (neither German nor democratic, and a Soviet satrapy terming itself a republic), treacly, innocuous drivel. The pianist caught my eye, bobbed his head, and tore into "Poor Little Robin," a forgettable Tin Pan Alley relic from the early fifties and obviously the only American music he knew. He was honoring two visitors from what must have seemed like Mars to him and his trampled-down fellow citizens. We smiled back at him, flattered and sad. Those three hours, intended as an innocent lark, depressed the hell out of Klaus and me for days afterward. Fuck you, Walter Ulbricht. And the T-34 Red Army tank you rode in on.

My Frankfurt life elevated my standard of living so far above my Toronto, Windsor, Detroit, and New York levels that I had to remind myself how artificial it was. Without Hank's compulsive generosity, I'd have had to live humbly: no Mercedes, no grand apartment in a grand house in an affluent neighborhood. No vast corner office furnished by Knoll. And no secretary whose sole responsibility was me—mine brought me a hard roll (*Brötchen auf Deutsch*) every morning. If Hank ceased to exist or was no longer the managing director of the agency, my life of privilege would implode within days, maybe hours.

Hank, never a diplomat and too busy solving advertising problems to be a politician, had attracted critics and enemies over his years with O&M. The consensus among his opponents was that he was a reckless spendthrift of agency money. Worse, he ignored the proper channels for expending it. What was deemed arrogance really wasn't. The White Tornado, as he was nicknamed, probably got reamed when the annual accounting was done. Hank took the bullets. He never whined about anything. In rushing to do the jobs of ten people, Hank raided O&M's piggy bank to buy people and time, cars and airline tickets—whatever speeded up a solution or fended off a crisis this week. He knew more than his colleagues and saw situations only he could solve. And he always believed that money was meant to ameliorate them.

Our relationship was so close, and so fruitful, that certain Bernhard critics in the New York office suspected favoritism unto the edge of ethical impropriety. From an outside perspective, the implications carried weight. If charged with being Hank's bum boy, who hugely benefited from his largesse by use of the brown nose, I must accept some criticism. My defense is twofold: First, I genuinely admired Hank and worked hard to earn his trust. He was smart. I learned more about advertising from him than from all other teachers combined. I was no goldbricker. Hank couldn't trust a lazy, no-talent wimp in the position I held. If I wasn't useful, or blanched at the prospect of hard work, I'd have been on the next plane home. Second, I took what I was given innocently. I had no means of comparing my situation with the prevailing standard because there *was* no prevailing standard. Mine was a one-shot assignment. I assumed, because Hank operated in the daylight and was incapable of sneaky dealings, that I was being paid and subsidized according to some set of rules.

It was only years after I left Frankfurt that I understood that Hank's largesse reflected his judgment of how he could run an agency effectively without a professional creative corps. He had inherited a dismally untrained team of copywriters and art directors. He had hit the ground running, without the luxury of picking and choosing from a list of qualified candidates. I was fast, fecund, absolutely loyal, and willing. Until creative professionals were found and hired, I filled the gap. Despite the emoluments showered on me to the point that some might say I was spoiled, I represented a bargain. Maybe a less agitated person than Hank Bernhard could have made a cheaper arrangement, but I ended up feeling no need to apologize. I labored long and hard in Frankfurt. And effectively. O&M got its money's worth.

I was billeted in three apartments in Frankfurt. The first two fell short: one because it was a wearying half-hour drive to and from the office and was in a neighborhood without residents, so a mite too quiet, verging on the creepy. The second was a tiny single room, but with a balcony overlooking Schillerstrasse, a busy little street with a cigar store selling Havanas directly across from me. My last Frankfurt home lorded it over Mendelssohnstrasse in the affluent Westend. I felt like an emperor—and not only because the building was a big, white, grand kaiserene hulk. High ceilings, oversized rooms, ten-ton Biedermeier armoires, and a desktop big enough to land planes on—the place felt several sizes too big for one person. Its magnificently equipped kitchen, and a dining room large enough to seat the kaiser's entire general staff, were wasted on me. Food held all the interest for me of One Hour Martinizing. No meal was ever prepared in the kitchen or served in the dining room. The bedroom was airy, and the thin coverlet stuffed with goose down did away with a top sheet. German winters can get cold, yet opening bedroom windows is a custom observed in most dwellings. (Germans have fetishized the value of *frische Luft* into near insanity. Booked into a New York hotel in the heat of summer, German visitors reach their rooms, set down their luggage, and rush to turn the air-conditioning off. The *Luft* isn't *frische* enough.)

On countless evenings I drove twenty miles to the affluent suburb of Kronberg for dinner with Hank and his family. Hank fancied himself a gourmet cook; the banging and cursing emanating from the kitchen testified to his intensity. The fact that dinner inevitably arrived at the table forty-five minutes late testified to his perfectionism. Perfectionism can sometimes be a pain in the ass.

Several times a week I dined at Café Kranzler, a musty survivor of at least one world war and probably the least hip restaurant in Hesse. The decor was haute German bourgeois circa 1910, summoning comparisons with old postcard views of grand hotel lobbies. The high-ceilinged dining salon, roomy as a barn and furnished in post-Biedermeier upholstered chairs and low round tables, exuded the sort of dignity that encourages hushed conversation. I wallowed in nostalgia for some vague, unidentifiable past. Waitresses in black outfits scuttled about. The house pianist and a violinist gently serenaded an elderly clientele with Franz Lehár and Sigmund Romberg light-opera songs and Viennese waltzes.

The Kranzler newsstand stocked the daily lifeline of American news, the Paris *Herald Tribune*, a legendary but by then feebly unenterprising newspaper. Daily news that had been cutting-edge in *The New York Times* two days earlier now had the cutting edge of a butter knife. The paucity of reliable American news, in that pre-Internet age when information circulated not in seconds but sometimes weeks, drove me to depend on British media. Whereupon I discovered that British journalism often tasted richer, wittier, and meatier than most of its American counterparts. *The Economist*, *The New Statesman*, and *The Sunday Times* (of London) *Magazine* amounted to a trifecta that satisfied my curiosity about the world while exponentially expanding it. My sopping-up of English journalism bred in me the sneaking suspicion that perhaps *Time* magazine wasn't the omniscient interpreter of the civilized world after all.

Life at Heumann, Ogilvy & Mather Frankfurt churned on through the months and then years. My lone involvement with our television advertising,* a small media element, involved sending two agency TV producers and me to London for a shoot. The studio we used, tucked into a small building on Wardour Street, was, like all film studios, crammed with a Collyer brothers maze of film-related paraphernalia. The star of our spot was Rotbart. (In addition to Mercedes, the agency handled Rotbart, Lufthansa, Shell Oil, and a few others.) The commercial featured a man at a bathroom mirror, stunned by the smooth closeness and affordability of the new Rotbart blade. A TV spot sucks up all the energy that can be drawn from a crew, and a timetable from hell aided the air of total confusion. Under the heat of lighting and the stress of getting footage in the can, filming a commercial becomes an expensive ordeal of boredom so sustained that, after three or four hours, it's impossible to care. Lunchtime was an opportunity to escape. My two companions, one a graying veteran of TV production and the other a smirking, repulsively chummy gofer, had used the studio before and knew just the place for a swell lunch. Off we went.

The Raymond Revuebar looked nothing like a restaurant, because it wasn't. An atmosphere of erotic gloom seeped from a passageway of drapes in pitch darkness. My companions now became my hosts and led me to our table. My questions about lunch were smilingly rebuffed; this, said the older producer, was a banquet of a superior kind. The tinny pit band's overture heralded the lifting of the curtain. An Amazon in feathers posed for a long moment, then

* Commercials on German TV could run only in clumps of a dozen or so, at two or three fixed times an evening. The order of placement was controlled by the broadcasters. This meant that campaigns couldn't be built through scheduling frequency to increase awareness and impact. Many advertisers decided to forgo TV altogether rather than piss away their budgets on scattershot pokes at the consumer.

proceeded to strut, bend, and gyrate slowly, while picking off her feathers to reveal a patch of golden-brown skin. Further picking and shucking followed. The band played mood music for people in the mood to contemplate sex. After fifteen increasingly suspenseful minutes, the Amazon stretched out on a chaise longue, naked as a jaybird and frozen in her pose.

England allows women to strip in public. The catch is that once she has attained total nudity, the woman isn't allowed to move a muscle or an eyelash. I sat and watched another eight or so comely ecdysiasts perform their exhibitions of the penultimate moment before coitus interruptus. Eight times was more than enough. The Raymond Revuebar killed my hunger for a few hours.

■ ■ ■

Advertising was my life. I gave my energies and hours to the cause of selling. I had so completely adopted the mercantile pursuit and the society and customs it spawned that I had isolated myself from other interests and other people. Yet Frankfurt was where my career as an artist leapt overnight from an abandoned failure, all but forgotten ten years later, to the equivalent of a home run in my first big-league at bat. My dedication to advertising, to Ogilvy & Mather, even to Hank Bernhard, was about to crumble.

All because my friend Brock Yates liked World War II military aircraft as much as I did. Yates, an automotive journalist and the nearest thing to Hunter S. Thompson I ever knew, crashed through life at speed. Brock founded the Cannonball Baker Sea-to-Shining-Sea Memorial Trophy Dash, a flagrantly outlaw sprint from New York to Los Angeles that attracted every nutbar car maniac in America. There were no rules. Miraculously, nobody got killed. But it was typical of Yates. He flicked an anarchic finger at convention everywhere he ran into it, earning such a reputation for aggression that his nickname was the Assassin. He wrote an article in the eighties, a blistering attack on Detroit's foot-dragging stupidity about automotive design, titled "The Grosse Pointe Myopians." Everything he wrote was a blistering attack on something or somebody.

Brock was also witty and decent (at least in person). We'd both grown up in the atmosphere of war, and as kids were besotted by the fighters and bombers that filled the skies. Something in my nature, and Brock's, generated an appetite for every scrap of information, every design detail and characteristic of scores of military planes. American, British, German, and Japanese planes piqued our curiosity. But so did Russian, Italian, French, Australian, Finnish, Polish—every example of every warbird extant. In the small Ontario town of Simcoe, I was recording my savvy by drawing planes; over in upstate New York, young Brock Yates was doing the same.

In early April 1970 I was admitted to a Frankfurt clinic for emergency surgery to remove a pilonidal cyst. One afternoon as I lay abed napping, a fat envelope arrived. Brock had sent me half a dozen pencil sketches: aircraft of the RAF, the Luftwaffe, and assorted belligerents, lovingly drawn, sprinkled with idiotic figments of an informed imagination.

Satire had found a new subject. I couldn't let Brock one-up me. By next morning I had sent off in return a sheaf of aircraft drawings, all of them ridiculous inventions but dead serious in the look, the purpose, and the nationality of each. Brock had kicked open a Pandora's box. The following weeks filled the air and our minds with airplanes of all nations. No country was spared; Brock and I cashed in on arcane knowledge acquired years before, knowledge patiently waiting to become nuggets of warplane-satire legend. We never talked about it, but it's possible, perhaps likely, that we thought we were satirizing fictitious airplanes. What we were actually satirizing were the stereotypes of each nation in their broadest, most caustic and vulgar form.

The exchange cooled off after a month. Brock had other fish to fry; I was finally pronounced healthy enough to leave the *Klinik* and waded back into the advertising fray. In late July a letter from Brock arrived in an envelope too flat to be carrying another spate of stupid-aircraft renderings. Inside was a single sheet of paper. Brock's distinctive scrawl said, "Hey McCall! *Playboy*'s going to make a humor piece out of those airplanes of ours, and you're illustrating it. Hurry—it's already on deadline!"

I didn't have time to write or call Brock and wax indignant over having my services subcontracted out. The assignment terrified me. I hadn't even thought like an artist in precisely ten years. Now I was virtually ordered to deliver eight tight color renderings of lunatic World War II military aircraft. Some workspace improvisation was necessary. For example, my drawing board was the coffee table in my apartment living room, so low that I had to bend over it. In a backbreaking siege, I sat hunched over my paintings hour after hour. Every minute I could steal—before work every morning, late into every weekday night, and every hour of every weekend—I gave to the project.

The article *Playboy* ran in the January 1971 issue I had titled "Major Howdy Bixby's Album of Forgotten Warbirds." That fluky idea, a transatlantic collaboration between a couple of amateur airplane buffs illustrated by a failed commercial artist who hadn't so much as lifted a brush in a decade, won *Playboy*'s humor award for that year. That success ripped open a seam of reflection previously buried under more immediate concerns. Doing that silly piece had been gratifying. More meaningfully, it had been fun—an emotion I'd almost forgotten during my recent career. The article and its absurd success revived a passion for drawing and painting I assumed I had neutralized years ago. One article in one magazine didn't prove to me that I had finally wearied of the madcap Bernard pace. Of carrying the Ogilvy & Mather banner in a vacuum. Of fixing and saving ads but never achieving anything beyond quenching creative fires. I was getting disenchanted with advertising itself.

Meanwhile, a sense of homesickness and isolation from the one culture I understood was rising. Three years were enough. My learning curve had flattened out, and staying longer would only perpetuate the tension, the frustration, and the inevitably mediocre outcome of trying to build a solid structure with inferior materials. It was time to repatriate. I dreaded telling Hank that I wanted out. I braced myself for an angry explosion, ready to grimly hold to my decision while Hank berated me for abandoning him, then as the detonation cooled, urging me to stay and see the mission through.

I guess I just wasn't cut out for dramatic confrontations. Before I could stammer my decision, Hank preempted me with a bigger bombshell of his own: He was leaving Heumann, Oglivy & Mather in December and returning to New York and to Ogilvy. I should think about doing so, too.

Gasp! That was late August 1970. The next four months were an easy downhill slope. Relief, the knowledge that all this Sturm und Drang would soon be behind me, loosened my psyche. It would not be a tearful leave-taking, for me or for the creative staff. My guilt at abandoning the creative department to the cobwebs and the rats was greatly assuaged when Hank hired Walter Lürzer and Michael Conrad, both German, a writing team from heaven who overnight turned around the agency's creative reputation from nothing to first-rate.

My final day arrived, a Friday shortly before the Christmas holiday. No elaborate leave-taking ceremony marked my departure. Relaxed at last, I fell in with a motley crew of copy and art people, first swilling beer in an empty office in the deserted agency, then adjourning for dinner at a restaurant favored by Frankfurt's demimonde.

By the end of dinner I was smitten by a beautiful young Brunhilde nearby at the table. I'd never been so beguiled. She was Emma. She returned my stare with a smile that could melt ingots. The chemistry between us was inexplicable. What it fomented was irrepressible. Instant mutual lust like this belonged in bodice rippers, not real life. Later, at the apartment where our little group had ended up, I went out onto the balcony to collect my thoughts and try to understand what was happening. Emma sidled up. This was no time for thinking. We embraced, writhing with mutual desire.

"I have to leave on Sunday," I whispered. "I can't stand the idea that I'll never see you again."

"There is all day tomorrow," Emma said.

I picked her up next morning. We repaired to my apartment and fucked like rabbits until nine that night. Years had compressed into hours. Every minute swept me further under her spell. Emma wasn't talkative. She didn't need to be. She seemed as torn as I was by having to part.

The taxi I'd called pulled up to the curb beside us. Emma said softly, "*Ich liebe Dich.*"

"I love you," I replied. "You're coming to New York as soon as you can. We'll take it from there. *Wiedersehen.*"

Sunday morning I boarded the Lufthansa 747 flight to New York, settled into my seat, and commenced to muse about how three emotionally empty years had been redeemed at the last possible moment. My life had reached its highest plateau. Even dour, ugly, empty Frankfurt was transformed. I mused in a state close to ecstasy all the way home to America.

My *Lampoon* piece imagined a proto-"Everything Store" stocked not with the gadgets we all need, but with the junk we all deserve.

Chapter 8

America Discovers Satire

It's December 1970. I dutifully put my seat up and push the meal tray shut as the Lufthansa 747 trundles to a gate at the International Arrivals terminal at New York's JFK airport. It's been a long nonstop flight from Frankfurt am Main. Customs and baggage pickup are painfully time-consuming. I check my watch: it's been an hour and ten minutes since we landed. I've survived an ordeal slightly less taxing than a month with an angry mob. Good practice for life in New York.

But the meaningful half of me is still back in Frankfurt. I'd met Emma on my next-to-last day in Germany. I couldn't believe my sudden good fortune. She was young and blond and, putting it politely, a full-figured fraulein. She spoke in a throaty voice. She looked you straight in the eye. Emma reciprocated my interest. And my passion. My final day in Europe, in Germany and in Frankfurt, was spent with Emma in my bed in the Mendelssohnstrasse apartment. I'd remember it for years as the best day I ever spent in Frankfurt. She flew to New York in late May and we commenced a leisurely cross-country drive to Los Angeles in a welter of sex and tourism. Then we drove back to New York. My chronic sense of emotional starvation had vanished. It was right to wallow in an idyll of love and freedom.

Of course it couldn't last. The great romance of my life evaporated by the end of the year. Emma had proposed that we marry and settle in Germany. Maybe we should have; it could have turned out swimmingly. I instinctively panicked, surrendering to a fear of commitment that had forever blighted my life. I stalled. After two months, Emma gave up. As fast as it had flared up, what had been so hot and so steamy cooled down. *Das Ende.*

As had been the case before when an emotional tsunami knocked me on my keister, the muse appeared to assuage the emptiness and pain of reality. Without requiring me to lift a finger, the Gods of Funny more than smiled down on me: they tossed me a life preserver to help me solve my career and my life. It was the *National Lampoon.*

▪ ▪ ▪

Humor in the American print world was a brittle wretch without a home. *The New Yorker*'s occasional humor pieces, by James Thurber, S. J. Perelman, Peter De Vries, and the like, shone brilliantly but cast a small glow. Mass-market magazines—*The Saturday Evening Post* and *Collier's*—ran sitcoms, safely bland. Adventurous humor had a brief heyday in the twenties and thirties in smallish publications: *Judge*, the pre-Luce *Life*, *The American Mercury*, et al. But all were killed by the Great Depression.

The *National Lampoon*, that Harvard-descended newsstand magazine, had clicked on its advent in 1970 and was booming. In my Frankfurt exile I had of course known nothing about it. But the second I came across an issue, my brain threw a party for my creative soul. This had never happened before: first shock, then burning jealousy. This troop of snotty college kids had sneaked in, rifled my prefrontal cortex, and now they were getting rich and famous by duplicating *my personal ideas of satire and parody.*

In 1968 Henry Beard and Doug Kenney graduated from Harvard, as did the third partner and moneyman, Rob Hoffman, who was admitted to the bar just in time to broker a deal. The *Lampoon* name was leased; Beard and Kenney moved to Manhattan. The *National Lampoon* was born.

America hadn't seen anything like it. Stinging satire! Wicked parody! Humor with brains! Crammed in were tits, farts, juvenilia—the postpubescent male readership demanded their candy. But the editorial guts of the *Lampoon* whizzed past the puerility of *Mad* and *Cracked*, overleaping hackneyed formulas that had served as the humor standard of American comedy sensibility (Bob Hope! Jack Benny! Cartoons in *The Saturday Evening Post*! Gimme a freakin' break!) that had reigned over the pages and airwaves since the death of vaudeville. This generation had grown up in a society in such turmoil that dried-up institutions crumbled under the pressures of change. The *Lampoon* blasted past the dim-bulb mainstream American humor tradition to create the first seriously post-stupid comedy forum of the era. Its fresh outlook reflected the sensibilities of an all-night Harvard dorm room bull session and the fun of pure mischief. It made the monthly magazine safe for all the geeks, polymaths, smart-asses, and autodidacts—all the misfits who'd been sharpening their parodic/satirical scythes in high school lunchrooms, upstairs bedrooms, and college cafeterias forever.

The magazine injected a powerful virus into the bloodstream of

America. It was more a serendipitous fluke than a shrewd plan. Half a dozen people came together at a critical moment of U.S. history and found a bully pulpit. Their various talents coalesced into something greater than the sum of their parts.

Doug Kenney exuded an ethereal mist through a pharmaceutical daze. But when roused, Kenney at the top of his form matched every living humorist anywhere. He was a midwesterner by birth and a free soul by choice. Henry Beard, on the other hand, had lived for most of his pre-Harvard life in private schools. All they had in common was humor. Both were fearsomely smart: neither felt that creating a clever humor magazine was their sole intent. A monitor in their brains was constantly checking the world zeitgeist; the monitor's alarm system would sound if the zeitgeist should register serious trouble. Some zeitgeist. Its detection system messaged a simple devastating fact: the early seventies sucked, and nobody was doing much to try to correct the malaise. No sentient American in that turbid time could ignore the shabby state of social and political life. Beard and Kenney sure didn't. They envisioned a satirical magazine to ridicule the primary villains: Nixon, Hoover, Kissinger, Agnew, Westmoreland; the political right wing; disco. A satirist's cup overflowed. The *Lampoon* made satire a viable presence and a commercial bonanza for the first time in American history, striking a chord that would outlive the *Lampoon* itself and that has reverberated through the culture ever since.

I knew nothing about who was running the magazine, or even if freelancers had a place there. I wangled an interview. Assuring myself that I had nothing to lose, I slid some wacky satirical pages—probably something related to cars (big surprise!)—into a used mailing envelope and jumped on the uptown subway from my cozy little Greenwich Village flat. Half an hour later, I stood in the

National Lampoon's reception area on the fourth floor at 635 Madison Avenue. "Reception area" overstates the three feet inside the front door. No receptionist was on duty, there were no chairs, and only a peek into a few offices sans nameplates. I stood for several minutes, trying to look blasé in case I was spotted as an interloper and attacked. Eventually a tall, skinny, mop-topped nerd with thick glasses and a formerly white turtleneck under a bunchy gray suit he could have worn for a month came out of an office. A pipe was so tightly clenched in his teeth it seemed to be holding his jaw in place. "Welcome," he said. "I'm Henry Beard."

He was Supernerd. The sanest guy on the premises. The smartest. The quickest-witted. The funniest. The most effortlessly prolific. And *fast.* Several times a year, a scheduled article isn't nearly finished and there's going to be a three-page hole in the middle of the magazine. Henry to the rescue: two days later he emerges from his dark, dank grotto of an office with his perfect parody of Dickens's *Bleak House*, complete with notes for the illustrator. Henry Beard and I meshed virtually on sight. My puny handful of samples seemed to excite his imagination. At least it excited him enough to offer me ongoing work. Our initial arrangement was for thirty pages a year, of some combination of writing and art. My first piece for *Lampoon* epitomized this arrangement: a brochure mock-up for the 1958 Bulgemobiles ("Too Great Not to Be Changed, Too Changed Not to Be Great!").

As we worked together in the first months, his off-the-cuff comments fed me fresh ideas, bolstered my confidence, and invariably enlarged what I'd seen as an okay idea into an ambitious piece. If I pulled it off, he'd suck on his pipe and say in a quietly reverent tone, "Sublime."

Henry did enjoy a certain advantage over *Lampoon* writers: he was born with three brains. One brain held an estimated 500,000 infobytes, growing daily with fresh info input. He spoke at machine-gun speed and seldom raised his voice. And perhaps most amazing of all, he patiently absorbed—while drawing out the best of their talents—the tantrums and hissy fits of a staff of born malcontents, ingrates, and prima donnas, all while keeping their respect. "As much a forum as a nightclub, a mini-campus whose entrance requirements were only that you should be overeducated and funny," Tony Hendra wrote of the *Lampoon* in his piercingly perceptive 1987 survey of humor, *Going Too Far.* It's still the most cogent description I know.

The magazine relied on a motley group of varied talents for most of its content. They weren't recruited so much as their talents adhered to sundry aspects of the *Lampoon* and ensured month-to-month continuity. Their individual contributions won them attention and admirers. But they were also working parts of the whole.

Occasionally I'd breeze into the *Lampoon* to drop off a piece. I found myself speaking exclusively to Henry and the genius art director Michael Gross and his right-hand man, David Kaestle, also a genius.

Maybe because they don't control the words and they never sign pieces with their names, magazine art directors are almost never celebrated, or even simply credited, for their epic contributions. *Lampoon* covers could make the magazine fly off the newsstand or render it a dud. The *Lampoon*'s most famous one, "If You Don't Buy This Magazine, We'll Kill This Dog" withstands comparison with any cover in the history of consumer publications.

The *Lampoon* naturally slopped over into my private and social life. I dined with most of the magazine's brain trust in myriad combinations in dingy Village restaurants, where the ribaldry and sheer antic energy, augmented with Molson's and cheap red plonk, generated article ideas and entire issue themes. I marveled at finding myself invited to hang out with an elite fraternity of gifted young talents as only a Canadian high school dropout, hanging on to the humor big-time by his fingernails, who now supped with Harvard men, Yalies, and a Cambridge grad, ever could.

My five years of close proximity to that clutch of Renaissance maniacs taught me an invaluable life lesson: spend every hour you can with people smarter than you, who make you feel dull-witted. Sometimes on my stopovers in the *Lampoon* writers' warrens, I'd get into conversations with tall, gentle Brian McConnachie. Brian never evinced the slightest desire to flail Washington's evils, America's broken promises, or headline events. He marched to a different drum—or perhaps it was a xylophone—working in eccentric directions, supplying the magazine with humor from Mogdar, the invented place he claimed as his own planet. "Cowboys on a Walnut Farm" intrigued Brian for years. He never felt he'd maximized the idea's potential. He was still pruning it a decade later.

Sean Kelly charged down from Montreal and wrung spot-on parodies from his black-Irish soul on everything from Catholic dogma to poetry of the Great War. Sean was no parlor wit: he was dead serious about humor. He also came armed with almost too much erudition. You came away exhausted from conversational encounters.

Tony Hendra was, like Kelly, a lapsed Catholic. Tony, he of the Cambridge purr and thick skin and a résumé as a nightclub comic, was a soft-spoken Brit on the outside and a pissed-off Yank inside. He waged verbal war against meat and religion, among numerous targets. George W. S. Trow, also a "Talk of the Town" writer at *The New Yorker,* composed send-ups of New York's precious art world and a strange piece about Marshal Pétain drifting into senility. He was a lively, original writer and the one *Lampoon* voice I didn't get. The feeling was mutual.

▪ ▪ ▪

I was ten years older than any other *Lampoon* regular. Henry Beard conferred the title of contributing editor on me; I contributed plenty and edited nothing. I chose to stay an outsider. This distancing of myself from Action Central fit a lifelong pattern. I was thus blind, deaf, and dumb to the wormy underside of this volatile assemblage. I never got to know and never sought to know who was banging whose main squeeze, or what nefarious plots the *Lampoon* publisher, Matty Simmons, was allegedly about to hatch against his ingrate wards. I was unaware, in the spring of 1973, that the *Lampoon* was putting on a live comedy show, *Lemmings*. I paid for my own ticket, well after opening night. (Call me Mr. Insider!)

Tony Hendra was behind the *Lemmings* production, which was an unqualified success. Alas, like the kid who didn't get an Xbox for Christmas but his little brother did, Michael O'Donoghue felt traduced: he demanded justice, in the form of his own extracurricular project. Michael's threats, tantrums, and will to win worked. He got his own radio show, symbolically several floors above the magazine at 635 Madison.

For me it proved a windfall. I owned a good pair of ears, a lifetime of listening, and a head full of radio ideas. An hour of radio devoured ideas like a sperm whale devours plankton. Out of my imagination, as fast as I could type, poured enough tight five-minute sound pieces to fill an entire *Lampoon Radio Hour* every week. Engineer Bob Tischler was under pressure to deliver sixty minutes of great radio per week, to run on a syndicated basis on stations in major markets. Every week he pulled it off.

I'd written a forties newsreel in weekly installments, with a stentorian announcer describing idiotic events against a tinny musical background, just like actual newsreels, relying on bits and pieces of footage and no original sound. New York radio rabble-rouser Don Imus stole the opening: "Megaphone Newsreels: Around the world, across the seven seas and right . . . into . . . your face!" I was so flattered to hear my stuff on the radio that it never occurred to me to sue.

I loved writing for the show. My work there probably had a higher batting average than any of my other creative pursuits. Alas, *The National Lampoon Radio Hour* lost sponsors and outlets at a rate that guaranteed a brief lifespan. More's the pity. Michael's idea of a radio show was, with its slashing and bashing, an aural version of its magazine parent. A knot of obscure young comic actors—John Belushi, Bill Murray and brother Brian, Chevy Chase, Christopher Guest, and Gilda Radner among them—were brilliant. They put more life into the scripts than the scripts had in the first place. By 1977, it seemed impossible that only a couple of years earlier, these future TV stars would have been hanging out on the *Radio Hour* floor, hoping to pick up a few bucks.

Brian introduced me to Polly Holihan, whom he befriended when she came aboard to work with Michael O'Donoghue on the *Lampoon Radio Hour.* Polly was a veteran of Dick Cavett's TV show. She was strong-willed, energetic, and witty enough to hold her own with Mr. Mike, a self-invented terror who transmuted his semi-hysterical misanthropy into satire nasty enough to make Lenny Bruce call the cops. The more I saw Polly, the more impressed I became. We spent time together that I found preferable to my fetish for solitude. The next step was cohabitation; the next, engagement, and two and a half years later, marriage. That was forty-three years ago. We seem to be good for each other.

■ ■ ■

My satirical bent perfectly jibed with the mission of the *Lampoon*. The difference was that while the *Lampoon* exposed and trampled contemporary bogeymen, their lies and misdeeds, I wandered back through time to uncover satirical fodder and ridicule the false promises of technology and the future. Henry gave me carte blanche and I took it, at an agreed frequency of thirty pages per year. I slaved to produce a nine-page brochure on behalf of RMS *Tyrannic*, the "Biggest Thing in All the World." "So safe that she carries no insurance"; decks stretching off to infinity; a mile-long dining salon; the dark, barren tunnel that was X-deck steerage quarters. I also took sweet, deeply personal revenge on Detroit's befinned fifties road hogs and their advertising in an eight-page brochure for the 1958 Bulgemobiles: "So All-Fired New They Make Tomorrow Seem Like Yesterday!"

Life had flung open the doors. I'd been waiting for a chance to strut my satirical stuff, and boy, did I get it. I'd work all day and through the night on a painting, goaded not by a deadline but my own passion. It was the peak of my creative career. The style that best expressed my view finally solidified.

■ ■ ■

The momentum of its exotic humor, its *quality*, kept the *Lampoon* churning ahead. The circulation numbers proved it. By 1974 the magazine could boast a million readers. Never noted or praised for prescience, I continued to beaver away in my own contented groove, blithely assuming that this blissful state was permanent. Until, goddamn fate, it wasn't. My abiding ignorance of the feuds, tensions, and shifting alliances simmering below the surface prevailed until the day in March 1975 when Doug and Henry jointly exercised a contract clause, collected barrels of cash, and walked out of 635 Madison forever.

It ranks as something less than Henry Beard's finest hour. Absent as usual, I later found out from a few attendees what allegedly had transpired. After taking his check but before exiting the office, he called a meeting in an open area roomy enough for everybody to gather. Standing on a desk in the hallway near his office, he confirmed the rumor that was now no longer a rumor. He and Doug had acted on a contract provision from 1969 that paid them, as agreed back when they started out, sizable sums. The money, Henry said, was payment for the six years of hell he was ending that day: the nights and weekends he'd lost; the times he'd had to step in and rescue a piece somebody had been too lazy to figure out. And then, in a final salvo that has become *Lampoon* lore, hostility poured from quiet, reasonable, ever-agreeable Henry. He purportedly said something to the effect of, "I've hated every minute of this damn job. Zero satisfaction. Nobody really helped. So I'm leaving for good. And I hope I never see any of you again."

Everybody wanted to, needed to, talk to everybody else. Who'd be in charge? Is the magazine broke after that huge payout? Which one was the real Henry Beard—the patient, calming presence who never raised his voice, or the sore, dour, angry son of a bitch who knew the *Lampoon*'s salad days were over and didn't care?

The shriveling of the *Lampoon* began immediately after Messrs. Beard, Kenney, and Michael O'Donoghue left. The self-styled Mr. Mike had quit the magazine a bit earlier, in a rage over—well, you name it and you'd probably be correct—and the outrageousness of his *Lampoon* work was lost. I swiftly realized that a *Lampoon* denuded of Michael, Henry, and Doug wasn't a magazine I wanted to work for. The young office assistant, P. J. O'Rourke, began his climb up the ladder when publisher Matty Simmons declared the shit-kicking Ohio doper the new editor. Popular he was not; O'Rourke had been kicked around by the *Lampoon* loyalists, who wrote him off as Simmons's toady, with a busy mouth and insufficient deference to the proud anti-Republican–free love–impeach-Nixon *Lampoon* aura.

By then, late spring of 1975, I was once more an unattached freelance, temporarily in career limbo. But plum assignments from high-riding *Playboy*, its adopted (and mercifully short-lived) Euroslut sister *Oui*, and *Esquire* chained me to the drawing board and bought a respite from the reckoning I'd have to face. Those freelanced pieces, "Mementos and Memories of the 1936 Cairo World's Fair," "That Fabulous Battle of Britain!," and "Zany Afternoons" (later the title of my first book) forced me to dig deeper, reach farther, and work harder than ever before. I needed to prove myself afresh as a satirical artist and prose writer. All three pieces were as strong in concept and execution as anything I've done.

Proud of them as I was, I knew those pieces represented brief blips in my post-*Lampoon* life, not a new career. With the *Lampoon* on its deathbed and no home for my eccentric art visible, I surveyed prospects for future work. Naturally, my assumption that money for rent and groceries would roll in every month produced collywobbles. It was scary, and on sleepless nights terrifying, to think about being jobless. I'd assumed that helpless state belonged to the distant past. Queasy insecurity felt like seasickness, and whenever I went walking, it was cautiously: What if fresh banana peels had been stuck to the soles of my shoes?

This augured for a shabby prelude to the imminent start of my married life. Polly and I married on a beautiful July afternoon, in the beautiful garden of the beautiful house we rented in Wainscott, one of the last Hamptons havens to stay remote from the beautiful people.

Many of the minds behind the *National Lampoon* populated the ranks at *Saturday Night Live*, including, very briefly, me. I'm on the bottom right. *(Courtesy Arky & Barrett)*

Chapter 9

Saturday Night Dead!

The summer of 1976 was splendid, except for the niggling matter of joblessness. Otherwise I was newly married, had few other attachments or responsibilities, and a plump fiscal cushion in the bank from the advertising days. Polly and I moved into a swish apartment on Central Park West, hired a decorator, and got a dog. I bought my first Mercedes (I'd had use of one at Ogilvy & Mather, but this was my first one in full). Hardly a breadline.

We had a bunch of good friends, but I wasn't avid to expand the list: solitude, sealing myself off from the world, seemed to me a rare luxury. If that sounds like a misanthropic grunt, come back with me to 101 Union Street in Simcoe, on a rainy July afternoon in 1947. Pack six kids into the second floor of a creaking old barn of a house. A cacophony has already erupted: Walter and Tom are both bawling, in an early preview of stereo sound, after breaking a few dishes for fun. Mike is gabbing on the phone with a crony. Alas, the household racket drowns out the Bunny Berigan record he's playing. Hugh is scraping the bow across what's left of the bridge of his violin.

Four-year-old sister Chris has started singing "Bobby Shafto"; she could be out to break her own record of singing it eighteen times without an intermission. I flip aside the book I've been trying to read. At moments such as this, I envy the Count of Monte Cristo.

It's now twenty-nine years later. I've followed the saga of the *Lampoon.* Publisher Matty Simmons, who hasn't given up after Beard and Kenney defected, taking the soul of the magazine with them, can't—and won't—believe the *Lampoon* is doomed. A million-circulation magazine that's lost some cachet can still survive: a new editorial slant, a new editor, and an infusion of fresh young energy were crucial.

▪ ▪ ▪

A brief interlude here—a noncommercial break—to catch up with the other McCalls. Mike is still in the navy, flying planes (we McCalls always find a way to go against the grain). Hugh recently started as editor of *Track & Traffic*, which I helped secure for him through my relationship with the boss, Jerry Polivka. Tom was in the navy, too. But unlike Mike he was actually on ships (well, submarines), working as supplies support. Walt moved from St. Thomas to Windsor, where he became a local reporter for *The Star.* My kid sister, Chris, married one of my best friends, John (Jno) Jerome, in 1966. Both were magazine editors who despised New York life and quit in 1967 to live like hippie pioneers in rocky, isolated northern New Hampshire. Their departure robbed me of lively company. I railed against the move; it took me a couple of years to square Chris and John's shucking of cosmopolitan Manhattan life for freedom and independence. Which they valued and I would, down the road a ways, noisily embrace.

John was that rarity, an intellectual Texan. He was tall and slim and looked like a cowboy. His taciturnity hid a sharp wit that never stooped to cruelty. Quiet in his manner, Jno was the shyest man and best conversationalist I'd ever met. He'd followed a zigzag path to reach book publishing and wrote only about what interested him: building a stone wall; rebuilding a 1950 Dodge pickup; the strange allure of mountains; the "sweet spot" in sports. He wrote poetically but adhered to reality, acquiring a devoted readership far from the mainstream. Enough readers were attracted to support John Jerome's work over a span of twenty-eight years.

▪ ▪ ▪

P.J. cleaned house. Into the trash went the literary element. Sex mattered. The editorial ambience dropped from faux Harvard to what you'd find in the auto-repair shop class of first-year boys enrolled in an unlicensed Arkansas trade school. The laughs were coarser. As in the Beard-Kenney era, females had only one major role: as photographic models showing their secondary sex characteristics. P.J. hired a crew of new writers headed by Chicagoan John Hughes, later Hollywood's darling for writing and directing a slew of warmhearted teen-agony movies. It worked: the magazine replaced its lost cachet with a nose-picker persona from O'Rourke's semi-redneck origins. The *Lampoon*'s heart was transplanted to Hollywood, where a single mammoth movie hit, *Animal House*, rerouted the magazine's major purpose to making movies.

▪ ▪ ▪

In autumn 1975, a young Canadian refugee from *Sonny and Cher*, *Laugh-In*, and other network TV shows, Lorne Michaels, was aiming to be more than just a writer. He wanted to produce and call the shots, from casting to script approval and the myriad other elements of a TV program. Michaels charmed NBC into giving him the opportunity to run a new show. In return, NBC got a phenomenon. Michaels insisted that his new show be live, boast no stars, and run in one of the least coveted network slots imaginable: eleven thirty on Saturday night to one on Sunday morning.

As it turned out, it didn't much matter whether the show was coming from the Hindu Kush, whether the week's star host was Idi Amin, or whether the musical guest was Kate Smith. Showbiz glitz was out. *Saturday Night Live* debuted in October. Within a month it was a hit. Within a year it was a sensation. The sophisticated slapstick style pioneered in the pages of the *National Lampoon* came off even better on television, adding movement and sound, with weekly musical acts that were a must-see lure for the younger generation.

Lorne Michaels looked more and more like a genius, toppling stale shibboleths. Example: A *live* show ninety minutes long gave television's old guard the willies. It forced cast members to navigate a tightrope in a milieu of nonstop tension. But a loosey-goosey young generation was forgiving of miscues; in fact, most believed a live TV show *should* stumble now and then. The *Saturday Night* crowd *relished* the odd gaffe: it made television more human.

The mouth-breathers would always have their comic books, but for many educated young people, the success of *SNL* deflated that appeal. Why get your laughs from a slow, clumsy, time-wasting medium like print? Never mind the fact that print forced you to pay to read it while TV was free, which led to America becoming a couch-potato nation. Except for PBS treats like a six-part documentary on the history of ink, network TV stuck to (moronically) simple ideas, expressed in (crude) simple words. You avoided having to learn anything: with TV, your one task was to turn the set on.

The *National Lampoon*, my central money source for five years, had been transmogrified into something cruder, aimed at kids. I no longer belonged. My alternative employment options shivered no timbers: stitching together enough assignments to underwrite Polly's and my New York lifestyle was impossible—a fantasy. Yes, I regularly wrote and illustrated light humor for *Car and Driver* and *Road & Track*, the Red Sox and Yankees of car magazines, but they needed only occasional japes. Beyond that, my universe was empty. The odd windfall assignment wasn't a career. I had to accept the fact that my artistic skills were too arcane to be trusted by most advertising art directors. Once again my imagination froze when the chips were down. I'd made no contacts that could generate a chain of tips and introductions, either in advertising or on the editorial side. My blinkered vision told me that one option remained.

A résumé needed to be prepared. I had an advertising career to make claims about; everything else in my employment history was crap. Any potential boss would slide his or her eyes down the page and discover, under the *Education* heading, proof of such incompetence that my fate would be sealed, as in, say, a tomb. My tactic in the face of probable defeat was ingenuity itself: write like a hack professor in a backwater college, someone striving to impress his betters with erudition and boldness so striking that I'd be hired just so they could have a latter-day orator around.

I decided after a month with no responses, either from editors or creative directors, that somewhere in the résumé there must have been a gaffe, a political hint, or some other wordage that wrecked my cause. That was the moment when I abandoned the formalities and pleaded with Michael O'Donoghue to get me an interview for a job as a writer on *Saturday Night Live*. I compressed my suitability credentials to a couple of points. One: I was a good writer in print and a professional artist who naturally thought in *images*. No minor plus for a show so dependent on a creative use of settings. Two: I'd been writing satire in some form since I was a kid. I was also that rarity in America: a humorist specializing in satire, the lifeblood of this new kind of TV comedy.

Mr. Mike broadcast his disdain for all network comedy and most comedians, Lenny Bruce excepted. Brooking no criticism, he felt Bruce was the one uncorrupted humorist, probably in the known universe. Over the years, O'Donoghue's uncompromising humor and his role-playing as a sharp-witted cynic made him a kind of front man—for the *Lampoon* but also as a Che Guevara for all comedic rascals. His jump from 635 Madison to 30 Rockefeller Center was momentous for both sides. He had become the poster boy for the *Lampoon*'s brash-brat reputation. That was okay with Mr. Mike, who relished (and burnished) his enfant-terrible image. Everything he wrote reflected outrage: an O'Donoghue piece never flattered his audience so much as beat it up. Lorne Michaels's hiring of O'Donoghue helped position Michaels as a pioneer of advanced TV comedy. O'Donoghue never pulled his punches. Out went fifty years of mass-audience American comedy. In crashed a new barbarian mode.

O'Donoghue and I had never had a fight or even cross words. He and his gal pal, Anne Beatts, dined now and then with Polly and me. Polly had helped Michael produce the *Lampoon Radio Hour*; his willfulness and daily tantrums, often aimed her way, failed to faze her. Once he realized she wouldn't take his guff, Michael backed off, although he still managed the occasional fond dig, as in his description of Polly as "a rich girl with no money." To this point I'd avoided asking Mr. Mike, as he styled himself, to get me in on the action, but now I shamelessly importuned him to use his influence on my behalf. I wanted an interview in the Comedy Xanadu with Lorne Michaels.

Mr. Mike came through. Two weeks later, on a hot, late August Friday afternoon, I drove into Manhattan from our rented Wainscott summerhouse to be inducted into the world of network television. Lorne Michaels was polite and undemonstrative, in the

Canadian way. I immediately played my Canadians-in-U.S.-showbiz card: "We Canadians seem to be taking over American comedy, all right!" My piercing insight elicited no response. I tried our common bond of growing up in Toronto. That and my bulletin on U.S. comedy becoming Canadian-heavy had bought me five minutes of "Auld Lang Syne."

We chatted briefly. There's a lingo used by senior showbiz types. Lorne knew it; I didn't. The interview went from tired generalities by me to Michaels's generalities in reply. He got up from his desk, the signal that our talk was over. I headed for the door. Lorne was offering me a provisional job. He had no budget for another writer, but I could come aboard at a mere token salary; if I showed promise by the end of the 1976–77 season there might be an opening I could fill.

No slap on the back as I left. Michaels was already on the phone to someone who counted. The interview and the half job was a personal favor to Mr. Mike; he entertained no conviction that this modest introvert would soon be deluging him with brilliant TV skits. My desperate need for employment had been satisfied—if you interpreted "satisfied" to mean supplementing a nothing salary with my own savings. I took the elevator down to street level, harboring feelings that matched its rate of decline. Lorne Michaels knew every TV comedy writer on the planet, and we both knew I wasn't one of them.

I was now a part, however modest, of TV's hottest entertainment property. Why, then, did this triumph of ambition feel so similar to the agony of defeat? I should have barged in, fire in the belly and smoke pouring out of my ears. Instead, I spit the bit. Polly tried cheering me up the weekend before my first day at *Saturday Night* in early September. I bucked up and used every erg of willpower to banish my self-image of the beaten-down dunce of 1951 that had never gone away, only skulked nearby, waiting to bring me down. The palliatives of money and relative success had smothered the pain of my early life. Willpower alone kept the pain and its partner, distress, at bay but hadn't abolished it. Those ancient bruises connived to return whenever actual progress threatened.

■ ■ ■

The *Saturday Night* offices occupied most of the nineteenth floor of the Rockefeller Center complex. Space was too tight for an office at my humble level. A battered desk in a long hallway would have to suffice, but at least the semi-dark corridor was lightly trafficked. I felt isolated but not alone: a fellow hallway denizen sat at a desk a few feet away. Tom Schiller was a video guy doing short comic sequences dropped into the show now and then. He used his frequent downtime to try writing live-action bits for the show. Maybe because he didn't wear the hot young performer's slick coating of cool, Tom was open and helpful—as in answering "Where's the john?" and other pertinent queries.

Some *SNL* cast members had been regulars on the radio show. John Belushi, the terrifying performer, was a gentle, sweet-natured civilian. I had written a sketch making fun of Belushi's Albanian descent; I showed him the script and he thought it was funny but asked me to kill it. He feared it would offend his Albanian-immigrant parents.

Belushi's frequent partner and cowriter, Dan Aykroyd, talked like an outlaw biker, usually in an aggressively loud, blustery voice. His energy was exhausting. His ideas—the ridiculous and ridiculously funny Coneheads, the blender that could turn a whole fish into soup—were original. Although we were fellow Canadians, this kinship never came up.

Chevy Chase looked Ivy League. He'd leave the show in a month or so, and seemed to be preoccupied with his imminent stardom.

He'd separated himself from his fellow cast members. Chevy was, from where I sat, the least popular guy in that close-knit group.

You couldn't *not* be a fan of Gilda Radner. Everyone felt protective of that needy soul: on camera, Gilda was hilarious, in control, a trouper who drew laughs whatever the role. Off camera was different: emotionally fragile enough to be in tears half the time, yet selflessly supportive of everyone who needed it. Jane Curtin came from a completely different world: affluent, suburban, settled. She was easy to talk to. How she got into the *Saturday Night* caravansary mystified me: she wasn't funny, didn't look weird, indeed was as straight as can be. And those factors, I realized, were just what the show needed: a figure the crazies could play off.

Laraine Newman transmitted a West Coast sensibility that perfectly fit exotic roles. I never contacted her essence. The comedy duo of Al Franken and Tom Davis had no easy time on camera; their real value was in the writing they contributed. Franken had a wider grasp of life than anyone else; if "intellectual" could ever be ascribed to somebody working in TV comedy, Al Franken was one. Maybe the only one.

Hundreds of fame-hungry writers would have gladly given their left testicle for the opportunity I'd been vouchsafed. I kept both of mine. I also kept a day-by-day diary. Impressions outweigh factual reporting, but the diary is a conscientious day-by-day record of that not-at-all-wonderful adventure:

Monday

Every step uncertain. Sit reading *Time* and the *Post* and looking engaged while people buzz all around, very busy. No typewriter. Schiller shows me around a bit, short talk to O'Donoghue, Beatts. See Michaels briefly. Overwhelming sense of confusion; standing at base of mountain whose top—the actual show—is obscured in mist. How to get from here to there? Suddenly, no idea. Hours drag. Weird schedule. Having done no work, hard to know when I can gracefully leave. Leave around 8.

Tuesday

Still no typewriter. More sitting around. Meet more people but feel keenly lack of "belonging" and have little to contribute to conversation. Borrow a typewriter, try to work out list of ideas. Work on Martin Bormann Amexco idea rest of day. Michaels suggests helping Alan Zweibel with "George and Cornelia" thing but he's done it. Help Schiller write end of "Paris" sketch. Itch to produce ideas strong. Had worked up a few ideas in the previous week in Wainscott and at home, now put them on paper.

Wednesday

Bring in ideas and show to O'Donoghue. He critiques them. Left with three or four possibles and a sharper understanding of what is likely to and isn't likely to work. Schiller slightly more encouraging but already clear O'Donoghue is tougher and better than anybody else. Make notes of what Michaels said re: each piece. Abandon Bormann thing. Meeting for run-thru in Michaels's office at 2. Self-conscious in the meeting—I have nothing to contribute. It is unexpectedly relaxed and friendly all 'round. Still feel complete outsider. Had brought portable typewriter from home but my new machine finally arrives. Learn how 1-to-1 parody not enough. Anything that would work on Carol Burnett, etc., not for this show. You can't be simply absurd. Have to cull ideas from real life, and twist them. "West Point Cheater Bowl" has possibilities. Resolve to show stuff around and not get too private. General pace and level of wisecracks and conversation is too quick for me. I feel sluggish. Say nothing funny. For a 41-year-old feel decidedly green and young.

Thursday

Had idea about "Eskimo in the R.A.F." Wednesday night and try writing it most of Thursday. Start out in high gear but gradually it becomes clear that this is simply a phrase, not an idea, and lacking any logical action or a real premise, it won't go anywhere. Schiller shows me around the set and associated mysteries. It is a maze. Everybody busy but me. Not relaxed. Keep working on "Eskimo" idea, but with sinking feeling. It will take more than that. Also thinking about Chinese Opera. A "good look," as they say, but again, no real content. Seeing and hearing other people's ideas makes me sometimes despair. Can I ever be that sharp? Not in the groove yet. Have to work through the pile of ideas I started out with in order to break into the right stuff. Beginning to grasp difference apt and inept ideas for skits. Much of my stuff only puns. Absurdist. Like radio material. This show demands more topicality. Every idea has to work harder. A matter of mental conditioning, too. My three years of hibernation, and three months in Wainscott, have left me somewhat dull and uninventive. The handful of ideas I'd had for articles or books seems suddenly very thin and paltry. Not enough stimulation. The demand for material on TV is insatiable and stirs your brains. You accelerate all aspects of the creative process. [My then agent] David Obst that night (Wednesday) describes fiasco of my book proposal at Random House and Simon & Schuster. A letdown, but not a very painful one in this context. I have new and more immediate worries. Word of David McClelland's suicide that night. [Marginal note: (Watch cassette of "Citizen K")]

Friday

Write "Weekend Update" things all day. Incredibly slow. Begin to perceive shape of these items is subtler than I'd thought. The joke has to be fast and at the end. Solzhenitsyn piece occupies hours. Traffic safety also. Chevy [Chase] is reasonably enthusiastic about these but I suspect he's being nice. Tension is clearly mounting as time for show comes closer. Office largely empty while I work. Don't visit set—too boring, too much time to do nothing while my energies are all throbbing. I'd burst. I am humbled, but not discouraged by Friday night. It will be harder than I thought. But it can be done, and after five days I've learned so much that it seems logical that another few weeks will get me where I have to be mentally. At which point I could contribute. Good ideas sometimes just arrive. No mechanical process is likely. They're close-knit, and I'm not yet part of the group. Partly my unwillingness to let go of my privacy and reticence. Have to mix it up with them or no hope of success.

Sunday

Necessary social intercourse with platoons of strange people, from first minute to last every day of every work week, is the hardest aspect to adjust to. This is exacerbated by the absence of an office with a door that can be shut to seal you off from all the static. I'm exposed continuously, and haven't yet been able to train my ears to filter out the extraneous.

Last night's show was I guess about average for SatNite, not terrific and not a total failure. The amount of energy, emotion, time, skill, money, and ego invested in those 90 fleeting minutes, though, was amazing. "Appalling" was my first choice of adjective. I stumbled out of the studio afterwards, wondering how these folks can muster the required industry and concern, etc., week after week after week, all for the sake of . . . that. That evanescent little series of pallid images on a TV screen. My panicky reaction at that moment was, I couldn't and can't. Most things don't matter. But TV . . . it *really* doesn't matter.

Yet why is it so hard? I quickly counter. And it is hard to make live TV comedy work, as last night's show by omission underscores. Worst of all creative worlds—a medium that is tripe, work that is unspeakably difficult and drudgery-laden.

But then I remind myself that this is the recognized best of its kind, and any other show would be even worse. I think part of the sense of letdown I feel—felt all week—connects with the nature of the illusion that this is TV and showbiz; the seediness, scuzziness, utter lack of glamour and fun and illusion, behind the scenes. The discovery of all that rusty, dirty, ordinary-looking machinery behind the magic can make you cynical. Everybody in TV is cynical, I find. From where they sit, it's inevitable. This seldom happens in print. The writer doesn't have to pull proofs or watch the presses. If there indeed is any such creature as a "natural" TV writer, I'm not him. The term "apprentice" in reference to my position on that show is all too accurate. My nagging question is whether the apprenticeship is worth living through; whether I really want to go where the acquisition of TV writing skills is likely to take me—that is, into more TV and more into TV. Unlike most of my colleagues, I didn't grow up in the fifties and sixties acutely aware of television and making plentiful room for it in my life and career. The medium isn't one I have studied or even thought about much when I didn't have to, which was all the time. I'm not sure at my age, with an almost spiritual loyalty to print, that I can now graft a TV mentality onto myself. And I begin to think that to succeed in this racket, you have to do just that. It's a knack to un-learn, not to write for permanence as you do in print. On TV, you can learn to get away with whatever works *at the moment*, without reference to any larger frame of reference. My linear training keeps tripping me up. I work too logically.

I'm also about the only non-doper, non-Village, non-Woodstock type in the general vicinity—an elderly bourgeois fellow with a wife and a clean apartment, even a dog. I felt so alien last night in the greenroom with all those types among whom it's almost a matter of professional pride to be strung out. Their, er, lifestyles and mine are so hopelessly separate. Depressing, that. Not because I feel I'm too late or too old, but the opposite—what the fuck is a fellow like me, who has grown up and who found what he wants and likes it, and has dismissed ratty clothes and the putdown as conversational currency and the whole tedious business of "hanging out"—what am I doing among all these barely-post-juvenile delinquents? Only way I'm going to win this issue is by sweeping along on such a high tide of unassailable talent that they'll just have to accept my middle-aged eccentricity.

The show just kind of happens by Saturday in the rehearsals. I am still baffled as to the exact route things take from the blank sheets in the typewriters on Monday to the final typed-up script issued late Friday afternoon. Who decides what, and why, are veiled in Rosicrucian-like secrecy. There's much quibbling and grousing about sketches that get dropped—they usually have 30 minutes more than the show needs. Sketches are rewritten and reworked virtually until airtime.

■ ■ ■

I'd never kept a diary, for the intellectually sound reason that the drama of my life was all in my mind, and arguments between the warring sides would be boring to read blow-by-blow years later. The *Saturday Night* diary was different. The major purpose of writing an entry every day was to talk to myself (because there was nobody to complain to), to answer broad questions, and to witness and record the strange world I'd stumbled into. Talking to myself also provided a candid look at what I was doing—for future reference.

Exactly mirroring my state of mind, the diary peters out once I abandoned TV writing as a career and *Saturday Night Live* as a job. By then, I had nothing to learn and had become bored by the elephantine process of staging a five-minute comedy sketch. I made no friends there. Common use of drugs was a way of life among the cast; I wasn't interested. That made me uninteresting. I came to the show over the transom, in the second season, when writers and actors had already formed relationships that had hardened. I was an interloper, needed by nobody.

The age difference penalized me: I was at least a decade older than everybody in the writing *and* cast cadres. That was deadly: my values had been shaped in a world not familiar to these sprouts and vice versa. The culture had speeded up tremendously: no good at all, when the show's very theme concentrated on the current me, not the now half-obsolete baby boom generation.

"Despair" is a word flung around too carelessly: the dark feelings we all experience in life, if you haven't actually checked out potential suicide locations, are depression. Extreme depression is close to despair.

Gobs of the stuff occluded my skull the Friday afternoon in mid-November when I decided enough was enough and walked away from *Saturday Night*, still in the early days of its second season. Enough internal rage at never having solved writing TV comedy. Enough guilt at lacking the initiative and the guts to force myself into that fractious family. Enough regret, mixed in with guilt, that

I had actually kept my distance from the writers and cast members I might have asked or, what the hell, *begged* to help me figure it all out. Those were only the obvious regrets; I'd keep digging up regret and guilt stragglers for years.

Polly sympathized, but only so far. That show, she said in the spirit of the loyal opposition, is the gravy train. A very few writers will ever get a crack at it. And here I was, announcing defeat after a lousy three months. I countered with my increasingly existential response. Ultimately, it wasn't my isolation or my sense of exclusion. I didn't and never could feel excitement about working in TV. I toyed with accusing myself of gutlessness in turning off the superhighway to *SNL*, but even with my guilt working overtime, I knew there was another side to it. I'd earned a niche in the world of illustration. It would be illogical to throw away something I'd been doing all my life, gotten good at, and loved. The possibility of making money as an illustrator was a long-term goal, if a vague one. But from my current position in the back of the pack, it wasn't exactly hardheaded reasoning to forecast big money waiting to be scooped up in the parking lot at the end of the rainbow.

The central issue in our lives dictated a strange interlude: materially, I'd never had it so good (and this was still from the larder of advertising). Yet how long could the Big Bad Wolf be hammering at our front door? My sense of prosperity and the comfort of living well—all of it was built on sand. Sooner or later the bank account would dry up and end this sunny mirage of well-being.

The next year lay fallow. I'd lost conviction, didn't know who I was. I wasted an opportunity by doing a piece (both the writing and illustrations) on the Battle of Britain—one of the best pieces I've ever done—and throwing it away in the pages of *Oui*, a magazine aimed at readers who found its parent, *Playboy*, too intellectually challenging.

We left Manhattan to start a family and try our hands at rural life.
One of them worked out; my daughter, Amanda.

Chapter 10

Appalachia North

I'd interred the *Saturday Night Live* experience in the darker corners of my memory, but it kept popping up like a guilty conscience. What could be done to shake the gloom that descended whenever I tried to foresee a life that worked? Passing myself off as a writer after my pratfall on a live TV show seemed almost criminally dishonest. The memory of a lifelong romance with words left a sour taste in my mouth.

Maybe a normal upbringing would have shaped my career and produced a normal artist. But only extreme conditions could produce the kind of artist I became. The seesaw effect of trying to decide between writing and art had been roiling my innards since boyhood. I settled it by defining myself as both an artist and a writer. That shut me up.

New York itself was beginning to feel alien. When you aren't being productive, the city has no place for you. The taste in my mouth was bitter. I couldn't have fun in New York now. I didn't deserve it.

I wasn't the first dummy to blame his screwups on where he worked. For me, depression—or its visible effects—gradually retreated, replaced by a fresh emotional state I invented: baseless optimism doomed to fail, or what psychiatrists prefer to call super hubris. This inspired a bold plan: run from the city that neither knew nor needed me, and hide. It was a plan that was, as a close friend remarked, "ten times wackier than before," not to mention career suicide.

I had insisted on buying a farm with a barn in Western Massachusetts's all too authentic re-creation of Yoknapatawpha County, a place where neither of us had ever set foot, where nobody we knew lived. Making drastically illogical decisions—like ours to leave New York and invest our life in a mythical paradise—rapidly swelled into full-fledged reality. The deciding factor for us was the endorsement of my polymathic friend Dan Okrent, who'd recently left a job at Harcourt Brace and ventured north to start *New England Monthly* magazine. He didn't try to stop us but lured us forward and right off the cliff. My official excuse for getting out of Manhattan was the shame of flopping at writing funny skits for the hottest comedy on TV. That, and we succumbed to the craze set off by *Blair & Ketchum's Country Journal* of trading in taxis and skyscrapers for gardening clogs and stone-mantel fireplaces.

The Okrents found a rambling old house in the pleasant little crossroads town of Worthington, Massachusetts. It seemed only natural that Dan's house abutted the local golf course. By the time Polly and I had started serious shopping, he and Becky were well settled.

Our progress was slow—no, it was fumbling and stumbling, a dictionary definition of naiveté. We hadn't even settled on the kind of house we preferred. Or where it would be. Or what it had to be—or not be—to suit our needs. Oh, and by the way, what were these needs? All our energy was poured into projects like what wood-burning stove to buy. Vigilant or Defiant? Their names were more suited to World War II fighter planes than a hot, squat metal box.

We ended up on a property near the town of Conway, Massachusetts, home of the much-lauded Librarian of Congress and poet laureate Archibald MacLeish. Why would a renowned man of letters choose to live in a town of rustics whose last brush with poetry was "Mary Had a Little Lamb"? Now and then he parked his Mercedes in front of the post office, dashed in to collect his mail, and drove off. I never worked up the courage to intercept him and ask this question.

An hour's worth of due diligence might have warned us off Conway as a McCall homestead. Socioeconomic factors alone should have saved us much later heartburn: no industry, no jobs, an elderly-heavy populace, and perennial vetoes on allotting tax money for education. A short drive through town would have served to turn us off. Conway shared its charms with any half-dead little burg in a Kentucky hollow. New England should have expelled it; "lackluster" is too fancy a word for a string of small houses, a sagging old bar, and a run-down hut that sold groceries, gasoline, and lottery tickets. Had we done our homework, the discrepancy would have whacked us in the kisser: neither of us was a polished intellectual, but neither were we of the mouth-breathing ranks. And the mouth-breathers held sway.

Sitting in Manhattan, seduced by myths of New England as the leitmotif of our new life, I envisioned dinner parties with tweedy academics. Cracker-barrel chats with salty old-timers. Meeting reclusive writers and artists to talk all night about Whither Creativity. And on and on, until reality melted into fantasy. But the cultural influences of Smith College in Northampton and Amherst College in Amherst faded at the city limits. Had Polly or I rooted out the facts, we'd have seen that our bit of heaven formed what could well be the northern end of Appalachia.

Nightlife was seriously lacking. Either the combined economies of Northampton and Amherst weren't robust enough to support more than a couple of mediocre restaurants or else dining out was regarded as putting on the dog. In Conway the locals' favorite social event came every Saturday evening, when vans and speeding pick-ups bounced up the gravel road in front of our house. A small mob convened at a beat-up shack in a clearing a quarter mile on: the Sportsman's Club, where members celebrated their working lives by firing their guns. Sometime after midnight, what sounded like a convoy of half-tracks barreled back down the gravel road, their occupants flinging beer bottles and insults at the night and the world.

It was 1978. Polly had just graduated from Columbia with a degree in social work and wanted to start her career, but the only employment available relegated her to a Dickensian halfway house on a side street in nearby seedy Greenfield, serving sad wrecks turfed out of state mental health facilities because standard measurements said they weren't crazy. Some she treated for alcoholism. As for the other residents, neither Polly nor Sigmund Freud could help: imperfect upbringings, broken families, bad-joke educations, and generations of poverty produced citizens unable to work and left to wander the streets. The best Polly and her colleagues could do was babysit their wards. And show them a little kindness.

Some residents did not reciprocate. One such person, thirty or so years old, was given to declaiming loudly, tantrums that escalated to a hyper condition wherein he muttered dark threats. He needed discipline. Polly began trying to talk him off the ledge but backed away, very slowly, when she discovered that this obstreperous young sorehead had recently cried for help in the most convincing manner known to the science of healing souls: by murdering his dad.

Meanwhile, twenty miles south of us, in Worthington, Dan and Becky were living the life we'd expected for ourselves: interesting friends, physical activities: turning a rough and bumpy patch of lawn into the best and possibly only croquet venue north of

Stockbridge; cross-country skiing; playing hockey on frozen ponds and softball games in local fields.

■ ■ ■

We approached our handsome old Greek Revival house with zest. Hardly an inch of High Meadow Farm (a name inherited from some prior tenant) escaped a cosmetic makeover. Built-in bookshelves flanked the fireplace. Light gray and silver wallpaper worthy of a Paris salon lined the entry hall. The house provided us the luxury of five bedrooms. Ours was lushly carpeted; guest rooms that wouldn't host an occupant for months were spiffed up with delicately color-coordinated bedspreads, carpeting, window treatments, and paint.

Misery descended on High Meadow Farm and persisted for most of our days there. Yet I had to grudgingly admit that our location offered certain pluses. Hardware-store calendars tried but only came close to reproducing the sylvan beauty we experienced from our late June arrival through most of November. Even the town basked in a kind of glow. Day after day for our first six months, staying indoors felt like a crime against nature.

Polly's green thumb, an offshoot of her rabid new passion for growing plants and an outlet for her blast-furnace bouts of energy, created a huge garden; we consumed most of its yield, which was topped by a crop of monster zucchini.

■ ■ ■

Cars have always mattered to me more than to most grown-ups—a statement instantly belied by the wheels I chose for our bucolic life. Together with the obligatory L.L. Bean wardrobe, the wood-burning stove, and a boxcar-size freezer for the fall venison haul, we'd also need the appropriate vehicle for country living. Back in 1978 the SUV was still in the offing, a sugarplum fairy dancing in Big Oil's eyes, and the pickup truck had yet to become the Marlboro Man of the suburban affluent. Americans deep into the black Lab/Agway/antique-refinishing lifestyle had the Hobson's choice of a station wagon or a station wagon, or another station wagon.

The station wagon perplexed me. Having never come within hailing distance of that creature, I did the smart thing and consulted an eminent automotive journalist for his station wagon wisdom. A foolish move: the automobile journalist of those days lived with the car he'd be reviewing for a few days. What it's like to drive a vehicle through the vagaries and vicissitudes of quotidian life is for those poor owners who actually have to keep it running to find out. Car journalists are in the commercial news business, atwitter about what's poised to burst onto the scene. This is a virtual guarantee that whatever they recommend will be too new to have established a record, pro or con.

I gritted my teeth and settled on a brand-new 1978 Ford Fairmont wagon. Polly and I often drove aimlessly around in it just for something to do, to get out of a house that felt more and more like a spiritual prison. The Fairmont was a lowest common denominator on wheels. It did nothing well, and I hated it because it was so dull. Dull to drive, dull to ride in, dull to contemplate sitting in the driveway. "Build quality" was still a slogan in Detroit in 1978 and was supposed to mean more than pieces falling off a car. What annoyed me most was how flimsy it felt, and for a V-8–powered vehicle, how gutless. Rattles and squeaks appeared after a thousand miles. The bench-type front seat was a monument to cheapness, as ergonomic as an electric chair. What it says about the American car buyer's standards in the late seventies that the Ford Fairmont was a smash hit in sales, Dear Reader can probably divine.

I had better luck with a spavined old 1952 Dodge station wagon, bought on an impulse. Like the loyal Saint Bernard trekking through snowdrifts to haul his sick master to safety, that Dodge—built like a brick smokehouse, fittings that were metal castings, the paint still shiny after twenty-six years—ran and ran, requiring only age-related fixes (a new fuel line and a new battery) and four new tires. Nothing could be done about the faux-useful "vacuumatic" transmission, which required the driver to change gears by lifting his foot off the gas and pray that this would result in a reassuring *clunk!* before the Dodge had slowed to a near stop.

▪ ▪ ▪

In late November came a brief snowstorm, and it dawned on us that a New England winter would alter our life. The weather deteriorated, fast. The color drained from the landscape. Snow and sleet started to make driving iffy. Freezing rain was a novel menace.

The dark moments always seemed to be darkest in the slack after-dinner hours. We spent New Year's Eve of 1978 alone in the living room, watching Jim and Tammy Bakker's *700 Club* on the one channel our black-and-white TV could pull in, while a sleet storm pelted the windows with what sounded like buckshot and the phone didn't ring.

"Never a dull moment" seemed to be the Okrent motto. "Never an interesting moment" could have been ours. Jealous envy could have but didn't arise as the Okrents prospered in their new setting and the McCalls floundered. I knew damned well that ninety-nine percent of our disappointment was our own fault. Nobody had forced us to choose this place; my lifelong custom of inadequate planning, shortsighted and too reliant on others for too much of the heavy lifting, was the real culprit.

The absence of friends was a continuing sadness. The imminent

Christmas season in our first year seemed a sound pretext to ingratiate ourselves with as many neighbors as we could identify by inviting them over. Thus we were the hosts of what might have been the first cocktail party ever staged in Franklin County. Polly laid out a rich spread of meats, vegetables, and hors d'oeuvres. She made certain that everyone had a plate. Cocktail napkins, swizzle sticks, scotch and bourbon, an ice bucket, and glasses for liquor and wine brought a Manhattan note of sophistication to this benighted backwater.

That had been a well-intended blunder. All guests had left by seven thirty. The scotch and bourbon, and the elaborate spread, had no takers. Beer was the drink of choice. One housewife said she'd never flown on a plane. Welcoming ourselves to the area wasn't only a bust, it was an embarrassment. New York was a hundred and eighty miles away. The difference in culture was unbridgeable.

■ ■ ■

But a bailout was looming for Polly and me. The successor U.S. agency for Mercedes-Benz was McCaffrey & McCall, a pale echo of Ogilvy & Mather. Its head man was David McCall (no relation), who had been copy chief at O&M. He'd so implemented David Ogilvy's rationalist philosophy that wags nicknamed the firm "Ogilvy East." Yet neither David McCall nor anyone working with him knew the automobile industry, its history, or Mercedes-Benz. Somebody at Mercedes-Benz of North America must have absorbed the Ogilvy doctrine and was smart enough to recommend the agency most closely resembling O&M. Thus did McCaffrey & McCall reap the windfall.

David and I arranged to meet soon in New York to discuss my role and related matters. The notion of a return to advertising stuck in my craw after all the righteous bad-mouthing I'd done about it after pulling away from the business and not only surviving but finding psychic rewards in doing what I believed I was born to do. Polly and I talked it out. On a points basis, New York scored over one hundred. Conway earned twelve.

Moreover, taking the job would settle us financially—slaying the dragon we feared most. That made the prospect of getting back to New York real. But trashing our folly and pulling up stakes was no overnight task. Should we sell the property? How could we find an affordable apartment in New York from a hundred and eighty miles away?

I should have written a list of issues and questions before meeting David McCall, but settling things face-to-face struck me as a speedier means of resolving issues than endless fence-sitting telephone negotiations. A pure bonus would be the chemistry test: Did he seem to be a guy I'd respect, admire, and be ready to follow?

An expensive East Side Italian restaurant was the venue. David was a red-faced WASP in a seersucker suit who radiated earnestness. I trusted him on sight. He was physically restless, spoke fast, and was as transparently honest as anyone I'd ever met. His sense of proportion differed wildly from Hank's monomaniacal focus. His balanced life meant time for his five sons, his political activities, and his recreations, i.e., tennis and golf. His first marriage had ended in divorce. His second wife died suddenly of a brain hemorrhage.

David had a well-furnished mind; I considered myself well-read, but he matched and often beat me to the latest political or historical find. I could only conclude that he must be a speed-reader.

The advantage in negotiating terms for my "consultant" role, it turned out, was all mine. David hadn't been ordered to retain my services, but he was quick-minded enough to sense that dragging his heels without a convincing reason would send MBNA the wrong message at the wrong time. The negotiating of terms proved swift and easy. I'm the sorriest dealmaker in advertising's annals, and it was part of David's charm that money and related negotiations weren't exactly his strengths. One could describe it the way Shirley Povich, the great *Washington Post* sportswriter, portrayed a trade of nobodies between the hometown Senators and the Chicago White Sox: "Both sides lost."

Thus did I find myself an advertising guy again.

I personally liked the McCaffrey & McCall creative group—to my private relief: if an asshole art director and a prima donna copywriter fight over an ad, or a brilliant idea veers off-strategy, the hellish tensions arising therefrom can screw an ad or a whole campaign.

I had no official standing as a consultant (commonly defined as the guy you bring in from out of town to borrow your watch to tell you what time it is). My role would be to keep creative work true to the brand's marketing strategy. And, arguably for morale purposes, to avoid being taken for an inconsiderate know-it-all: a ticklish task indeed.

Meetings are the bane of any industry divided into separate disciplines that must regularly interact. I sat through hundreds of them, dealing with media, research findings, and myriads of bland details. I squirmed in my seat as hours ticked away. By that time I'd taken on the "informal" duties of chief copywriter. This was to circumvent the resident copywriters—eager fellows all of them, but hopeless amateurs in treading the fine line that separated good copy from wretched, inaccurate word clusters. Justifying a steep sticker price for a car that looked minimally styled, its power a fraction of that offered by a Detroit luxobarge, an interior designed primarily for comfort and driver efficiency demanded that every line of copy combine common sense and competitive fire.

Interacting with the advertising department in the Mercedes-Benz main U.S. office in Montvale, New Jersey (eventually labeled the Death Star by disaffected agency people), ate chunks of time.

Gimlet-eyed Mercedes executives expected a thorough, sophisticated knowledge of cars—and especially those produced by Mercedes-Benz. This was a must for the creative team and a virtual job qualification for new writers. The belief that technology was paramount had to be the core of every ad; writers who strayed from that claim weren't writers who stayed.

▪ ▪ ▪

Bob (until he upgraded himself to Robert and told his secretary to tell the agency) was MBNA's advertising manager and one of the most brilliant people I ever knew in that curious industry. At the same time, he could also fairly be termed a bully, a paranoiac, a sadist, and a saboteur of his own well-being. A lonely egoist. The McCaffrey & McCall creative group were ready to fall on their swords for the Three-Pointed Star. Robert-formerly-Bob was the obstacle. He organized a nest of flunkies—as outspoken a team as Trump's cabinet. Advertising was voodoo to his Mercedes overlords: left to operate with minimal supervision, Robert-formerly-Bob was free to exercise his worst instincts. Had MBNA used a personality test for hirees, Robert-formerly-Bob wouldn't have made it out of the waiting room.

The myth of smooth, reasonable "teamwork" to bring the ad department and the agency into an efficient, mutually rewarding symbiosis disgusted me more than any other aspect of client-agency relations. It comes down, literally, to the bottom line. The client pays the agency. If the client sees an intractable problem with its agency, such as bad chemistry at high levels, weak advertising, or the feeling that the initial client-agency bond has withered over time, then there needs to be a rejuvenation of spirit on both sides. Other factors may be in play, too—such as another agency that's producing more memorable work than the present firm seems capable of matching.

The honeymoon phase becomes nostalgia. The account is placed in review. The present agency, already a loser, is too boring, its brainwork inadequate to new challenges; its presentation flops and the account goes to the more creative outfit. The new agency is giddy. At the celebratory dinner, the chairman of the winning agency raises his glass and invites everyone present to join him in a toast—to something about the importance of teamwork.

The depredations of Robert-formerly-Bob's regime have become too blatant, have embittered and damaged the efforts of too many loyal agency people. David McCall feels he can take no more. On a hot July afternoon he drives out to Mercedes-Benz headquarters in Montvale for a talk with senior executive Hans Jordan and spills the beans. Meanwhile, Robert-formerly-Bob happens to be lunching with a visitor from Stuttgart and a couple of senior agency people. The headwaiter comes to the table to tell him he is wanted urgently in Montvale. He leaves the restaurant and is never heard of again.

▪ ▪ ▪

The agency was invited to visit the Mercedes-Benz works in Stuttgart once or twice a year. Courtesy demanded senior-level representation: by my reckoning I made at least a dozen visits. New creative and account staff, green as an Irish parade, soaked up every German experience. At least one agency visitor decided to speak a phonetic imitation of the German language at dinner—unaware that his hosts regarded the discordant gibberish of every such attempt as yet one more demonstration of American bad manners, condescension, and ignorance.

Our genial hosts inevitably commenced their hospitality orgy with a mandatory dinner on the first night of our visit—more a test than a treat. Most of the American invitees had had no sleep in a day or two. Strict protocol meant that everyone at the table—probably twenty altogether—kept his mouth shut until the ranking Mercedes host and the head representative of MBNA had clinked glasses and said *Mahlzeit* ("Enjoy the meal"), releasing the party to drink and, eventually, to eat.

No sooner had the group reached the hotel than a kind of tour-guide-cum-babysitter was herding everybody onto a bus that would take them out to the factory in nearby Sindelfingen. There, bone-weary visitors faked fascination watching engines dropped from above to the correct waiting car, then manhandled into place. An hour of trudging on concrete flooring with no respite for their feet left even gung ho Americans blurry, yawning, and aware of knots in their stomachs from breathing air that consisted of what seemed like fifty percent automobile paint.

Monotony ruled on these trips: same hotel, same room, same breakfast in the gloom of winter mornings before dawn's early light. Then in a convoy to—I never knew where, until our car stopped. There weren't all that many choices. A weird feeling of something akin to despair overcame me one gray January morning when our small visiting delegation was driven half an hour out of town and herded into what could be called a blockhouse: the foundry where engine blocks are cast.

Foundries are dark satanic mills at the best of times. But early on a winter morning, when you haven't slept since leaving New York and your diurnal clock knows it's actually midnight yesterday, your concentration wavers. Drag-assing around the foundry, pretending to listen to your tour guide when all you can think of is a warm bed (now exactly ten hours away at the earliest), your self-protective instinct takes over and forces you to think about anything but that warm bed. You shake your head violently to scatter those yearnings and return to reality. By the time the footsore factory visitor reaches the paint booth it's been three hours; the thrill of all these behind-the-scenes glimpses has palled.

Spirits revive when the afternoon's final activity is a visit to the huge domed styling center. We've been granted the secret privilege of inspecting a new model, one not yet in production. It's something of a kick, walking around a new car that the rest of the world is waiting for. Herr Bruno Sacco, the head of design, is gruff and formal. He wastes no time on small talk. His responsibilities are immense. Bruno Sacco is the keeper of the flame. In his hands he holds the image of the cars, and through them of the company. The challenge is to balance the temptations of a blank drawing pad with the necessity of keeping faith with the brand personality: a new model that breaks with tradition would jeopardize the familiar, vital "Mercedes-ness" that undergirds the meaning and the value of every car that rolls from the factory into the world.

Italian-born Bruno Sacco is an old Mercedes-Benz hand. His critiques of Mercedes—and other cars—convey the sensibilities of a serious, ardent student of automotive design who thinks not in short-term annual changes to stimulate short-term sales but in how a Mercedes-Benz of today exudes values that have never changed.

▪ ▪ ▪

Three years in, I sensed that McCaffrey & McCall was beginning to change. And not for the better. First, the agency was sold to those pirates of commerce, the Saatchi brothers in London, for cash and promises of creative support the Saatchis never honored, and probably never meant to. As chairman and principal strategist of the agency, David McCall had the right to do whatever he wanted with it. But despite his genuine belief in a democratic management style, he kept this transaction secret from his loyal staff.

Shortly after the Saatchi deal—and again not bothering to ask anyone who knew him, including me—David hired Hank Bernhard away from Ogilvy & Mather for reasons that continue to puzzle me. He gave him the grand title of vice chairman, and nothing much to do. Not knowing Hank or what he was like, David hadn't realized he'd just sent a wolf into a kennel full of puppies. Hank thrived on combat and wanted power. In every way imaginable, he and David were oil and water. Their fraught relationship lasted little more than a year and helped poison the atmosphere of the agency from the top down.

Had I ever lifted my nose from the grindstone and looked around me, I would have detected flaws that eventually proved fatal. David's almost neurotic optimism blinded him to the sensitivities of his senior creative people. Ignoring the notorious bugaboo of nepotism, he allowed his sister Peggy—who lacked any of his charm or other attributes—to run the J. C. Penney account. The most gregarious of men, he kept his distance from Peggy and she from him. I can't remember his ever mentioning her name; she was never seen in his office, the agency's nerve center. Was this bad blood from some ancient family feud? Was it David's natural generosity, mixed with guilt about his success and paying for it by giving a sibling a job? I never knew, and I knew enough not to ask.

David stocked his namesake agency with mediocrities in every senior position. Mediocrity begets mediocrity. The team he had assembled lacked fire in their bellies. The talents at his agency drifted away until it was a weak, colorless blob. If David hadn't fooled himself and run the place on the basis of his strong personal delusions, then McCaffrey & McCall might have survived.

I fell into a routine, driving to New York on Monday mornings and back to Conway late on Thursdays. My Manhattan digs were lavish: a room in the UN Plaza, a boutiquey new hotel serving United

Nations visitors. (The UN itself was right around the corner.) Hotel life in New York suited me; I'd stroll over to the UN Plaza after work, order the finest cheeseburger known to man from room service, and luxuriate in bed, reading a book.

My Willy Loman life in New York did much to quell my dissatisfaction in living the crummy country life. Phone calls home wiped the delight off my face, fast: my gain was Polly's loss. Depressed to the brink of tears when I wasn't there to share our failed dreams of rural life, she had no company in that big, echoing house, night after long night. I was forced to face a fact: my otherwise bulletproof wife harbored a genuine phobia about being left alone in the silence of a gloomy old house in the epicenter of nowhere.

How could I rewind Polly's desperate plight and help make her life at least bearable until I could invent another way of earning a decent livelihood? My meek suggestions sounded feeble even as I spoke: read the entire oeuvres of all your favorite writers; brush up on your Italian; scope out a nearby YMCA and use the swimming pool. To which suggestions Polly responded with a variety of derisive snorts.

Farmwife Sophie Hart from next door phoned one summer day. "We got three kittens we're *drownding*," she rasped. "So if you want 'em you better hurry!" In minutes Polly had dumped three cats—one orange, one black, one beige and white—on the kitchen floor. Goldie, Tommy, and Tuffy had arrived, in all their softball-size wiggliness.

■ ■ ■

Franklin County had been dirt-poor since the Civil War: a woebegone northern spur of Appalachia populated mainly by hardscrabble farmers, laborers, and sixties-era hippies lying low. Our lack of rapport with Conway remained from first day to last. But in the end, the town failed to live up to the idiotic delusions by which we judged it.

What finally budged us out and back to New York happened around dinnertime on a sullen mid-March afternoon in 1980. Polly's car pulled into the driveway. A minute later she burst into the kitchen area where I was sitting on a couch, browsing *The Boston Globe.*

I managed to get out "How was your—" when Polly barked, "Guess what—I'm pregnant!"

The celebration was muted: this pregnancy was Polly's fourth after three miscarriages, none of which had made it past the first trimester. This run of abrupt failures had mystified Polly, a healthy thirty-seven-year-old who'd given up smoking and didn't drink. When the pregnancy surpassed that previously sad milestone, Polly took that fact as a positive omen. Because I didn't care for another gripping drama ending in sorrow, I joined the positivity team.

Park Avenue obstetricians had examined Polly after her run of miscarriages, and no cause seemed obvious; the simple explanation, she heard from her relays of medical experts, was that birth was a serious and mysterious thing. "So keep on trying, Polly," went the advice, "and one of these days you may get lucky."

Polly had gone to a doctor in Greenfield once we were settled in. His examination yielded a heretofore unremarked clue: her supply of corpus luteum was low. This meant that when the fetus in the womb reached a certain weight, the sac it occupied wasn't strong enough to support it. Invariably, a miscarriage resulted.

So Polly began a drug regime to increase her corpus luteum supply, and it worked. She went to term, and our daughter arrived without incident. Chalk one up for the country way of life.

Pregnancy instantly reordered our minds, our priorities, our values, and the habits of our lives. Those lives now meant more than daydreaming: we wouldn't stay in this backwater a minute longer than needed to take our prize to thrive in civilization. A fresh wave of action bestirred even me. We would rent out the Conway house and rent an apartment for ourselves back on the Upper West Side, real estate permitting. (For reasons that can only be attributed to the power of necessity, we succeeded without much incident in letting out our Paradise Abandoned to a pleasant younger couple beckoned by the same call we'd succumbed to.)

The dark, stuffy, and never other than creepy attic was plundered for its treasures and its junk, in the standard country-to-city ratio of one part treasure to twenty parts futureless flotsam, lugged to the municipal dump.

By October 19, the baby was overdue. An hour after driving to Greenfield, during lunch at Herm's, Polly took a sip of her coffee and announced, "My water just broke." My 1980 Mercedes 300D wagon far exceeded the power limits of a diesel in a mad sprint to the emergency entrance of Greenfield's sole hospital. Overpowered by the significance of this moment, both excited partners now fell silent, realizing that our quotidian existence, our individual lives, were turning upside down.

This wasn't the comfy pondering of our choices anymore. We had just entered the realm of real time as Polly was rushed from the hospital entrance to wherever births are managed. Our snobby plan to arrange for a drug-free childbirth was jettisoned as soon as the doctor recommended a cesarean birth. The baby's position in Polly's womb wasn't precarious; still, a risk existed—so, given the shaky state of two first-time parents, we said no thanks to the fashionable natural procedure.

The reality of childbirth pulled us onto a higher plane. The atmosphere changed. The McCalls, calmer than they'd felt in months, now saw themselves as stable graybeards. Around suppertime on Monday, October 20, 1980, we greeted the arrival of a nine-pound, seven-ounce gift. Joyous relief flooded my parched system. It was all my emotions could handle to simply admire this miraculous creature as she was lifted from her mother's belly, weighed, wrapped in swaddling, and then officially handed over to her mom.

We named her Amanda Christine McCall, after a spirited competition waged for months. An unsurprising name, given Dad's pressure to keep all McCall names traditionally conservative. So although we toyed with classy, original names we stuck with Amanda. A classy name, but lacking the singular charms of our first choice, Havana.

The medical center's rule was that fathers change to hospital greens—for bacteria neutrality, I suppose. Later that day, when I retrieved my civilian pants from the locker, they had been lightened by fifty bucks in cash. *So what?* I said to myself: suddenly life was too exciting to waste time on trivia.

The small Greenfield hospital supplied a bevy of pleasant surprises. Nurses and staff were efficient and friendly, a meaningless sort of compliment until the chips are down and the patient needs a kind word.

▪ ▪ ▪

One dark and stormy night six months earlier, Polly had glimpsed a shadowy figure moving slowly along the gravel road leading to the highway. On closer inspection the figure revealed itself to be a big, rough-coated black dog. He was limping. Protruding from his chest was a thin stick—he'd been walking the trail up on the ridgeline and had a mishap stumbling downhill.

Polly whisked the exhausted dog down to the local vet. The dog suffered the insult to his system more stoically than most humans—me, for example. The vet said the dog was half Labrador, half some similar breed. He exhibited no cringing or flinching. Fear never clouded his liquid, trusting eyes or ruffled his calm nature. His personality endeared him to us. He sat patiently in the rear of the station wagon, and by next day he had settled into our midst, a part of the family.

The renters agreed to keep him at the house and care for him until our return in the spring.

He was crazy with joy when we pulled up to the house. A full summer followed; then it was time again to leave. Departure day arrived on a cool October afternoon. Packed into the wagon were three cats, two pugs, Polly, our baby, her babysitter, a bunch of black plastic garbage bags stuffed with quaint utensils, and me. A big country dog, we were advised, would be unhappy in the city. I checked my rearview mirror as we pulled away; there was the dog, lunging after us. He kept up the chase until exhaustion forced an end to the pursuit. I glanced back for a last fleeting look at High Meadow Farm. There he sat in the middle of the gravel road, exhausted. I knew dogs could be trained to imitate human emotions, but until that moment I never realized that a dog could express disappointment, confusion, and a sense of betrayal.

■ ■ ■

Coming back to New York City reversed every aspect of our durance vile in Western Massachusetts. It took a couple of weeks to synchronize. Polly traded her Nurse Ratched house-mothering duties in Greenfield for a re-return to Columbia University and her rudely interrupted pursuit of a master's degree in social work. I went back to advertising. My plan/dream to haul myself up to the status of a literary lion and an artist of fame and fortune got sidetracked even before I got to New York. We needed money and lots more of it. The sole route to a stable income, I thought, was advertising, and I would operate under this assumption through two Reagans and most of a Bush.

All the while, in case it hasn't been established over the course of this book, I'd kept up with my artwork. Liz Darhansoff, my friend Dan Okrent's book agent, wised me up on publishing and what it could mean for me and my work. I'd cobbled together a myriad of reasons based on my own low self-regard and semi-moronic grasp of the industry why I'd never have a book with my name on it. Everybody in Letters was an Ivy League graduate who'd read every good book in print, knew the night-shift hatcheck girl in every bar in town, and crewed on the second-place spot in the most recent America's Cup race.

But behold! My first book, *Zany Afternoons*, its title provided by young Ben Pesta for an earlier, much-briefer collection that appeared in the January 1975 issue of *Esquire*, was released at the start of the 1982 Christmas season. The American reviews topped Canadian critics' responses (apparently they took umbrage with some of the good-natured ribbing from a distant countryman). Similar treatment has followed with every subsequent book I've published.

Canadians resent critical satire, more so when it comes from the USA. And when the critic is a Canadian expat living in the USA, the blow is tripled.

Zany Afternoons is 123 pages of childish wackiness that captures some of the joy of finding my career after years of fecklessness. But joy hardly gushes from those pages. Much of the content is dark. Still, the creator was as happy, as productive, as masterful of his material as he'd probably ever get.

Seventy-seven *New Yorker* covers and I'm still flabbergasted.

(Courtesy of Bruce McCall and The New Yorker*)*

Chapter 11

Under the Covers

After a decade-plus in the ranks of McCaffrey & McCall, I realized I'd had enough. Not just enough of that agency, but of advertising altogether. This had been true since the early 1980s, when I'd started to get some traction with my humor pieces and artwork. To a more confident person, publishing a book, appearing on late-night talk shows, and having your work featured in national magazines might be sufficient proof of one's creative merits. But I was not yet convinced.

As I saw it, just because you're on the ice for a long time doesn't make you Wayne Gretzky. Even if everyone in the stands knows to the number how many goals you've scored, if you don't see yourself as a player, you might as well be trying to skate in flip-flops. (Speaking of ice, this metaphor is starting to show some cracks, but you get the idea.)

When I finally mustered the guts to flee the corporate world and get going on the career I wanted, whatever fears I'd had were, at that point, less scary than living the rest of my life as an adman. So in 1993, after nearly forty years with one foot out the door of the ad industry, I finally dragged the other one out, ending it all not with a bang but with two weeks' notice. I was fifty-eight years old when my real creative life began, at least as far as I'd understood it.

▪ ▪ ▪

In the months after I left McCaffrey & McCall, I wrote and illustrated pieces for *Car and Driver, Forbes FYI, Vanity Fair, The New York Times*, Toronto *Globe & Mail*, and others. As assignments continued to come in, I realized I hadn't made a terrible mistake leaving the adbiz. My real mistake had been allowing myself to be trapped there for so long.

▪ ▪ ▪

I've bored people to tears describing my childhood fixation on *The New Yorker.* By this time, those printed pages stapled together to form a magazine had frozen into an icon. A lifetime's admiration had hardened into something so far beyond and above that I had long since abandoned the ambition—even the hope—of ever seeing my name in its pages. I dared not even try. Mysterious supermen, Ivy Leaguers, clubmen, dinner companions of the great writers in the English language wouldn't deign to talk to a vulgarian upstart from nowhere, without an education to speak of. Better to get what pleasure I could from reading it every week than to try horning in where I didn't belong, only to have my reverence smashed by reality.

I'd been intrigued by *The New Yorker* since the age of eleven, when I found some 1931 issues tucked in a closet off our living room. In fact, issues of *The New Yorker* were scattered around every living room in every house or apartment the McCalls occupied.

Exactly why Dad had lovingly packed away those fifteen-year-old copies, he never said—we didn't indulge in that kind of table talk at dinner, on car trips, or anyplace else he'd be vulnerable to personal questions. Both my parents read the magazine front to back, as they were supposed to.

The New Yorker. It figured in my dreams before I knew what made this then-drowsy magazine so special. Because Dad and Mother were avid readers, I longed for their acceptance and reasoned that perhaps our mutual admiration for *The New Yorker* was the link I'd been hoping for. Dad, however, wasn't interested when I tried to get his attention, and Mother ceded such matters to him. Still, after I'd excavated those issues from the closet, I began surreptitiously reading the magazine.

I remember reading a profile of the flamboyant archcriminal Legs Diamond all the way to the end. As I worked my way through issue after issue, I gradually detected a streak of something running through the magazine, something behind the words or even within them. This comforted me. Half a century later, when my first piece was published, this quality was still there. No single word covers it. Wit? Intelligence? Elegance? Grace? Sophistication? The distillation of all of these. In time I developed admiration both for the magazine's literary and artistic contributors—Vladimir Nabokov, John McPhee, Roger Angell. It seemed wildly improbable that I would one day follow them into the magazine's pages, and from the pages to the covers.

So, in 1980, when I wrote a piece that seemed passably *New Yorker*-ish, I wavered for weeks before finally summoning the courage to send it to Liz Darhansoff, my agent, to pitch to the magazine. Titled "Browsing," my submission featured my favorite literary form—satirical image captions. They included a soldier relieved of his nose in a World War I army camp; President Gerald Ford's preferred footwear; and a taxonomy of weevils, to name a few of the twenty-six. When the magazine agreed to publish it, I was alarmed and elated. I still can't believe my name appears on the contributors page and, now, on the *New Yorker* website, where the entirety of my oeuvre waits patiently to be drawn out of the crypt by the magic of search queries.

▪ ▪ ▪

Fortunately, I always managed to work from home. I only had to show up at the office to drop off work or meet an editor for lunch. I'd learned after many years of working in offices every day that this arrangement was self-protective, one of the best things about my new freelance career. Not having to attend meetings or join clandestine overthrow-of-management plots hatched in the men's room saved a lot of time. Working at home kept me from being trapped in hallway klatches with nothing to say and fifteen minutes to say it. It also let me work at my own pace and tune my radio to whatever crap I chose.

I was free to organize my stuff—tubes of gouache paint that could cost $12 and up, arranged in a spectrum of light to dark, along with big, fat, manly tubes of Permanent White, which I could mix with all colors that needed a lighter effect. (I eventually renounced this toning-down and accepted working with bright colors that were so shocking to a timid thirteen-year-old that I'd avoided seeing vibrant color, even in my own art.)

▪ ▪ ▪

I can't teach a subject that I learned from a self-taught instructor (me), yet I educated myself to a level of skill that earned me a good living. A penchant for art is rewarded by the pleasure of doing it. It needn't be prizeworthy to thrill its creator, either. Catching the play of light in the frothy waves of a violent sea can stimulate feelings in the artist that are simply electric.

No one has ever claimed that the finest art in the world has already been painted. Maybe you're too old and strapped for time, or maybe you just lack the semi-suicidal lust to invest psychic energy in a hopelessly stupid cause. But somewhere, in the basement of her parents' ranch house in the Denver suburbs; in a tiny bedroom in the 18th arrondissement of Paris; and in the kitchen on an Argentine farm where she's babysitting a three-year-old while burnishing the chalk portrait of her father astride his palomino—someone is taking the same chances I did. Good luck!

▪ ▪ ▪

Here is a story no one would want to tell, but it happened, so I will. Then we can get on with it.

I smashed my right shoulder to bits early in 2014. Recovery took three months. It was the only serious health issue in my life, aside from that dustup in Frankfurt. Let loose from the hospital, I looked forward to getting back to my normal routines. I celebrated the retrieval of my former life a week or so after my discharge by lunching with friends. Afterward, Dan Okrent and I trekked north on Broadway. We crossed Eighty-Sixth Street, and shortly thereafter Dan peeled off for his apartment on West End Avenue. I decided to walk the rest of the way. My body needed the exercise.

Walking east from Broadway, I stopped for a moment at Amsterdam, aware of a subtle change in my gait. No pain, only a strange new way of walking. It had to be connected to three months of no exercise. What else could it be?

I was tipping forward and walking on my toes. Until this point, willpower had always been enough to let me wrest control back from any physical malfunction. (Did someone or -thing brainwash my feet? I wondered.) I was woozily off balance by the time I reached Columbus. A bunch of probably-not-typical Trinity School boys across the street were joking and laughing at my struggle. What if the little savages came over and beat the stuffing out of me? Fortuitously, a lost little dog rounded the corner. My boy torturers succumbed to their adolescent attention spans and moved on, probably to pull leaves off the trees in Central Park.

I now felt more than woozy. By Central Park West, I had lost nearly all balance and had to grab lampposts to keep from sliding down to the sidewalk. Our apartment building sat on the next corner. The longest walk of my life was one city block. I wanted to collapse on the street. At the door of the building stood a middle-aged couple chatting with Joe, the day doorman. With my last reserve of energy I wordlessly barreled past everybody in my path and stepped/fell into the elevator.

Thus in 2014 I was diagnosed with a mild case of Parkinson's disease. No big deal; "mild" meant no tremors or uncontrollable muscle spasms. My drawing and painting skills would be unaffected.

Until it was revealed to me that all early Parkinson's cases are mild. It progresses for the rest of the sufferer's life, and no treatment has been found to stop or reverse it.

My contributions to *The New Yorker* have tailed off over the past five years or so. Until then, my output was prolific: more than a hundred "Shouts & Murmurs" pieces and seventy-seven covers in the course of forty years.

Novelists tend to shun the compressed "Shouts" form. Those eight hundred words have to start working with the first sentence. The end comes up so fast that the closing line should go *snap!* or your story will dribble off, forgotten before the reader is finished with the magazine. My only advice to wannabe Shoutspersons is vague but truthful: Look for a subject anywhere, anytime. That's it. Think of yourself as a blotter. I've had "Shouts" ideas watching a perfume commercial on TV and while sitting in a doctor's waiting room as a nasty hubby and his hateful wife duked it out.

This little discussion is way longer than eight hundred words. Which reminds me: the most important thing by far about writing a "Shouts" is . . . discipline! And the most important factors in enforcing that discipline are . . . editors! (Although I worked from home, the spatial autonomy did not exempt me from the usual editorial rigors.)

My first editor, for my first piece, "Browsing," was Dan Menaker, who was invariably perceptive and hilariously self-critical. (Nor was it an act: Dan was dead serious about his moral failings; his irrepressible wit saved him from being a bore.) To put it as tactfully as I can, he was not a fan of William Shawn, the magazine's editor for a total of thirty-five years, and never accepted the widespread belief in the editing genius of this strange little man. When something had to give, it wasn't Mr. Shawn.

Next came Veronica Geng, a collaborator as much as an editor. She was smart and charming and laughed more than anybody I'd ever worked with—and at all the parts of a piece I thought funny. A genius! In retrospect, I nominate Ms. Geng as the most talented anyone who ever wrote a "Shouts & Murmurs" entry. She did only a few; her interests extended way past humorous tidbits. I knew zilch about her private life, and found out about her role as amanuensis to Philip Roth long after we had worked together.

Veronica represented the heady literary world to me. Her seriousness about literature and humor was unique. She was an intellectual. I knew I was lucky to work with her as my editor for a couple of years. Then, suddenly, there was no Veronica. She didn't confide in me at all. Wasn't in her office but was too no-nonsense a character for hypochondria. Asked what was wrong with her, her colleagues said simply, "She's sick." Was she ever. She was seriously ill before she left the office, and I never knew why. Brain cancer, I found out after she died far too young.

Gwyneth Cravens was a close friend before she was my editor. Serious about life but funny by nature, she made me laugh when we worked on a "Shouts" in her office, for too brief a time. One day she was gone. Gwyn had effectively given her life to . . . nuclear energy. She researched the field, wrote a blockbuster on the subject, and began giving lectures and attending scientific conferences. As far as I know, Gwyneth found her calling. Good for her.

Chris Knutsen had been Dan Menaker's assistant. He was young, with blondish hair and a gregarious manner that must have cheesed off a lot of his *New Yorker* colleagues. Chris wasn't technically my editor, but he edited my "Shouts," cheered me up during my swoons, then left me dangling over the void when he left the magazine.

Then Susan Morrison was given to me, despite a workload onerous enough to make a stevedore cringe. She made time for detailed editing. She gave me great "Shouts" ideas. She became a close and valuable friend. Meantime, as a single mother raising two daughters, Susan was successful there as well. Today her duties at *The New Yorker* have ballooned, but she continues to read every line I write. She rejects more submissions than all my previous editors combined. Susan also serves as president of the Century Association (formerly Century Club), the first woman to hold this position. In her spare time she's writing a biography of the first Canadian in television history to merit the status of wunderkind in the U.S.—the individual popularly known as Lorne Michaels.

In 1987, Si Newhouse, of the Condé Nast family that owned the magazine, selected Tina Brown—editor of the revived and hugely successful *Vanity Fair*—to replace Robert Gottlieb, who'd replaced William Shawn as editor (Gottlieb stayed on for about five years). In doing so, Si ignited a revolt. "Flashy," "aggressive," and "ruthless" were the milder terms used by the Shawn-era holdouts when Ms. Brown arrived.

My personal history with Tina was perfect: she okayed everything, never turned down a "Shouts," and seldom ordered changes. She green-lighted my idea for a piece about why so many European automobile stylists were Americans. I was stupidly ignorant of the Iron Curtain–era paranoia among carmakers about their future models being trumpeted in the media, a violation of their policy of maximum secrecy. It turned out to be a disastrously empty story. Tina could have, probably should have, reamed me out for being so utterly unprepared and for squandering the magazine's money on a fiasco. She never uttered a word.

I must swallow my dudgeon when I recall the silly and sometimes vicious gossip her advent inspired. She made some judgment errors; the Roseanne Barr issue was a howler. But Tina also got the magazine into the black and boosted circulation. Among her host of talent-spotting triumphs was the current editor and prolific writer, David Remnick.

Remnick came from a newspaper background, and it shows—he's fast, accurate, honest, and values and encourages strong writing. He gets to the office early and leaves way past dinnertime. Remnick is a polymath, a guy who can talk to anyone as intelligently about boxing and electric guitars as he can about ISIS or the Kremlin. Over the years he has also proven to be a tremendously kind and loyal friend (and I'm not just saying that because he is, as I write this, deciding whether or not a cover of mine will run).

■ ■ ■

I published my first *New Yorker* cover in July 1993, and my last (for now) in January 2020. I'd hoped to keep on until I smashed William Steig's all-time record number, 117. It wasn't to be. As the Parkinson's gradually ruined my ability to draw and paint, I saw Barry Blitt's style so capture the political zeitgeist of America that his cover count skyrocketed in the space of six years to exceed mine. My proud record of seventy-seven covers will soon render me a forgotten also-ran. Boo-hoo.

The magazine's remarkable art director Françoise Mouly has overseen all my covers. Part of what persuades me to declare her remarkable is her intellect. A single conversation reveals a myriad of topics with which she's comfortable. Topping her list of issues demanding agreement, but often prompting good old-fashioned argument, is politics. International, national, and municipal. She respects France but she loves America. Her quiet voice charms the listener by pouring French into English and combining them with an accent that would make a Parisienne jealous. She and hubby Art Spiegelman (the *Maus* Man) could between them fill the air on a twenty-four-hour radio network.

Let's say you've pitched a kids-in-the-park cover idea. Within a week it has generated at least three entirely different concepts. You'll have interpreted each of these concepts in three rough sketches—the basic composition of the picture and the position and relative size of the central figure or thing, or in this case both.

Before email, I'd send all sketches to Françoise via the Gutenberg-era apparatus known as the fax. (In the technology gap between the late eighties and early aughts, the Before Email Era, I'd also use the post office or a messenger.) Any one of these means saved the time it would take to go all the way downtown to discuss which sketch, or sketches, deserve to be amplified to "comp" form. "Comp" is short for "comprehensive," the old-fashioned term now largely forgotten in the ubiquitous trend to compress words into info-blobs for faster-and-faster-and-faster communication.

After Françoise has received said fax comes the phone call with the word on how it hits. It usually hits. Françoise has seldom flatly nixed a cover completely. Acceptance from her is tantamount to high praise: her eyes are foolproof. In fact, she has frequently given extra oomph to a cover by suggesting (never ordering) a change in perspective, inevitably leading me to admit "I wish I'd thought of that."

Timing for cover appearances varies. Usually there's no reason to alter a scheduled date, but there's always the chance that some hiccup may force a change: a national tragedy, for example, that so focuses public attention that not acknowledging it would appear arrogant, uncaring, or out of touch with the zeitgeist—or all three. Such circumstances, given the pressures inherent in weekly publication, may result in a cover that's crude, less developed, or so heavily symbolic that the average reader quickly forgets it. But *New Yorker* cover artists routinely rise to the occasion and frequently surpass themselves. A disaster's emotional punch often allows a solid, sensible artist to come up with an ideal image—case in point, Françoise and Art Spiegelman's solemn, all-black post-9/11 cover. *The New Yorker* has had a lineup of clutch hitters forever.

▪ ▪ ▪

My favorite cover illustrations aren't likely to be your favorites. The artist's view is the reverse side of the coin, the end product of the idea. What I see first is the struggle that ultimately produced it, a tug-of-war that could take another book to explain. Some covers have come to me so full-blown that I'm more copyist than agonized creator. Some are the opposite: mean tiffs with my brain that persist until an idea has turned into a drawing that is then painted.

Certain of my covers betray the sense of confusion I felt as the process developed. A good cover is so smooth, so finished, that it hardly seems painted. It looks so natural; what was the fuss behind it? You don't want to know. But if you do . . .

The Blimp That Fell to Earth

August 16, 1993

Tina Brown let it be known that the next week's cover must be a humorous take on the deflation of a small blimp and its flopping onto the roof of a West Side apartment building. (Nobody was killed or injured, so no lawsuits could be expected.) I was keenly aware of my amateur status; had indeed painted like an amateur and lived in the status cellar. I sat at my drawing board, attempting to solve a riddle: painting a dead blimp, I believed, would result in readers young and old barfing or falling asleep—hopefully not both. Eventually, after a four-hour thinkathon that concluded at four a.m., the solution arrived: a straight-faced rendering of a blimp parking lot, with blimps arriving and departing. Large glass walls reflect the blimps.

King Kong Call

January 23, 1995

A dream delivered this image to my brain in my sleep one chilly winter night in the country. It was so clear and intact that it had only to be transcribed. Shortly after it ran, I received a phone call from a very pleasant elderly lady, who told me how much she'd enjoyed it. Just before the end of the call she said, "Oh, by the way—my name is Fay Wray."

Landmarks Commission to Meet in Special Session

April 1, 1996

The Land of the Pharaohs injected itself into my bloodstream in the Egyptian section of the Royal Ontario Museum in Toronto on my first visit, in 1946. A mummified corpse was the main attraction (can't beat a dead body for drawing crowds), but the hieroglyphics intrigued me more: pictures as language, but a language you can't decipher. The Egyptian decorative tradition froze everything and everyone in identical one-dimensional poses. Every year, another ancient Egyptian tomb was found in some desolate place a long way from the Great Pyramid. These discoveries suggested a new vision for playing with scale. Fascinated during a Manhattan construction boom by old buildings demolished to dust, I looked for commercial signs buried in the gloom since 1899.

Lobsterman's Special

August 4, 1997

The old switcheroo—in this case, a lobster family digging in at their table, while humans, wrists and feet bound, gurgle helplessly in a holding tank. Painting this cover flooded me with pity and disgust. Since then, I haven't been able to stomach a lobster dinner.

Easter Morning

April 5, 1999

Françoise asked me to think about doing something with the huge new exhibit of prehistoric creatures that had just opened at the American Museum of Natural History. I immediately decided to paint an outdoor scene, the best way to identify the museum. Dinosaurs and other monstrous creatures seemed overfamiliar. Birds, less so. And because the scene needed movement, and birds flock, that was that. Pterodactyls were goofy-looking, nasty-tempered flying thugs. I drew a flock of pterodactyls grubbing for rats, cats, and small dogs on the sidewalk in front of the building early on a Sunday morning. In fact, Easter Sunday morning. Pterodactyls didn't normally don rich purple coats, but the Artist felt that would better represent Easter.

I don't like to rattle the Art Mart by recommending one of my paintings as a "personal favorite" and thereby setting up a run, hiking prices already condemned by art sellers and buyers as "a blatant fraud." But I must tell the truth: "Pterodactyls" is my all-time favorite. I live a ten-minute stroll from the "Natural" (a fond nickname from the same loonies who tagged the Statue of Liberty "Stat" and the Chrysler Building "Old Walt"), but that day it looked like rain. I drove my car down Central Park West to Seventy-Seventh Street, U-turned, stopped the car facing north, and commenced to draw the Natural for half an hour from behind the wheel. I drove back up Central Park West to my cross street and parked in the garage. No rain the whole time; isn't that always the way?

Photo Opportunity

May 8, 2000

Everybody knows that image of famous photographer Margaret Bourke-White perched behind a steel eagle's head on the Chrysler Building, sickeningly high above Manhattan. I painted a cover satirizing the scene: an angry steel eagle's mate, lifting photographer and camera (and beret) to float helplessly in midair. The joke was on me: almost nobody knew that famous shot. The cover was confusing and pointless—a flop, and a warning to never overestimate the reader. Even the *New Yorker* reader.

Polar Bears on Fifth Avenue

January 13, 2014

The two mature polar bears guarding the main entrance to the New York Public Library, a wintry replacement for the more summery lions, were donated by the man called "Polar Pete," the Arctic legend who also runs Polar Bear Farm, a six-thousand-acre refuge where he hides out when chased by a pack of polar bears. The pair sitting at the main entrance to the library are the only identical twins ever known among the species. "Sure, they're cute, but those rascals are even harder to train than octopi," snorts Mrs. Polar Pete, the world's sole licensed polar bear wrangler. "Took six months to get those two to sit and stay sat," she bitches. Their sense of smell is so acute that one or the other—or both—will pounce on anybody passing by on the sidewalk who happens to be carrying a piece of meat in a bag. Their appetites are so avid that passersby sometimes toss them steaks even before they can pick up the scent and pounce. "It's a small price to pay," observes one veteran butcher. "Your polar bear is a carnivore. Better to let it gnaw on a chunk of meat than gnaw on you!"

The World Tomorrow (triptych foldout cover)

May 18, 2015

I had no grand vision of the idea of "Innovation" through history, so when Françoise gave me three successive pages—a foldout—on which to cover the matter, I panicked. Where to begin and where to end? And considering I had to work without using words, how would I convey the scale of the subject, even with a triptych? (Innovation itself isn't self-descriptive; it can be applied to anything.) I arbitrarily began the picture on the far left panel. Just as arbitrarily, the discovery of fire seemed a symbolic dramatization of the beginning of invention. That provided the image I used to cap the piece: the fiery launch of a rocket to a distant planet. Between the two fires lay several centuries of developments. There's no timeline to progress and no universal agreement on which innovations were decisive, so my own, personal triptych comprised the events most relevant to what I saw as meaningful in history, from Copernicus to Bob Dylan, the printing press to the personal computer.

■ ■ ■

Life in general has treated me better than I deserved. As a kid from nowhere, with no education, no guidance, no money, no formal training, I should have had no dreams, let alone an expectation to fulfill them. But to my continued astonishment, I've maintained a nearly four-decades-long romance with *The New Yorker* and accomplished the only dream I never knew I had: to be an artist. Plenty of kids who don't take art classes or get diplomas or have parents who encourage their artistic talents still end up as artists—growing up poor and unworldly doesn't sentence you to a mediocre, artless life (if it did, we wouldn't even have the Beatles)—but it certainly doesn't help. I don't think being coddled by familial love and money would have necessarily made me a "better" artist, but it might have helped me see that I was one a few decades earlier.

If you ignore the value of your calling out of fear—regardless of what kind of fear it is—your greatest fears will likely come true: you will abandon your true calling.

For most of my life, I'd felt a lack of connection. Lack of connection to my parents, to the place I grew up, to the schools I attended, to the offices where I worked. But in the years it took to get here, working alone in my studio, I've felt a greater sense of connection than I had in all my life—to the world at large, and to myself as an artist.

Acknowledgments

This book owes its existence to the friends who stood by it (and me) through its long arc of production: Adam Gopnik, Sandy Frazier, Dan Okrent, Michael Kimmelman, Bruce Handy. Many other friends and colleagues have offered support and company throughout this protracted period: Ron Chernow, Lisa Ford, Graciela Meltzer, Andy Borowitz, Mark Singer, Roz Chast, Patty Marx, Paul Roosin, Richard Thompson, and Erik Nelson; the group—more of a polite gang—with whom I shared many lively lunches at Cafe Lux: Dan Barry, Dan Okrent, Michael Kimmelman, John Weidman, Chip McGrath, Marshall Brickman, and of course Cafe Lux's benevolent Lynn Wagenknecht. The late great editor Dick Todd, taken far too early, and the magical Ricky Jay, who at this very moment is probably reaming out somebody Up There for whisking him away before his time. To Lynn Povich and Steve Shepard for their friendship and kindness.

My friends at *The New Yorker*: Françoise Mouly, Susan Morrison, and David Remnick; my generous, talented, and exceedingly patient editors Doug Pepper at Penguin Random House Canada and Jill Schwartzman at Dutton, New York. My agent, David McCormick, for his support throughout this long process. Thank you to John Kennedy for his help winnowing down the selection of covers written about in chapter 11.

My daughter, Amanda, who oversaw every turn of events from day one and led this untethered group down the long trail of this book's completion. My wife, Polly, generously proffered support, editorial comments, and more than a few meals, despite the pressures of her own demanding career and my own demanding personality.

This book exists because of everybody mentioned here. But before closing off my thanks, a few words of praise, admiration, and affection for two unsung heroes behind the project: My sister, Chris Jerome, copyedited (and so much more-ed) this book. She is sweet-tempered, industrious, funny, smart, and an excellent bullshit detector. And Jaye Bartell, a man of great editorial talent, patience, and an ability to make so many problems just go away. This book is his creative monument.

About the Author

Bruce McCall began his career in a commercial art studio, switched to journalism and then advertising, and began writing and painting humorous subjects in the seventies, first with *National Lampoon* and ultimately for *The New Yorker*. McCall has published six previous books, including *This Land Was Made for You and Me (But Mostly Me)* in collaboration with David Letterman. He lives in New York City.